Systemic Violence

Systemic Violence:
How Schools Hurt Children

Edited by

Juanita Ross Epp
and Ailsa M. Watkinson

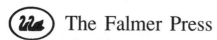 The Falmer Press

(A member of the Taylor & Francis Group)
London • Washington, D.C.

UK   The Falmer Press, 1 Gunpowder Square, London, EC4A 3DE
USA   The Falmer Press, Taylor & Francis Inc., 1900 Frost Road, Suite 101, Bristol, PA 19007

First published in 1996

A catalogue record for this book is available from the British Library

Library of Congress Cataloging-in-Publication Data are available on request

ISBN 0 7507 0582 5 paper

Jacket design by Caroline Archer

Typeset in 10/12pt Times by
Graphicraft Typesetters Ltd., Hong Kong.

Printed in Great Britain by Biddles Ltd, Guildford and King's Lynn on paper which has a specified pH value on final paper manufacture of not less than 7.5 and is therefore 'acid free'.

Every effort has been made to contact copyright holders for their permission to reprint material in this book. The publishers would be grateful to hear from any copyright holder who is not here acknowledged and will undertake to rectify any errors or omissions in future editions of this book.

Contents

Contents

Annotated List of Contents

Although the family and the school are two critical institutions that serve to socialize children, they often compete with and blame each other for the shortcomings or the attentions of children. Rather than seek out the rich possibilities and connections that could result from their common interests in the well-being of children, they separate and isolate themselves from one another and struggle for power and status in the eyes of the child. As a result, boundaries are set up and children are caught in the complex intersection of these two spheres of influence — one which nurtures and accepts them unconditionally and the other which categorizes and evaluates them according to prescribed standards. This atmosphere of dissonance, resentment and mistrust creates an unexamined form of systemic violence.

Part 2   Schools and Violence

In many instances, our youth are growing up to accept physical or psychological conflicts as part of the everyday school milieu. The students' perceptions described in this chapter differ greatly from those of their teachers and administrators. Efforts to deal with school violence must have as their focus a clear understanding of and compassion for children and the struggles that they are facing in what often seems an increasingly hostile world.

Understanding literacy in ethnically diverse classrooms often illuminates the intersection of an intricate mesh of power relationships among peers that thread gender, race, and ethnicity with systemic violence throughout day-to-day interactions. In an ethnographic study of primary learners, the dynamics of collaborative learning groups illustrated that between and among racially mixed girls, bullying was discrete and pervasive. Interventions that focused on a culturally sensitive curriculum helped to build a cohesive classroom community to ensure inclusion for all learners.

A pedagogy in which students can speak critically about their experiences and their relationships with others is more difficult to arrange than one would expect. This chapter is an examination of the realities of the lives of Grade 5 girls in an inner-city school. In their world, it is possible for the text of a conversation to have grave impact on them, in very real ways. The consequences of a conversation, with other students or with teachers, might include the possibility of apprehension by social services, 'getting burned', or being betrayed. Self-disclosure had the potential to change their lives in dangerous ways and they were unwilling to take that risk.

8 *Masculinities and Schooling: The Making of Men*
Blye W. Frank

This chapter is based on a study in which adolescent males were interviewed concerning their perceptions of masculinity. They spoke of authority, domination, the continuous struggle around power, responsibility, control, freedom, and the social privilege of being male. They also spoke of competition, violence of varying degrees against other men, women, and themselves, and sexuality. The ways in which schools reinforce accepted interpretations of masculinity contribute to violence in sports, harassment of girls and other boys, and the continuation of privilege for those who 'measure up'.

Part 3 Pedagogy: Violation or Vindication?

9 *Argument as Conquest: Rhetoric and Rape*
Lisa Jadwin

Is argument a conquest? By removing conquest metaphors from their contexts, we can defamiliarize metaphors that combine to create the larger 'conquest' image that characterizes argumentation. These metaphors work in two ways. First, they put a specifically sexual twist on the familiar progression of hypothesis, proof, and conclusion and incorporate the paradigm of male twentieth-century novels. Second, they glamorize the violent usage of 'appendages', not simply against an opponent, but against that opponent's will. Argumentative teaching strategies may severely inhibit learning for various members of the class.

10 *Men's Minds and Women's Matters: Digging at the Roots of Androcentric Epistemologies*
Sandra Monteath

Although particulars of cultural stories that keep women in their place may vary according to women's class, colour, and culture, the epistemic metanarrative is remarkably consistent about its exclusion of all women as 'true' knowers and of women's experiences as true knowledge. Thus women who pursue formal education may find themselves half in one world, half in another.

11 *Literacy Tasks and Social Change: Voices and a View from Somewhere*
Lorraine Cathro

Personal power means having your experiences, as an adult learner, accepted and validated within the educational setting. Personal power means being helped to learn the academic Discourse of the discipline and then being encouraged to critique it. Narrative must be validated as a legitimate and valued way of researching and writing within academe. Mentorship through sharing knowledge and power requires that instructors make the rules of academic Discourse explicit.

Part 4   Legal Violence

12   Suffer the Little Children Who Come into Schools
Ailsa M. Watkinson

Educational professionals generally consider teaching to be a 'caring profession', a training ground for instilling democratic principles. While children are compelled, by legislation, to attend school, their rights and freedoms are more at risk in school than out of it. Attempts to change the inequities and injustices are often rebuffed by an education profession bolstered by draconian legislation, their own code of ethics and judicial deference.

13   Postscript: Making Central the Peripheral
Juanita Ross Epp

A starting place in addressing systemic violence may be through renewed connections between formerly dichotomized entities — the home and the school, the affective and the cognitive. By moving topics which have traditionally been peripheral to the workings of the school to make them a focal point of the curriculum we can provide a forum for teachers and students to name and understand the underlying violence in their daily lives.

Preface

This book is a considered reflection on a phenomenon that first came to our collective attention at a conference on school violence. While many at the conference were
discussing the legal implications of 'zero tolerance' policies (in which violent children are evicted from the school system), some of us were examining the schools
themselves as complicit contributors to, and as continuing sources of, violence.
Systemic violence includes a wide spectrum of negative practices including intrus-
ive authoritative administrative structures, individual applications of inappropriate
discipline, and placid acceptance of school practices which exclude and damage
segments of the school population.

Educational systems are the products of the societies they serve and, as such,
become the vessels in which new generations are distilled into replicas of their
predecessors. The good and the bad of our culture are encouraged and enhanced
throughout each child's formative years. Many positive outcomes have been the
result of compulsory schooling. Democracies have evolved, science and technology have moved into new eras and many children have been encouraged to reach
individual goals while becoming thoughtful, contributing, citizens.

But our school systems have not been successful for all students. There are
students who do not benefit from public education. Many of them plod quietly on,
not recognizing their own failure to thrive. Others silently drop out, unable to cope
with the exclusion that they experience. A few express their alienation through acts
of violence. When this happens, school authorities focus attention on individual rule
breakers rather than on the reasons for the outbursts. All of these responses are connected with what we have called educational systemic violence.

The contributors to this book used a definition for systemic violence that
includes any institutionalized practice or procedure that adversely impacts on individuals or groups by burdening them psychologically, mentally, culturally, spiritually, economically or physically. *Educational* systemic violence includes any practice
or procedure that prevents students from learning, thus harming them. This may take
the form of conventional practices that foster a climate of violence, or policies which
appear to be neutral but which result in discriminatory effects.

The contributors used a variety of approaches, topics, and research paradigms
in their reflections on systemic violence but have reached similar understandings.
Systemic violence is caused by many things, but is often related to standardization,
exclusive pedagogical practice, or the use of punishment. The resulting dehumanization, stratification and abuse are described in Chapter 1, which serves as a framework for the remaining chapters.

The rest of the book is divided into four parts. Part 1 consists of reflections on attitudes and structures that allow educational systemic violence to occur. The assumptions that sanction systemic violence begin in the uneasy alliance between parents who are forced, sometimes reluctantly, to deliver their children for public education, and school systems which are sometimes equally reluctant to accept them. This becomes the battleground for the 'politics of childhood' (Chapter 2), which has resulted in various types of institutional abuse which continue in various forms into current practice. The uneasy home–school relationship augments a complex struggle between societal beliefs in the sanctity of family privacy and the need to intervene in suspected instances of child abuse (Chapter 3). Chapter 4 is an examination of the incompatibilities of the expectations of home and school as described by teachers who are also mothers.

Part 2 focuses on the aspects of systemic violence which impact on particular groups of children. Chapter 5 is an attempt to redefine violence by examining it from the students' point of view. Chapters 6 and 7 are similar to each other in that both are studies of the in-school lives of girls from minority groups, but different from each other in that their authors reach radically different conclusions. Minority girls are doubly likely to be affected by systemic violence and these examinations of the role of the school in teaching and protecting female students provides a troubling picture. But boys are not immune to the effects of systemic violence, especially in a world which values traditional concepts of masculinity above all else. The analysis in Chapter 8, of how hegemonic heterosexual masculinity affects adolescent males, is equally disturbing.

In Part 3, we reflect on the dual potential of the school as a site of healing or as one of continuing harm. Particular focus is placed on the masculine underpinnings of scholarly language (Chapter 9) and androcentric epistemologies (Chapter 10). The use of narrative as a tool for social change is the focus of Chapter 11.

The final part, includes a chapter that describes how systemic violence is embedded in the legal rights of schools, and how the rights of students are often viewed by the courts as secondary concerns. Chapter 13 is a revisitation of the themes of hope and change as they emerged in the twelve analyses. An awareness of systemic violence may enable us, as practitioners and as researchers, to reflect on the down side of compulsory education. However, we do not advocate its abandonment, rather we present current realities in order to work toward the day when public education will be a positive force in the lives of all children.

1 Schools, Complicity, and Sources of Violence

Juanita Ross Epp

Violence: Physical force or activity used to cause harm, damage, or abuse.
(*Webster's Dictionary*, 1988)

In this book it is argued that educational systems are complicit in the abuse of children through 'systemic violence' and that this complicity, and the students' reactions to it, contribute to other forms of violence. My colleagues will, in future chapters, focus on specific aspects of systemic violence — exclusionary practices, toleration of abuse, discriminatory policies and the like — but it is my job to set the canvas. Systemic violence has been defined as any institutional practice or procedure that adversely impacts on individuals or groups by burdening them psychologically, mentally, culturally, spiritually, economically or physically. Applied to education, it means practices and procedures that prevent students from learning, thus harming them (Epp and Watkinson, in press).

'Harmful educational procedures' should be a contradiction in terms. However, even successful participants in the education system recognize the potential for systemically inflicted damage. The term 'systemic violence' gathers together the fragments of doubts and suspicions that make us distrustful of the compulsory education system. It reminds us of the incidents that were 'just not fair' and the situations that seemed fair on the surface but failed the test of equity. It describes the taken-for-granted 'common sense' (Ng, 1993) pedagogical approaches and educational practices that lead to success for some but to failure for others.

Systemic violence is not intentional harm visited on the unlucky by vicious individuals. Rather, it is the unintentional consequences of procedures implemented by well-meaning authorities in a belief that the practices are in the best interests of students. Systemic violence is insidious because those involved, both perpetrators and victims, are often unaware of its existence. The students, accustomed to learning about the world in positivistic terms reflecting a 'white wealthy reality' (Carnoy, 1974, p. 365), do not see their own 'failure' in any other terms. When students are not capable enough or compliant enough, the failure is not shouldered by the school as a failure to provide a meaningful educational experience: the blame is shifted to the student for lack of industry or ability — or to the parent for lack of a positive environment or for failing to support school initiatives. The students most damaged by systemic violence are removed from school, or remove themselves, and suffer the lasting disadvantages of an incomplete education. They accept the personal blame and economic detriments associated with academic failure as their own. The irony is that when students who are compelled by law to attend school are failed by the school system, they accept responsibility for the institution's failure.

From the school administrator's point of view, when students drop out of school, it is often deemed to be 'for the best'. The students' behaviors have often been disruptive and their marks are usually poor, so their removal can be seen as an improvement in the environment for those who remain. Sometimes students respond to systemic violence in violent ways, and administrators are forced to remove them. In these cases, school authorities feel vindicated. They can focus on the students' acts and justify their removal as necessary to preserve the harmony of the school building. They see no need to examine the circumstances to ascertain whether or not there was systemic violence predicating the students' actions (Lee, 1994). Occasionally, when the results of systemic violence are particularly obvious or disastrous, school personnel stop to question the role that they have played. A student suicide, for example, will cause authorities to pause to consider their complicity. In one case, the suicide of a Grade 7 student who had recently been suspended caused a special kind of grief for the administrators and teachers in his school (Sakiyama, 1996). Their intention in upholding school policy had not been to cause the child harm and there was no way for them to ascertain the effect that implementation of school policies had had on the child's life.

What makes systemic violence 'systemic' is the fact that there is no-one to blame. People applying the violence are only a part of a larger process. Administrators and teachers do what is expected of them. They follow protocol, they maintain standards. They do what they believe to be in the students' best interests (Miller, 1990b); it is the protocol itself that is sometimes damaging.

Complicity

Perhaps the most useful beginning for an examination of systemic violence is in the commonalities shared by critical pedagogy and feminist pedagogy. Critical and feminist pedagogy share a belief in 'self and social empowerment' as elements of 'broader social transformation' (Gore, 1993, p. 7). They both pay attention to student experience and voice and raise concerns about teacher authority (Gore, 1993, p. 7). These issues are also important to people concerned about systemic violence.

Work on systemic violence is also linked to advocacy literature in which there are calls for inclusionary education for traditionally excluded groups of people — special needs students, economically deprived students, students from minority groups, girls and women, or gays and lesbians. Ellsworth (1994) suggested that disadvantaged students might include all students who are not 'white, heterosexual, Christian, able-bodied, intelligent, thin, middle-class, English-speaking and male' (p. 321).

Although the disadvantaged are more likely to be affected by systemic violence, even the privileged can suffer damaged self-concepts in competitive learning environments and experience dampened creativity in oppressive classrooms. Systemic violence is visited upon all students, but does not damage all children to the same degree. Systemic violence constricts and directs many student behaviors, but is especially damaging to those who are too creative, too sensitive or too discerning. Even children who fit the confines of 'privilege' find themselves being punished for defiance of senseless rules and for acts of rebellion against meaningless curriculum. All students are subjected to tedium in lesson delivery and to an expectation that they will sit still and perform tasks that often appear to have little value for them. Teachers may justify this as preparation for future jobs, and they will be supported in this view by administrators and parents (McLaren, 1986, p. 224), but conformity and routine can be mind-numbing and could hardly be classified as a meaningful learning experience. The intentional exposure to boredom and repetition is a part, but only a small part, of what is systemically violent in our schools.

Systemic violence is found in any *institutionalized practice which adversely impacts* on students. To be damaging, practices do not have to have a negative impact on all students. They may be beneficial to some and damaging to others. Many practices that are systemically violent are assumed to be beneficial to students in general, but the processes that some students find 'nurturant and protective, providing them with a sense of security . . . [are for others] a manifold system of oppression and condemnation' (McLaren, 1986, p. 219). For example, a marking system which provides positive reinforcement for only a few good students often has an adverse affect on other students. Intended to encourage the others, to inspire them, and make them want to 'win' the next time, this practice often has the opposite effect. The response is likely to be a wadded-up project in the garbage, a muttered acceptance of personal inadequacy (or dislike of the winning student) and a vow to try no more. Systemic violence occurs when the positive impact on some students is only possible through the negative effect it has on others.

The effects of systemic violence are exacerbated for disadvantaged students because their experiences in school are quite different from those of privileged students, even though they may be sitting in the same classroom. Systemic violence sometimes takes the form of colonialized knowledge, that is, the acceptance of a pre-ordained set of curricula which reflects the history, values and expectations of the dominant society while denigrating as untrue or lacking in value the experiences and heritage of disadvantaged students (Darder, 1991). The social hierarchy differentiates student experiences in terms of both cognitive and behavioral skills (Bowles and Gintes, 1976) as classroom interaction encourages different outcomes for different students. Middle-class males are encouraged to be aggressive and to use critical thinking skills, while girls and minority students are taught to be passive and 'civilized' (Bowles and Gintes, 1976; Sadker and Sadker, 1994).

Damaging as the colonialization of knowledge (Darder, 1991, p. 5) is to disadvantaged students, its detrimental affects are not felt exclusively by them. The school system teaches all children that they must 'compete with each other for the few positions at the top' while ignoring its own potential as a site in which children could be encouraged to work together 'to improve their collective condition' (Carnoy, 1974, p. 365). This trains all students for the reality of the current economy without offering them any alternative views for the future. It also conditions some students to be accepting of their own eventual 'failure'. A meritorious view of success disempowers students to the extent that few place the fault or credit where it belongs, with an education system geared to perpetuate stratification (Darder, 1991, p. 5), all the while proclaiming equal opportunity.

Systemic violence encourages disadvantaged students to disappear from the school system and from competition for economic success, but the effect on the 'successful' is also troubling. The damage to the privileged takes the form of the ingrown isolation of 'sexist, racist, elitist, ablist and heterosexist' (Ellsworth, 1994, p. 306) attitudes. Privileged students believe that they have achieved success because of personal ability and superior intelligence. Separated by their own disdain from most of humanity, these individuals pay the price in terms of fear, vulnerability and self-doubt. Unable to understand their differences, they build walls to keep others at a distance and chain down their belongings in fear. The price of privilege can be isolation (Kaufman, 1987).

Often those working within the school system do not even recognize this alienation. Administrators and teachers who cannot perceive their own biases cannot see the systemic violence happening around them. The negative ways in which disadvantaged students respond to systemic violence encourage the privileged to assume that the inequities are the fault of the disadvantaged. Thus privileged students remain unable to recognize an uneven playing field, especially if they are standing on it. Eventually the privileged learn to view attempts at equity as invasions of their personal rights (Thornhill, 1995).

There are so many aspects to education that it is difficult to focus on particulars in seeking sources of systemic violence. The daily activities of education may be endemic with violence, but systemic violence can also be manifest in particular incidents. Many of us have walked away from our own elementary education with generally positive memories mixed with the odd painful experience. I teach aspiring teachers in an after degree BEd program. When my students are asked to remember the worst incident of their educational experience, and share these incidents in small groups, they regularly comment on the emotional residue that the exercise touches in them. They are surprised that a long ago, half forgotten moment can still affect them with such force, and they are a little embarrassed by the tears that sometimes attend the exercise. When individuals look back at the pain of an education, can they distinguish among simple mistakes, intentional hurts, and systemic violence? To focus the search, I propose three basic sources of systemic violence: standardization, pedagogical practice and punishment.

There But for Fortune: Standardization

Most people in positions of authority within the education system are not people who suffered debilitatingly from the effects of systemic violence in their own educations. Those who have suffered systemic violence are unlikely to want to have anything to do with schools and are even less likely to have stayed in the system long enough to have the qualifications necessary for them to re-enter it as professionals. Thus educational institutions are peopled by individuals who have accepted the positivist ideology, that is 'an empirical analytical method of inquiry that incorporates the notion of quantifiable objective facts and neutral observation' (Darder, 1991, p. 6). Most teachers and principals believe that there is a 'standard' that can be applied to students and to student learning. Inclusive policies, intended to allow 'disadvantaged' students more access to education are often scorned as a diminution of this standard.

Standardized Tests

The word standards is a code-name for 'an amalgam of current prejudice and the choices of this particular culture' (Lessing, 1972 cited in McLaren, 1986, p. xvii). The idea of a standard is based on the improbable premise that students of the same age will have similar abilities and backgrounds and that those abilities are measurable. My own first memory of a standardized test takes the form of a picture test in which we were instructed to circle the appropriate object when the teacher read the word. The word was 'icebox'. My experience did not include an icebox so I got it wrong. (That is why I remember it.) I now understand that standardized tests are 'necessarily embedded within a cultural frame of reference' (Samuda, 1995, p. 294). Much later, after my 'high IQ' had landed me a spot in a university, my wariness of IQ testing was confirmed by something called the Chitling IQ test. In it I was asked questions about Black American culture and failed miserably. My failure was not surprising, considering my background, just as the failure of others in the 'real' IQ tests is not surprising considering theirs. But I was lucky, in my case the test was not being used to assess my potential as a scholar as it is for them. The only difference between us is that my origins are in the dominant culture.

Another way in which standardized tests are biased is in their dependence on timing as a means of discriminating intelligence. The mistaken assumption that a quick response is the best response (Samuda, 1995, p. 295) makes timed tests biased against the poor reader, the slow thinker, and people who want to reflect on answers and assess the alternatives before going on to the next question. Timed tests create both a gender and culture bias (Sadker and Sadker, 1994; Samuda, 1995). The first time I did the Miller's Analogy test I had not learned the importance of speed. I was shocked when I was told that the time was up because I had completed only about two thirds of the paper. Fortunately, that proved to be enough to get me into graduate school. Years later, when I applied for a doctoral program, I was advised to take the test again to bring up my score, but to first buy the practice book and study for it. This brought my score up 15 points. Was this an intelligence test? All it proved was that I had the connections necessary to find the appropriate practice book.

Cultural Bias

Standardized tests, as we know them today, are based on the Army Mental Test devised by Carl Campbell Brigham early this century. The test was devised to sort soldiers — to determine appropriate ranks and tasks for new recruits. Brigham believed in the intellectual superiority of northern Europeans and felt that there was a need to prevent the 'continued propagation of defective strains' in the population (Sadker and Sadker, 1994, p. 152). It is not likely that his test reflected a balanced class and cultural component. By 1915, Columbia University feared that it would be inundated by the children of refugees. Brigham, now a professor at Princeton, adapted his Army Mental Test and called it the Scholastic Aptitude Test. Its use ensured that only certain kinds of people were admitted to Ivy League Colleges (Sadker and Sadker, 1994, p. 153).

Standardized tests today are reputedly less racist, sexist and classist. They are developed to reflect the kinds of knowledge taught in school (Rudman, 1995, p. 307). The irony of this method is that test constructors — by surveying textbooks and including concepts articulated in course outlines — are unwittingly reflecting and perpetuating the bias already present in our school systems. By using the schools as the basis for test construction, test constructors are compounding the effects of exclusionary curriculum and unidimensional teaching practices (Sadker and Sadker, 1994).

The gaps in standardized test scores among minority groups and white students and between males and females persist (Sadker and Sadker, 1994, p. 139). Although Samuda (1995) reports that the 'theories of genetic inferiority, cultural deprivation, and psycholinguistic deficit' have 'lost their respectability', overcome by a 'barrage of withering and devastating logic' (p. 296), they are not gone. Although we know that standardized test scores do not prove intelligence but rather indicate a test bias in favor of knowledge and test-taking skills of white males (Sadker and Sadker, 1994, p. 140), student placement decisions continue to be based on them — not only at the university level, but also throughout elementary and secondary school.

The natural outcome of standardized testing is tracking or ability grouping. Once a student has been assigned to a particular track, his or her place in the social order has been established. Children assigned to classes for the 'less able' or the 'less intelligent' are handicapped not only by the type of education they get — which is inferior in terms of 'curriculum content, type of instruction, degree of selection, frequency and type of teacher–student interaction and available educational resources' (Darder, 1991, p. 16) — but also in terms of the options open to students upon graduation. The assignment to a particular track also affects teachers' expectations for the students' success. Children considered to be intelligent (with a high IQ) and articulate are expected to be successful and will usually fulfill that expectation. Similarly, students considered dull and unmotivated just as consistently live up to the expectation for failure (Ryan, 1981). Disadvantaged students are further disadvantaged by the fact that teacher expectations for their success or failure have a stronger influence on them than on privileged students who are more likely to be influenced by parental expectations (Darder, 1991, p. 18). All of this contributes to a compounded disadvantage for students placed in anything other than the academic stream.

What is Normal?

Much of what is systemically violent is found in the constant comparisons that school personnel make among similarly aged students. Our schools are arranged around the premise that all children need to learn the same things and that they need to learn these things at the same time in their lives. For generations, students have been forced, through compulsory attendance legislation, to present themselves for an education at an arbitrarily determined early age. Upon presentation, children are placed in batches with similarly aged children and given a more or less standard curriculum.

The compulsory nature of schooling and the use of age-graded classroom units assumes that children of the same age are able to learn the same things and that they will share similar interests and abilities. The systematic use of standardization practices, the use of common curriculum, standardized tests and routine methods of instruction, all facilitate the classification process necessary to fit students into categories and classrooms. However, the same processes shape the child into someone who is able to fit those classifications. As Ball has observed:

> Through surveillance, observation, and classification [we] normalize children but do not seem to acknowledge or even understand the point that the developing child is an 'object' produced by those very same practices. (Ball, 1990, p. 12)

The assumption that there is a 'normal' developmental pace, and a method by which to measure that development, leads to the use of labels to identify students who do not proceed at that pace. The children who do not assimilate information and develop skills at the same time as their peers are dubbed as 'developmentally delayed'. This designation prevents students from being treated as individuals and often leads to their removal from the 'regular' classroom. They are stigmatized by the use of labels which set them apart (Monteath and Cooper, in press). All children are different and special but the labeling process attaches a stigma to that reality. In some cases, these differences are considered deviant to the extent that children are taken from their parents to become wards of the state. The Eugenics movement of the early part of this century used labels to justify many forms of violence. As Martineau will argue in Chapter 2, some of these abuses are still with us.

Students who are not identified as 'different' and remain in the classes for 'normal' students are not guaranteed that they will be spared systemic devaluing. If a student is unable to 'perform' (think about that word) on par with other students of a similar age, he or she can be 'failed'. There is a tendency in our culture to ask children, not how old they are, but what grade they are in. Children understand that age is the real question, and they respond with, 'Well, I am in Grade 7, but I failed Grade 2.' Before we know anything else about the child, we know his or her sense of failure.

The systemic violence of standardization, then, is visited upon children in several ways. It is based on testing and testing procedures which convince students that they are 'below average' without making them aware of the real meaning of average. They are not aware that the sample used to determine what is 'average' is usually limited to students with a white, Anglo-Saxon heritage. The majority of students are not 'average' and nor should they expect or be expected to be. Perhaps the most systemically violent aspect of standardization is in the conformity that it demands from all students. The need to be like others not only damages the personal psyche of individual students, it discourages the collective creative process. Much of the damage is done, not by the testing and assignment of grades and labels, but by the daily 'ritualization' (McLaren, 1986) of the acquisition of knowledge.

Looking for 'Me' in Meaning: Pedagogy

As society becomes less and less able to quantify, let alone assimilate, knowledge in the computer age, it becomes more and more ludicrous to defend a standard curriculum. Yet the 'banking' system of education, described by Freire (1970) in the early 70s is still the most prevalent approach to education found in our schools. Teachers continue to 'talk about reality as if it were motionless, static, compartmentalized, and predictable' (Freire, 1970, p. 57); teachers persist in their discussions of topics 'completely alien to the existential experience of the students' (Freire, 1970, p. 57); and pedagogical practices are often 'managerial rather than educative' (McLaren, 1986, p. 220). The 'banking' system is closely tied to the positivist view that knowledge is detached from the individual, that learning is impersonal and that learning outcomes are reproducible in similar forms in large groups of children. The standardization of curriculum and the ritual transmission forms of teaching continue to alienate and damage students.

The issues of pedagogy were obviously important to a group of junior high school students who were asked in focus groups to identify what it was about schools that made them angry (Johnson, 1996). Students listed hundreds of things that made them angry, but they were all connected to one of four categories: teaching practices, evaluation techniques, power relationships, and matters of equity (Johnson, 1996, p. 120). As Johnson suggested, all of these are related to each other. The poor teaching practices resulted in inequitable evaluation procedures and all of these were based on power relationships and matters of equity.

Neglect of the Affective

A reassessment of Maslow's (1968) hierarchy of basic needs, which was developed using a mostly white male sample, might encourage us to spend more time on 'belonging' and less on 'self-actualization'. Basic to our current systems of education is an assumption that students can focus their minds on material to be learned without involving the affective parts of the brain. The compartmentalization of the cognitive and affective is abusive in three ways. First, it assumes the same level of affective stability for all students and an equal ability to suspend the affective in favor of the cognitive. Secondly, it implies that there is more value to the cognitive and that the affective; that is, the elements of learning which are associated with the personal, are less worthy of development than are cognitive elements. Thirdly, by ignoring the affective, educators tacitly condone abuses and inequities of the students' experiences. These three assumptions have various damaging affects depending on the background of the student.

The rejection of the affective places unparalleled value on objectivity and reason. The children who do not come from an abusive background are affected by the lack of emphasis on the affective in that they are discouraged from becoming in touch with their feelings. They learn to scorn and fear emotions when others display them. This cultivation of cynicism, although reputed to be valued in business, does not produce well-rounded individuals able to productively relate to other people.

Boys in particular are encouraged to neglect their affective possibilities and concentrate on the more valuable and negotiable cognitive abilities. The retardation of the affective is most prevalent in male students as they are the ones most likely to be able to subvert the affective long enough to concentrate on the cognitive. They get good marks but pay the price in personal understanding. The expectation that they will be dominant is an unfulfilled promise of patriarchy (Orr, 1993) and many young men carry unresolved childhood traumas associated with power and control. A curriculum focused on cognitive learning does not provide outlets for developing self-understanding. (See Frank, Chapter 8.)

The children who have been abused, either in school or in other areas of their lives, are even more vulnerable to damage through the separation of the valued cognitive and the devalued affective. For them, the separation of the cognitive and affective is less possible. They are often unable to focus on the cognitive because they are overwhelmed by the affective, so they do not do well in school. Furthermore, they accept the blame for not being able to do the cognitive work. They think that something is wrong with them; they internalize the responsibility for both the abuse and their own inability to cope with it. The lack of attention to the affective in our schools teaches children to mask their feelings and disown their emotions:

> I had not been taught to critique the world as it appeared to me. Instead, years of uncritical, rote learning had taught me how not to know. (Brookes, 1992, p. 2)

Ignoring the affective also exacerbates abuse problems in other ways. Children look to adults to help and protect them. As long as the affective is disallowed in school, teachers have no access to information about the abuse that the child is experiencing. As Tite found in the research reported in Chapter 3, most teachers would rather not know. Many teachers believe that their responsibility to the child ceases with the development of the cognitive. By ignoring the affective, and by not providing an outlet for the examination of affective responses, school personnel unwittingly convince their students that the inequities and abuses that they are experiencing are normal and acceptable, for, if they were not, would not the authorities in their lives condemn and correct them? (Brookes, 1992).

It is ironic that a curriculum adapted to include the affective would probably increase cognitive understanding. Teachers and students would see benefits in cognitive abilities if students were able to connect information to their personal lives and use information in meaningful ways. Attention to the affective would also encourage students and their teachers to recognize practices that are abusive and incidents which are abuses of power. If children were taught how to recognize abuse in their own lives, they could understand that they are not responsible for the abusive actions of others. Teachers and students 'together seeking reality' (Freire, 1970) could also examine the dominance and submission structures in other aspects of society.

The purposeful neglect of the personal is fueled by and contributes to a dehumanized society. As long as facts, words and numbers are treasured, and personal feelings are subverted and discouraged, children will continue to become adults who believe that facts, words and numbers are the most important aspects of life. Pedagogy has long been geared to what Perry (1970) has described as a 'Type 2' learner — someone who assumes that all knowledge is known or knowable and that there is always a right or wrong answer. The mastery perception of learning is ideal for the transmission of dominant cultural values but is damaging to students from other backgrounds and to those who recognize the limitations of this format. A 'Type 4' learner (Perry, 1970) exhibits an alternative understanding of knowledge, recognizing learning as a life skill to be applied to personal and professional problem-solving. Children who refuse to memorize, who question teaching practices and insist on alternative interpretations of text can be frustrated within the school system and serve to frustrate their teachers. Such students fail the obedience component of pedagogy.

A Question of Obedience

Once we become aware of the damage that abuse of authority can do to a young life, it is necessary to rethink the absolute and automatic immunity that has traditionally been afforded to those in authority. The only way to protect children from abuse by authorities is to teach them to question authoritative actions and to understand the dynamics of power-based relationships. Concerned parents and teachers encourage children to evaluate authority figures and to comply only with demands that are reasonable and reasoned. Such training has its drawbacks because many teachers are unused to reasoned defiance, and a school-aged 'critical thinker' is likely to be viewed with suspicion.

As more and more students reach an understanding of the potential for abuse, they become more and more wary of authority. This may lead to a series of scuffles over minor issues and result in a confrontational atmosphere in the classroom replete with daily power struggles. Students and teachers can find endless issues of contention. The wearing of hats, swearing, the size of poster paper, the process of collecting papers, the ritual of checking homework assignments — any one of these has the potential to become a serious disciplinary issue. When students step over the 'line', school authorities believe that they must stop defiance when it starts — before it becomes a problem. They become entrenched in their righteousness and the students become equally entrenched in theirs. Students are rarely winners in this power struggle (see Watkinson, Chapter 12, this volume), as disobedience can cost them the right to attend school — and all the attendant rights that that includes. The power of the teacher as gatekeeper to success is often wasted and abused in attempts to maintain control.

A major difficulty for school officials faced with disobedient children is dealing with those parents who have failed to do initial obedience training or, worse, have encouraged reasoned non-compliance. School authorities often assume that parents want strong discipline and conformity because, in the current school structures, these translate into good marks. Parents are expected to encourage students to fulfill the school's requirements in order to attain the honors, such as self-esteem and university entrance, that are the school's to bestow. Parents whose attitudes to authority differ from those of the school may be considered by the school officials to be at best ignorant or uncooperative, and at worst unfit parents. (See Abbey, Chapter 4 in this volume.) The authority of the school as the seat for the dispensation of societal norms serves to overwhelm objections from individual families. This is especially true if the family is not of white, middle-class origin.

In issues of obedience, the question of classism is not far from the surface. Parents who are alienated from the school system are not in a position to protect their children from systemic violence. Whether a reluctant gifted child or a misdiagnosed autistic child, many children do not have the protection provided by the threat of parental intervention. When systemic violence happens to these children they have no-one to defend them from its damage.

Incidents requiring irrational compliance make some students keenly aware of the potential for abuse among those who hold power. Many accept this as the way the world works, but others defy authority when it is used without respect and sensibility. Once students have learned that people placed in positions of authority cannot always be trusted to do what they have been entrusted to do, the relationship between student and teacher changes. Some school practices are indefensible, yet legal power resides with the school. Children who have been raised to be critical thinkers do not understand compromise. Unfortunately, these children are unlikely to win their cases. (See Watkinson, Chapter 12 in this volume.) They find themselves barred from the school with their grievances unresolved. When these students become dropouts, they and all of society suffer, for lack of schooling affects their potential contributions to the future.

For Your Own Good: Punishment

Compulsory education, which operates using grades based on age groups, requires teachers to attend to the needs of large numbers of children who are all at approximately the same developmental level. At the kindergarten level, it requires the tying of thirty pairs of shoes and the finding of thirty sets of mittens. In the primary school, teachers must deal with thirty students competing for similar resources — swings, basketballs, paint boxes or computers — all at the same time. By the time the group has reached middle years, teachers are expected to educate thirty people going through similar life changes and intensified peer pressure. It is little wonder that draconian methods of control in the classroom persist. Most punishments are intended to enforce obedience; in the child being punished, and in the others by example. Teachers may not privately approve of punishment, but they may be forced to apply control measures because there are no alternatives. It is the teachers' duty to preserve a safe learning environment, and this usually means teacher–student conflict is resolved using punishment and other administratively sponsored means of control. Add to this the boredom and repetition of routine rote learning, and it is little wonder that teachers and students have disagreements. The physical make up of the classroom and its context necessitate the maintenance of order by force.

Control

When students are gathered together in classrooms, there is obviously a need for some method of control, and the authority of school personnel to punish students is backed up by law. School officials are entitled to 'correct' students — even if correction requires physical violence. In Canada, this is written into the Criminal Code. Section 43 states that:

> Every schoolteacher, parent or person standing in the place of a parent is justified in using force by way of correction toward a pupil or child, as the case may be, who is under his [sic] care, if the force does not exceed what is reasonable under the circumstances. (Martins Annual Criminal Code, 1996, p. 86)

Principals and teachers have the legal right to insist that students fulfill even senseless assignments if they believe that it is for the students' 'own good' (Miller, 1990b). Although the teacher's right to strike children is assured, many school boards have outlawed the practice through local board policies. But punishment, whether it is physical or whether it takes other forms, remains an important aspect of education.

Alice Miller's (1990a, 1990b, 1990c) analysis of punishment as a form of child abuse, deconstructed the processes we use to control children and also examined our personal motives for continuing to use punishment. Miller (1990b) suggested that those who believe in punishing children for their 'own good' are basing their actions on a deeply rooted misunderstanding of things that happened to them when they were children. Miller views society's acceptance of authoritative methods of punishment as part of a cycle of abuse.

The cycle is started when well-meaning parents, who have been punished by their own parents, punish children. The punishment is incongruent with other beliefs that the parents have previously espoused and is, therefore, incomprehensible to the children. The punishment and the parents' values are in conflict. On the one hand, the parents claim to love the children and want what is best for them. They have set up the rules of fairness to mean that big people do not hurt little people. But, with the other hand, often quite literally, the parents are breaking their own rules. The children respond to punishment by rationalizing away the inequity and contradictoriness of the situation. They assume that the punishment was deserved, that the punishment was justice, and that adults must do this to children because they love them and want to prevent them from becoming bad people. The anger and the pain of the moment are sublimated by these more noble arguments. Years later, when these children find themselves in a position of authority over other children, they then have a residue of anger, resentment and righteousness to dole out on the next generation. Thus the cycle is continued. The right to punish is carried on into the next generation without thought for the fairness of the process or consideration of other methods to deal with misdemeanors.

The use of 'teacher power' (Gordon, 1974), in which teachers use authoritarian methods to control students, often results in a negative cycle which is ultimately damaging to the child but is equally damaging to the teacher. Punishment may elicit compliance from some students but it results in acts of aggression from others. The spiraling power struggles waste time and drain energy. Students drawn into these power struggles learn to use power: 'They are likely to become tyrants, and, in their tyranny, disrespectors of the feelings, needs, and property of others' (Gordon, 1974, p. 212).

Negative experiences with power relationships have different effects on males and females. Boys who are subjected to unequal power relationships with adults may seek to re-establish their own dominance through violence against others. Girls are more likely to turn that violence on themselves through various self-destructive behaviors (Steinem, 1992). But for both genders, criminal behavior may be the delayed result of bottled up childhood aggression:

> Biographies of criminals . . . give us plenty of information on the origin of criminal behavior . . . If parents fail to respect and satisfy their children's needs, their sons and daughters will later transfer their claim to other people and institutions. Using violence or manipulation they will attempt to force the world at large to respect and satisfy their, by now perverted, needs. (Stettbacher, 1991, p. 107–8)

Rather than contributing to the cycle of systemic violence, the schools could serve as instruments to help children come to terms with their anger and their unresolved feelings. This would allow 'affirmative feelings, which are not based on denial or feelings of duty or guilt, [to] emerge' (Miller, 1990c, p. 23).

Reflections on School Punishment

Miller (1990a) contends that, in order to interrupt the punishment cycle, adults must examine their own pasts in order to understand what happened to them during their childhoods and to evaluate their interactions with children. As Miller described it: 'Only those who are themselves victims of such deeds and allow them to remain repressed are in turn in danger of destroying other lives' (1990a, p. 191). Brookes (1992) also insisted that education should facilitate the personalized interpretation of life experiences to enable students to recognize and deal with abuse, injustice, and inequality. Only when students have come to terms with these issues will they be equipped to deal with cognitive understanding.

If beginning teachers are to become aware of the potential dangers of an unexamined past, there is a need for a process through which they can reflect on their own educational experiences. In my class, education students have an opportunity to describe critical incidents from their own school experiences and reflect in small groups on the emotions, motives and themes arising from these stories. The process was originally intended as an exercise in relating personal memories of school to current teacher practice. It was not intended as an examination of power and punishment. However, these themes are startlingly pervasive in the stories students tell. I have collected their stories as a series of incidents, as yet unpublished elsewhere, that I will refer to by number here.

The students are routinely amazed at the intensity of emotion that they feel in recalling these incidents. As one student commented: 'Today when I think back on this event that happened over 14 years ago, I still get a knot in my stomach' (Incident 55). Others were surprised to think that the things that had happened to them might be abusive. Students who had failed classes or who had been forced to repeat grades were particularly vocal about the power they had regained by revisiting the experience through this exercise. Many students had never before questioned the actions of the adults involved in the incidents and had assumed personal blame for failure. Several spoke of the 'redemptive' power of speaking about these experiences from the safety of adulthood:

> It was extremely emotional to both read your own and listen to the others' worst school experience. I could identify with the pain and embarrassment experienced by the others, and in a way, you realize that you are not alone. However, I find the whole thing frightening, because of the obvious effects these experiences have had on our entire lives; the complexes developed and the intensity of feeling remain. (Incident 73)

Elements of Punishment

It is probably not surprising that many 'worst school experiences' involved punishment. The physical aspect of punishment was evident; there were strappings, ear pullings, cheek pinchings, and bottom slappings. There were also incidents in which teachers disregarded students' privacy and personal spaces and used other methods of control that may have been equally damaging. Students reported being humiliated, singled out, embarrassed and excluded.

Sometimes it was the way in which the punishment had been administered that was disturbing. One student described a punishment that she had witnessed:

The teacher and the student were standing at the front of the class and she
was using all her strength when she strapped the boy's palms . . . his eyes
were filled with tears. He was so humiliated and the teacher kept hitting.
(Incident 47)

Students often resented the public display more than the punishment itself. One
Grade 5 girl was hit with a stick on the buttocks in front of the class (Incident 64).
Another reported: 'I felt embarrassed and hurt because she did this to me in front
of all my classmates' (Incident 58).

The most unsettling part of the students' stories was the range of minor infractions that had provoked the punishments. One student was strapped because
he had not completed his homework for several days (Incident 47). Another missed
assembly for the same reason (Incident 53). Students were hit for not singing loud
enough (Incident 60), talking (Incident 62), not understanding the math assignment
(Incident 63), and not drinking their juice (Incident 54). Two Grade 1 students were
spanked in front of the class for laughing together after completing their seat work
(Incident 57). Students in one class had their 'fingers smashed on the desk' for not
holding the pencil correctly (Incident 61). The memories of these recent graduates
were laced with images of adults striking children for rather trivial offenses.

Sometimes students were mistakenly punished for things that they had not
done. One student was pulled out of a line and sent to the principal's office for
talking. The culprit had been the girl behind her who owned up to it. The student
found out that the other student had confessed, but neither the teacher, nor the principal, apologized (Incident 12). In other incidents, children were falsely accused
of swearing (Incident 36), faking injuries (Incident 27), name calling (Incident 4
and 102), and hitting classmates (Incident 93).

The punishment was exacerbated when the students were unsure what they were
being punished for (Incident 58) or didn't know how to correct their errors. The
student left behind to redo her work during an assembly explained her frustration:

I know I was supposed to do my assignment over again, only this time
to do it right. But, how was I to do that? What I did the first time was
what I thought was right. What was wrong with it? At least tell me that.
(Incident 53)

Power struggles often culminated in threats of removing the student from the class.
One teacher reduced a student's biology mark from 82 to 49 because she had not
rewritten the question and did not use full sentences in her answers. When she
approached him, he told her that he expected half the class to be gone from his
class by Christmas and that if she were to 'continue in this irresponsible manner,
she would be one of them' (Incident 49). Another student asked for help after she
had failed the first mathematics exam. She was told that she was never going to 'get
anywhere in education or make anything of herself' so she might as well drop math
right now.

For many students the painful experiences were the result of being centered out because of their 'special needs'. One student, diagnosed as hyperactive 'was sentenced to remain in the corner of the classroom with a bookshelf dragged in as a barrier between [him] and the class' (Incident 52). Some students' memories included punishment for being too successful. In one incredible story, a student in Grade 5 was given an independent study unit to work on. When she finished early and tried to hand it in, the teacher refused to accept it. She was summoned to the principal's office, lectured for working ahead, and told to do another project but to keep pace with the class!

Student responses to these incidents were vehemently held feelings of anger directed toward individual teachers and the school system itself. Some responded with self-hatred or were turned against learning. Others described a wish to flee. For example, the child who was strapped in front of the class for not having his homework done, sat quietly down for a few minutes and then ran out of the room after yelling a few profanities. As his classmate described it: 'The teacher acted so surprised at the boy's action' (Incident 47). Usually students just bottled up the emotion in order to 'hate the teacher from that day on' (Incident 59). Sometimes the punishment resulted in taunting and ridicule from other classmates, which made the students hate both their teachers and their classmates (Incident 52).

The most tragic cases were those that mirrored Alice Miller's (1990b) argument concerning the internalization of blame. Whether the punishment was deserved or not, children learned disgust for themselves. They felt 'insecure and stupid' (Incident 69):

> All I could figure was that I must be stupid or bad. Why else would she punish me this way? Either she didn't like me or I'm dumb. But I honestly thought that she did like me. I must be dumb. (Incident 53)

The students recalling these incidents were obviously not so repulsed by them that they stopped learning or abandoned education. They survived long enough to acquire at least one university degree and were committed enough to education to consider it as a career. However, even in these people, the memories of punishment had affected their careers:

> The school system has served to kill my love of learning, and my pride in my work and myself. It has slowly turned me into a machine whose spirit has been lost in the battle to be the best.

Sources of Violence

The policies and practices associated with standardization, exclusive pedagogy, and punishment, prevent learning and may also foster a climate of violence. The same practices contribute to dehumanization, stratification and abuse, which are systemically violent and cause students to respond in violent ways. Sometimes the violence is aimed toward teachers and administrators, but more often it is directed toward fellow students or the self.

Dehumanization

Systemic violence begins with the expectation that all students of similar ages should and can learn the same things. Children are placed with large groups of similarly aged students and teachers are forced to adopt methods of control and routine that would be better left to the military, the workforce, or the penal system. The sheer number of students contributes to teacher and administrator detachment, but dehumanization is further assured by the conviction, on the part of school personnel, that their job is to aid in the cognitive development of students and that the development of the affective is better left to the home, community, or church. The reality is that for many children these three institutions no longer exist.

The school environment is often based on a military orderliness intended to control large groups of similarly skilled students. Influenced by both military and business expertise, schools adopt oppressive bureaucratic structures (Watkinson, 1993). Teachers can do little to change that environment; they take a job, expecting to act *in loco parentis*, and find themselves acting like jail guards. In a quest for conformity, students are monitored in their coming and going, they are required to carry hall passes and must seek permission to leave the room. Their activities are directed, and timed, and their learning is scheduled into periods of work followed by short breaks. Such regimentation requires rules and punishment and administrative models that rely on differentiated power relations. Managers and supervisors are replaced in schools by principals and teachers and the students assume the role of workers — doing the bidding of the overseers or paying the consequences (Watkinson, 1993).

Routinized delivery of education ritualizes inattention to individual needs. The grade by grade, standard course by standard course, application of Eurocentric curriculum does little to recognize the individual. The dehumanization of the bureaucratic school manifests itself in a poisoned environment that is not only lacking in concern for the individual but also fosters alienation and harassment. This results in 'common-sense' violence, violence that is accepted because it is hidden behind the 'banality of normal and ordinary actions and practices which render [it] invisible' (Watkinson, 1993, p. 17). In spite of the regimentation and attempts at control, student-to-student harassment is rampant, partly because administrative officials are unwilling to intervene (Larkin, 1994) and partly because the activities are accepted as 'normal'. Many activities that make students feel uncomfortable, and which they reject as personally intimidating, their teachers call 'normal' activities because they happen so often. When, as a parent, I complained about 'pantsing' (a practice in which children grab other children's pants and yank them down in public), I was told it was 'normal' because everybody was doing it. 'Normal' is not the same a 'right'.

Dehumanization is also found in the separation of cognitive development from affective development and in bureaucratic structures intended to keep students 'in their places'. Teachers are encouraged to treat students as faceless, voiceless entities whose individual differences and difficulties make no difference to the implementation of norms and rules. Individuals lose their importance and, in the process, the importance of people is denied.

Stratification

Dehumanization affects all children in the school system but is even more damaging to students who are 'other'. When children learn that there are people who are privileged and people who are 'other', they learn that sexism and racism are normal. A critical examination of all aspects of life — the processes, situations and circumstances encountered on a daily basis — would be necessary in order for students to learn the balance that is the basis of the distribution of resources. This would require deconstruction of much that is considered 'normal' in our school systems. The definition for 'normal' provides a distorted picture of human offspring which includes aspects of society that are culturally relevant only for a small, Eurocentric, male portion of the population. This standard serves to label and discard most of the population and even stigmatizes many white males.

A diagnostic labeling process assumes that students who qualify for these labels are more like each other than they are like other children and serves to stigmatize them in ways that impede learning (Monteath and Cooper, in press). There are monetary values attached: students with labels command more in government funding and access to public resources. School systems rely on labels and the processes associated with them to provide special programs and to ascertain funding entitlement. This may or may not be in the best interest of the children involved.

Official labels are not the only labels in use in our schools. Individuals are described as 'a little slow', or a 'disruptive element'. Teachers accept the stereotypes associated with 'good students' and 'scholarship material'. This more casual ordering is also dangerous because it allows for the further stratification in classist, sexist, racist and heterosexist ways.

Privilege for some students means the withholding of resources from others. The skewed allocation of resources has been accepted as 'common sense' (Ng, 1993) for so long that it often goes unnoticed and unchallenged. Male athletic programs use a disproportionate amount of school resources. Science, mathematics and technology programs continue to grow while music, art and domestic sciences are cut back. Privilege can also be reflected in our classroom routines, rituals and relationships. Teacher time and attention, opportunity for speech, access to positive reinforcement are all resources that can be distributed unevenly. Unequal allocation of resources, whether physical or ephemeral, systemically withholds from some students the learning opportunities enjoyed by others.

These practices are manifested in small day-to-day incidents intended to promote learning rather than to retard it. The effect, whether intentional or not, is systemically violent. As long as teachers are unwilling to intervene in 'normal' practices, which ghettoize and dissociate children, the common-sense racism and sexism of our adult lives will remain unchanged.

The separation by privilege is sometimes a very subtle unintentional process. For example, most teachers are disbelieving when they are first introduced to Sadker and Sadker's (1994) premise that girls are short-changed in schools. The Sadkers can demonstrate bias and do when they get the chance, but the bias is so subtle, so 'common sense' (Ng, 1993), that most people do not notice it. Teachers who are unaware of their own biases cannot be expected to identify similar biases in the students they teach. In fact, when teachers attempt to 'interrupt patriarchy' (Lewis, 1993) by examining the classroom for androcentric bias, discussing the implications of patriarchy with students, and using inclusive practices, they are often accused of having a female bias (Lewis, 1993). Tactics of critical education are difficult to carry out in a context in which most teachers do not realize or accept that bias exists.

Systemic violence is particularly pervasive in the lives of students who are coming to grips with a sexuality that is not unconditionally accepted in our society. Children who have homosexual tendencies are seriously scarred by the way they are treated in school and by the way homophobia is encouraged (Harris, 1993). This is damaging to children to the extent that many young people who believe themselves to be homosexual may attempt suicide because they fear rejection by family, classmates and teachers.

Abuse

School complicity allows the systemic violence of dehumanization and stratification to continue. The processes that uphold these aspects of violence are underlying factors in the continued acceptance of physical, emotional, psychological and sexual abuse of children both in schools and in society. School officials are responsible for child abuse on two levels.

On one level, schools are responsible for child abuse because they ignore and thereby condone abuse that happens to children outside of school hours. They ignore abuse by reporting only the cases that must be reported, the ones that are so blatant that they cannot be ignored (see Tite, Chapter 3 in this volume). They condone it by not talking about it in school, by filling the curriculum so full of other things that there is no place for personal understanding of abuse. By failing to provide a forum in which abused children can learn what it is and why it happens, they make it impossible for children to recognize abuse when it does happen. The damage of abuse is not only in the abuse itself, it is in the internalization of the guilt, fear, self-loathing and helplessness that attend it. If children are not allowed to talk about abuse, what it is, whose fault it is, and how it continues to happen, they will store the hatred and anger until it erupts in various destructive ways.

On another level, accepted school practices and procedures are of themselves abusive. Traditionally and legally, teachers and other school authorities have the right to use physical violence to uphold their authority. The power to physically punish children has been diminished as individual school jurisdictions have adopted policies against it. However, the right to punish remains and children continue to be publicly castigated and subjected to other forms of humiliation. The systemic nature of abuse is more than the physical and psychological uses of power to control children. Systemic violence also involves the use of competitive marking systems and exclusive pedagogy to diminish children's senses of self and to demean by omission the cultures and traditions of those who are 'other'.

Systemic violence is subtle. Students complain about aspects of it but author-itarian child rearing is so fully entrenched in our culture that few of us, even the children most affected by it, are willing to condemn it. It has 'worked' for hundreds of years. It has helped to stratify, control and organize our society for generations. It has become so endemic to our concept of child rearing that those most affected by it embrace it as the right way to treat children and claim the right to repeat the abuse on their own children. Students who have been taught to accept authority, even over the force of reason and respect, are ripe for abuse. The affects of abuse are felt by everyone. The pain inflicted on the child does not end there, it is enacted on all those who encounter that child in the future.

When we respond to violence in schools, if we respond at all, it is to the chil-dren who are violent. When a child forces another to do his or her bidding, we call it extortion; when an adult does the same thing to a child, it is called correction. When a student hits another student it is assault; when a teacher hits a student it is for the child's 'own good'. When a student embarrasses, ridicules or scorns another student it is harassment, bullying or teasing. When a teacher does it, it is sound pedagogical practice.

Many school boards have recently adopted violence policies that spell out the consequences for students committing violent acts. Most ascribe to a 'zero tol-erance' rule that states that any act of violence will result in a suspension from school. Students who break the rules are not welcome in school. The events and activities leading up to the act of violence are not important; they are often not even recorded. It is the reaction that gets the attention. The child who responds in violence to racist taunts is more likely to be expelled than is the child throwing the slurs. A child who is pushed into a corner and responds in anger is considered just as violent as the student who is an aggressive bully. Zero tolerance dispenses with them all (Lee, 1994).

Students' reactions to systemic violence are seldom acted out in immediate and physical terms. That is why it is so difficult to establish a cause and affect relationship between systemic violence and the kind of violence that happens in school. Responses to systemic violence may be acted out in the form of defiance, neglect of duty, withdrawal, or addiction. Students may become self-destructive, courting dangers, closing doors, and ignoring opportunities. The violence to others is more overt, and more likely to be connected to teacher actions. Children may respond by harassing teachers or their peers. They may damage property, or write graffiti on school walls. Some of them may respond with verbal and phys-ical attacks on teachers and administrators. These children are quickly excluded from the school system before they can do any more harm.

The lessons of exclusion and privilege that students learn in school and the student's placement in the hierarchy of intelligence will have repercussions not only for those children but for our society. School placements and school records play an extremely important part in the opportunities that people get in life. High school dropouts are often the abused or the disobedient who have chosen to take their chances with poverty rather than be pushed around. Unfortunately, that chance taken with poverty is a longshot and poverty usually wins.

Systemic Justice

Systemic violence is carried out through a progression of assumptions that begin with a belief that it is possible to standardize students, student abilities and student expectations. This belief allows school officials to stratify students, ignore individual differences, and standardize treatment. This is done in the belief that students will benefit, that they will learn valuable lessons, in spite of the power struggles necessary to enforce this standardization. Not only does this system retard personal development and the fulfillment of personal potential, it also fails society. Children who have been arrested in their development by damaging practices in the school system do not contribute to society in the ways that they might have done had the school system lived up to expectations. If schools are to fulfill their potential as catalysts in the creation of a more equitable society, educational systemic violence must be addressed.

In this book we advocate systemic justice. We want a system in which all students are treated honestly and fairly and in which all students are able to reach a positive, fulfilled adulthood. Addressing systemic violence at the system level would require a critical examination of the values and interpretations of everything that happens in schools: an examination of the things we teach, the way we teach them and the way we evaluate that teaching. It would require us to look at who is included and who is excluded and at the processes of exclusion. It would necessitate a thorough rethinking of what education is, the goals of our school systems, the processes used to meet those goals and the outcomes associated with those processes. In order to do a complete 'problematic' (Carr and Kemmis, 1986) assessment of our education systems, we must begin by allowing students the privilege of critical pedagogy.

Systemic justice would require attitudinal changes at every level of education and commitment on the part of all school personnel. The rethinking of school structures would, of necessity, be a collective process. As individuals, we can begin in the hope that we will eventually be joined by the critical mass necessary for change. Our children deserve it.

References

BALL, S. (ed.) (1990) *Foucault and Education*, London, Routlege.

BOWLES, S. and GINTES, H. (1976) *Schooling in Capitalist America*, New York, Basic Books.

BROOKES, A. (1992) *Feminist Pedagogy: An Autobiographical Approach*, Halifax, NS, Fernwood Press.

CARNOY, M. (1974) *Education as Cultural Imperialism*, New York, David McKay.

CARR, W. and KEMMIS, S. (1986) *Becoming Critical: Education, Knowledge and Action Research*, London, Falmer Press.

DARDER, A. (1991) *Culture and Power in the Classroom*, Toronto, OISE Press

ELLSWORTH, E. (1994) 'Why doesn't this feel empowering? Working through the repressive myths of critical pedagogy', in STONE, L. (ed.) *The Education Feminism Reader*, New York, Routledge.

EPP, J.R. and WATKINSON, A.M. (in press) *Systemic Violence in Education: Promise Broken*, New York, SUNY Press.

FREIRE, P. (1970) *Pedagogy of the Oppressed*, (M.B. Ramos, trans.) NY, Herder and Herder.

GORDON, T. (1974) *T.E.T.: Teacher Effectiveness Training*, New York, David McKay.

GORE, J. (1993) *The Struggle for Pedagogies: Critical and Feminist Discourses as Regimes of Truth*, New York, Routledge.

HARRIS, L. (1993) *Hostile Hallways: The AAUW Survey on Sexual Harassment in America's Schools*, Washington, DC, American Association of University Women Educational Foundation.

JOHNSON, D. (1996) Sources of student anger in schools. Unpublished master's thesis, Lakehead University, Thunder Bay, Ontario, Canada.

KAUFMAN, M. (1987) 'The construction of masculinity and the triad of men's violence', in KAUFMAN, M. (ed.) *Beyond Patriarchy: Essays by Men on Pleasure, Power and Change*, Toronto, Oxford University Press, pp. 1–29.

LARKIN, J. (1994) *Sexual Harassment: High School Girls Speak Out*, Toronto, Second Story Press.

LEE, E. (1994, June). Zero tolerance for the violence of racism. A paper presented at the Canadian Society for the Study of Education XXII Annual Conference, Calgary, Alberta.

LEWIS, M. (1993) *Without a Word: Teaching Beyond Women's Silence*, New York, Routledge.

MARTINS ANNUAL CRIMINAL CODE (1996) Aurora, Ontario, Canada Law Book Inc.

MASLOW, A. (1968) 'Some fundamental questions that face the normative social psychologist', *Journal of Humanistic Psychology*, **8**, 2, pp. 143–53.

MCLAREN P. (1986) *Schooling as a Ritual Performance*, London, Routledge & Kegan Paul.

MILLER, A. (1990a) *Banished Knowledge*, New York, Double Day.

MILLER, A. (1990b) *For Your Own Good*, New York, The Noonday Press.

MILLER, A. (1990c) *The Untouched Key*, New York, Double Day.

MONTEATH, S. and COOPER, K. (in press) 'Lethal labels: Miseducative discourse about educative experiences', In EPP, J.R. and WATKINSON, A.M. (eds) *Systemic Violence in Education: Promise Broken*, New York, SUNY Press.

NG, R. (1993) 'A woman out of control: Deconstructing sexism and racism in the university', *Canadian Journal of Education*, **18**, 3, pp. 189–205.

ORR, D.J. (1993) 'Toward a critical rethinking of feminist pedagogical praxis and resistant male students', *Canadian Journal of Education*, **18**, 3, pp. 239–55.

PERRY, W. JR (1970) *Forms of Intellectual and Ethical Development in the College Years: A Scheme*, New York, Holt Rinehart and Winston.

RUDMAN, H. (1995) 'The standardized test flap: An effort to sort out fact from fiction, truth from deliberate hyperbole', in ROBERTS, L. and CLIFTON, R. (eds) *Contemporary Canadian Educational Issues*, Toronto, Nelson Canada.

RYAN, W. (1981) *Equality*, New York, Pantheon Books.

SADKER, M. and SADKER D. (1994) *Failing at Fairness: How Our Schools Cheat Girls*, New York, Simon and Schuster.

SAKIYAMA, C. (1996) Children's response to death. Unpublished master's project, Lakehead University, Thunder Bay, Ontario, Canada.

SAMUDA, R. (1995) 'Assessing the abilities of minority students within a multiethnic milieu', in ROBERTS, L. and CLIFTON, R. (eds) *Contemporary Canadian Educational Issues*, Toronto, Nelson Canada.

SEARS, J. (1992) 'Educators, homosexuality, and homosexual students: Are personal feelings related to professional beliefs?' in HARBEC, K. (ed.) *Coming Out of the Classroom*

Closet: Gay and Lesbian Students, Teachers and Curricula, Binghamton, N.Y., Harrington Park Press.

STEINEM, G. (1992) *Revolution from Within*, Boston, Little, Brown & Co.

STETTBACHER, J.K. (1991) *Making Sense of Suffering*, New York, Dutton.

THORNHILL, E. (1995, June) Confronting race, breaking silence, shifting paradigms: Locus, voice and praxis. A paper presented at the XXIII Annual Conference of the Canadian Society for the Study of Education, Montreal, Quebec.

WATKINSON, A. (1993, June) Inequality and or hormones. Paper presented at the XXI Annual Conference of the Canadian Society for the Study of Education, Ottawa, Ontario.

WEBSTER'S DICTIONARY (1988) Baltimore, Harbor House Publishers.

Part 1

School Complicity in Child Abuse

2   Dangerous Liaison: The Eugenics Movement and the Educational State

Sheila Martineau

eu·gen·ics (yu jen'iks), n. (used with a sing. v.) a science concerned with improving a breed or species, esp. the human species, by such means as influencing or encouraging reproduction by persons presumed to have desirable genetic traits. (Random House Webster's College Dictionary, 1992)

The Eugenics–Education Alliance

By the early twentieth century, the educational state and the eugenics movement in Canada had formed a partnership of Puritanical proportions, inflicting a tyranny of social controls and devastating the lives of disadvantaged children who were capriciously classified as *feeble-minded* and unfit for breeding (Curtis, 1988; McLaren, 1990; Weber, 1958).[1] Eugenicists used both environmental and hereditarian arguments to popularize their politics, until their elitist careers finally ended in disgrace along with the eugenics-based 'final solution' of the Nazi Holocaust (McLaren, 1990). The alliance between eugenics and education represents a *dangerous liaison* in Canada's history, a liaison that is recurring today.

Eugenics emerged as a social welfare movement in Canada between 1885 and 1945 (McLaren, 1990). Prior to this period the educational state was constructed in the mid-nineteenth century, from about 1836 to 1871, during our turbulent transformation from an agricultural to an industrial economy (Curtis, 1988). The eugenics movement arose in response to the arrival of European immigrants who comprised the predominantly Catholic lower classes of early industrialization. The Protestant mission of the eugenicists was to protect the public health and improve the 'master race' by controlling the immigrant masses. In this context, poor and immigrant children were the objects of an inquisition imposed by eugenicists through the compulsory educational system (McLaren, 1990).

The Politics of Childhood

This chapter is a social critique of the eugenics–education alliance from the perspective of the *politics of childhood*, a concept that acknowledges the capacities of children and that 'revisions' children as political actors, not as just the politically acted upon (Thorne, 1987). Such a perspective requires addressing child abuse and neglect, and child labor and exploitation. It also advocates the inclusion of children and youth in public planning, promotes their active participation in community projects, and advances a culture of children's rights and responsibilities (Martineau, 1996). The politics of childhood locates the possibility of children's agency in a post-structural analysis that 'defines discourse and structure as something which can be acted upon and changed' (Davies, 1993, p. 11). Facilitating the agency of children and youth across classes and cultures conflicts with the re-emergence of the eugenics–education alliance for example, the linkage of school, health, and social services in inner-city schools and the medical diagnosis of *attention-deficit disorder* in children (discussed later in this chapter). Embedded in this conflict is the *possibility* that if the present can be used to explicate the past, the past can be used to illuminate the present (Foley, 1991; Saran, 1985; Somers, 1992). This seeming circularity intersects with linearity, neither of which can or should be dismissed (much as we may try).

My social critique, in the form of a bibliographic essay, focuses on the *violence against children* perpetrated by educators and eugenicists. This violence is viewed from the insight that children are 'complex actors, strategists, performers, users of language, [and] creators of culture' (Thorne, 1987, p. 101). Children can become particularly politicized under adverse conditions, and paying '[a]ttention to children may expand our overall notions of "the political"' (Thorne, 1987, pp. 99–100).[2] When children's re/actions to adversity are viewed negatively by adults as rebellion, aggression, disobedience, conduct disorder, or failure to conform, then children's political agency (and passive resistance) interacts with adult violence in systems of domination. The eugenics–education alliance is a system of domination and a seat of child abuse and neglect sanctioned by social policy and constituted by the good intentions of educators and eugenicists.

Symbolic Violence

The eugenics–educational alliance was, and is, intermingled with immigration and the maintenance of class and cultural inequality. The maintenance of inequality is defined as 'the rate of return on educational capital', euphemistically expressed as *symbolic capital*. The symbolic capital of the educational state is realized through *symbolic power* — the power to name, to constitute or construct knowledge — which manifests in *symbolic violence* — the power to impose arbitrary, and to arbitrarily impose, expressions of social reality through the 'instruments of knowledge' (Harker 1990, pp. 94–5).[3] The political power of the early educational state was invested in the social policies of the eugenics movement when eugenicists conducted their experimental examinations on the minds and bodies of poor immigrant children in the *class-rooms* of compulsory education.

Compulsory schooling theoretically afforded all children an education. But in an era when the corporal punishment of children was a disciplinary norm, the educational state's symbolic instruments of knowledge manifested in the corporal punishment and emotional humiliation of children. In Britian, compulsory school attendance exposed the now visible plight of abused and neglected children living in poverty and raised the concerns of early educators (Behlmer, 1982), while these same educators exercised violence as a learning tool and a disciplinary weapon. The imported British school system informed the educational state in Canada, and it was educated elites who formed a eugenics movement to 'discipline' the ignorant and immigrant masses.

The 'Doubleness' of Discipline

Discipline is a word of multiple meanings; it is both noun and verb, and represents at least a dozen different applications. Education is a discipline and we are disciplined through education. The rhetoric of discipline often masks child abuse, and child abuse too frequently masquerades as discipline, in public and private realms. A useful distinction between discipline and abuse is the perceived difference between *instructive* actions and *abusive* actions. In the educational state and the eugenics movement, abusive actions were conflated with instructive actions such that symbolic power and symbolic violence manifested as state-sanctioned child abuse and neglect; and corporal punishment and emotional humiliation, among other abusive indignities, were reconstructed as instructive disciplines and educational techniques.

In this educational context, the 'doubleness in a word like "discipline"' informs the link between power and knowledge (Hoskin, 1990, p. 51). In a Foucauldian analysis, discipline is central to the power–knowledge apparatus of the educational state; it is the 'examination' through which the superimposition of power and knowledge upon minds and bodies may be understood (Hoskin, 1990, p. 51). Education and the educated eugenicists were invested in a technology of surveillance that objectified children through a form of class and cultural 'appraisal' that sorted the normal from the abnormal and reflected the religious dualism between good and bad (Ball, 1990, pp. 159, 161). The obsessive examination of minds and bodies that marked modernism, and the classifications of immigrant children as unfit and inferior, manifested in the label of feeble-mindedness.

Feeble-mindedness

In 1919, professional botanist and burgeoning eugenicist W.L. Lochhead wrote:

Many defects such as feeble-mindedness, epilepsy, deaf-mutism, and disposition to tuberculosis and other diseases are undoubtedly inherited, and to put no hindrance to the breeding of unfit and degenerate persons exposes our country to the gravest risk of regression, especially when it is recognized that the population is being largely recruited from inferior stocks. (McLaren, 1990, p. 13)[4]

The British government shipped 80,000 unwanted 'orphans' to Canada between 1868 and 1925 in the interests of economic expediency. Many of these children were then 'farmed out' to farming families as slave laborers and abandoned by Canada's 'child-savers' to new forms of abuse and neglect (Parr, 1980). At the same time, the growing needs of industry were met by the immigration of European peasants who provided cheap factory labor and lived in the imposed poverty of urban slums and ethnic ghettos. The immigrant poor were perceived by the eugenicists as *inferior stock unfit for breeding* and the full force of the eugenics–educational alliance was brought to bear on them and their children.

The compulsory classrooms of the educational state provided the scientific laboratories in which eugenicists examined the minds and inspected the bodies of children, particularly those living in poverty. Questionable IQ tests and medical exams were used to identify the *future unfit*; immigrant children from the lower classes — especially those who did not yet speak English — could be, and frequently were, classified as feeble-minded (McLaren, 1990).[5] Abused children with behavioral difficulties were also classified as feeble-minded, a label which was in itself extremely abusive. Feeble-mindedness was used to deprive already disadvantaged children of a full education, to incarcerate them in industrial schools, and to institutionalize them in hospitals for the 'mentally deficient'. Children so classified could be abused simply because they were believed to be feeble-minded.

The eugenicists conflated feeble-mindedness with immorality. Victim-blaming enabled eugenicists to find feeble-mindedness and inferiority in the dualism of im/morality; anyone who was deviant, different, or delinquent was perceived as immoral, and feeble-mindedness was used to explain their immorality. In this way, even victims of sexual assault could be construed by eugenicists as 'morally retarded' (Gordon, 1988, p. 230). Such myopia justified the incarceration of the so-called unfit and feeble-minded. The battle between child reaction–resistance and adult power–violence locates child abuse at the racist and classist core of this eugenics–education alliance.

Constructing Child Abuse

Historically, what constitutes child abuse in any time and place is socially constructed (Hacking, 1991). The western construction of child abuse has generally rendered it invisible through a *culture of denial* (within the middle class) while locating it as a consequence of poverty through a *culture of blame* (against the working class). In our culture of denial and blame, child abuse (like eugenics) swings back and forth between visibility and invisibility.

In Larry Wolff's (1988) psychoanalytic 'archaeology' of this phenomenon, he excavated four sensational child-abuse cases brought before the courts in 1899 in Vienna.[6] Wolff found that those with the symbolic power to construct the meaning of child abuse — judges, juries, lawyers, prosecutors, parents, reporters — perceived it as both *too horrible* and *too familiar*. Then and now, if child abuse is too horrible, it must be denied; if it is too familiar, someone else must be blamed.

Ultimately, the 'particular monstrosities of [these] cases were presented as only excessive variations on the accepted patterns of nineteenth-century parental discipline' (Wolff, 1988, p. 193). Wolff's startling explanation of the Viennese experience resonates with Alice Miller's 'poisonous pedagogy', which locates child abuse in traditional parenting, where the power of adults over children is often misused and its abuse usually unpunished (Miller, 1983).

The Viennese cases provide a too horrible and too familiar picture of our own collective failure to protect the well-being of our children. They reflect the Victorian underpinnings of the educational state and the eugenics movement in Canada and its effect on the lives of children. Our culture of denial and blame is mirrored in the sentiments of the English educators who were horrified by the child abuses committed by others, but blind to the abuses they administered themselves in the name of discipline. The same may be said concerning the men and women in the eugenics–education alliance in Canada.

Our contemporary understanding of child abuse is that it inflicts deliberate harm and deprivation of potential; it perpetrates and perpetuates unresolved shock and trauma; and it is rooted in authoritarian adult–child relations (deMause, 1974; Hacking, 1991; Hendrick, 1994; Herman, 1992; McGillivray, 1992; Miller, 1983; Miller, 1986). Child abuse (whether physical, emotional, sexual, or verbal) comprises a complex of abuses that affects both mind and body (regardless of the dominant form of abuse), is deeply sexed and gendered, and takes different forms in diverse class and cultural contexts (Martineau, 1993). Although child abuse is defined by shifting perceptions of what constitutes child abuse, the abuse and neglect of children — whether recognized or not — always has real material consequences of harm and trauma.

Abusive adults are ever present; it is how we define and identify child abuse in the context of the public interest that is subject to reconstruction (Hendrick, 1994, p. 242). To perceive child abuse purely as a social construction (as Hacking seems to do) is perilously one-sided and lacking a material analysis. Extended to its logical conclusion, constructionism could claim that child abuse does not really exist. This perspective depends upon sustaining a polarization between essentialism and constructionism that privileges the latter. To disrupt this dualism, I draw on post-structuralism and Diana Fuss's deconstruction of the essence–construct binary in *Essentially Speaking* (1989).

Fuss claims that oppositions are not only interactive but 'co-inherent', and that essentialism and constructionism (or anti-essentialism) are 'co-implicated'. In other words, 'essentialism is *essential* to social constructionism' (Fuss, 1989, p. 1) and vice-versa. Our social constructions are based on what we identify as essential, and what we claim to be essential is socially constructed because we cannot separate the natural from the cultural. In this sense, the material and the structural co-inhere. Deconstruction demonstrates that 'what a concept or category . . . claims to exclude is implicated in it' (Young, 1990, p. 304). Thus, the essence of the social construction of child abuse can be read as the real harm and trauma caused to the minds and bodies of children, the historical recognition of which informs our social constructions of child abuse.

The post-structural lens brings into view the possibility of children's agency in social–structural change; children's agency that, in systems of power and domination, may antagonize adult violence. This lens also illuminates the material essence of our social constructions; in the case of child abuse, this essence is harm and trauma inflicted in the tension between children's agency and adult violence. Here we find immigrant children classified as feeble-minded by the eugenicists and hopelessly entangled in webs of morality and immorality, power and violence, and harm and trauma.

Educators did not perceive corporal punishment as abusive because they believed it was instructive. Eugenicists did not see the label of feeble-mindedness as abusive because they believed it was biological. Returning to Wolff's Viennese court cases,

> [c]hild abuse was the thing that was simply unbelievable in 1899, and in excusing himself, and 'all of us', the prosecutor posed, and dismissed, the issue of general responsibility . . . The forms [patterns and procedures] were the deeply set mental structures of the nineteenth century. Those were the forms that determined what was self-evident, and what was simply unbelievable. (Wolff, 1988, p. 150)

In Vienna, the criminal conviction of one was the vindication of everyone; the religious sacrifice of one was the salvation of everyone. Such covenants both shape, and are shaped by, public perceptions. The classification of feeble-mindedness in children today would undoubtedly be challenged as the socially sanctioned practice of child abuse and neglect (yet we are not seriously questioning the medicalization of attention-deficit disorder in millions of children). Feeble-mindedness was the primary link between the compulsory education system and the 'public health' policies of eugenicism perpetrated against the children of the 'unfit'.

The Eugenics Movement

> The Canadian eugenicists were not monsters or simple-minded reactionaries. Some were no doubt mean-spirited; others were compassionate and idealistic. Most saw themselves as progressives who were seeking to wed science, medicine, and social welfare . . . In their enthusiasm to change the world they plunged into the discussion of a host of issues — immigration, education, public health, intelligence testing, welfare, feeble-mindedness. (McLaren, 1990, p. 166)

Dr Helen MacMurchy — physician, hereditarian, and humanitarian — was a key political figure in the eugenics and child welfare movements in central Canada. MacMurchy was a school medical inspector from 1906 until her retirement in 1934, a period of almost thirty years.[7] 'clearly convinced of her own superiority', she believed that social inferiority was synonymous with 'innate biological inequality' (McLaren, 1990, p. 30). Her description of feeble-mindedness is, at best, feeble:

> She openly conceded that though feeble-mindedness was difficult to de-
> fine, it was easy to recognize. MacMurchy used the term 'feeble-minded'
> to refer to the higher-class mentally retarded who could be mistaken for
> the normal. They did not have the physical stigmata of the moron or imbe-
> cile and so could even fool the ordinary physician. How did the expert
> spot them? Obviously, asserted MacMurchy, *social failure was the clearest
> indication of mental deficiency* [italics added]. The solution to a host of
> social problems lay, she concluded, in rounding up such incompetents and
> subjecting them to custodial care. (McLaren, 1990, pp. 107–8)

MacMurchy's description conflates the cultural and the natural and embodies our
culture of denial and blame. At the time, however, eugenics theories advanced by
hereditarians 'seemed to make good sense to many Canadians preoccupied by what
they took to be the dangers of racial inefficiency, social inadequacy, and ill health'
(McLaren, 1990, p. 9). These 'dangers' were projected by White Anglo-Saxon Prot-
estants (middle-class WASPS) onto working-class White Catholic European immigrants who could barely speak English (if at all) and who were seen as social failures.
Illiterate immigrants and their children were, by MacMurchy's assertion, mentally
deficient. The tautological thinking of those invested with symbolic power was that
the early capitalist conditions of extreme poverty and widespread disease visited
upon the working class were the consequences of their own moral, mental, and
physical degeneracy. But the 'forcible control of the reproduction of the feeble-
minded' (McLaren, 1990, p. 44) reproduced immigrant poverty and disease.

The medicalization and individualization of these 'social problems' involved
school inspections, medical exams, and mental testing of children, resulting in predetermined outcomes based on eugenic assumptions about race, class, immigration,
and poverty (McLaren, 1990). Arbitrary classifications of feeble-mindedness were
a priori deemed to cause poverty, disease, and social ills. The eugenics emphasis
on 'race betterment' and the 'breeding of the fit' blamed individuals for social problems and prescribed social controls as social solutions:

> Like moths to a flame, eugenicists were inexorably drawn to the issue
> of sexuality. The reproduction of the degenerate, the irrational breeding
> of the feeble-minded, the swamping of Canada by prolific aliens were all
> subjected by hereditarians to morbid analysis. (McLaren, 1990, p. 68)

Canadian eugenicists 'raised the spectre of society being menaced by the marginal . . . [and] swamped by the feeble-minded' (McLaren, 1990, pp. 165, 138).
Working-class immigrants who were declared intellectually inferior were victims
of the symbolic power embedded in the progressive policies of economic efficiency.
This progressive assumption that social ills were caused by unfit and immoral
immigrants was both cause and consequence of society's fear of the feeble-minded,
a fear that affected the lives of thousands of children. MacMurchy feared that the
feeble-minded might be 'mistaken for the normal' (McLaren, 1990, p. 107), but her
own views were also 'mistaken for the normal', with tragic consequences. In the

name of eugenics, adults living in prosperity committed gross abuses against children living in poverty, abuses that were normalized through the racist rhetoric of *race betterment*.

The crux of the eugenics–education alliance in ferreting out feeble-mindedness was the IQ test administered to school children. These ethnocentric tests 'confused innate intelligence with an appreciation of bourgeois norms' of the cultural elite (McLaren, 1990, p. 92). Cultural and language difficulties earmarked immigrant children as social problems. Furthermore, teachers attributed deviant and delinquent behavior to mental retardation, and they 'unwittingly participated' in the perception that non-English-speaking immigrant children living in poverty were unfit (McLaren, 1990). Eugenicism offered a scientific panacea of biological solutions to social problems through a grab-bag of bio-social engineering.

In 1959, C. Wright Mills wrote that private individuals and public institutions are interactive, that personal troubles are related to public issues, and that the past is integral to understanding the present. Today, we are again confronted with biological determinism, which, among other things, throws up political smokescreens that blame marginalized groups for perceived economic and educational deficits.[8] Like the cyclical re-surfacing of child abuse examined by Wolff, eugenics did not so much disappear in 1945 as temporarily sink out of sight. Just as the history of western childhood sinks and swims in a deep sea of abuse and neglect (Pollock, 1983; Shahar, 1990) so the history of western 'progress' rides the recurring tidal waves of eugenicism.

McLaren did not anticipate that his generous explanation for the early eugenicists would be chillingly reproduced in the eugenics of the 1990s:

> For the middle class, of course, it was a comforting notion to think that poverty and criminality were best attributed to individual weaknesses rather than to the structural flaws of the economy. This explains why so many otherwise intelligent humanitarians supported the labeling, the segregation, and ultimately the sterilization of those they designated subnormal. (McLaren, 1990, p. 37)

His characterization of the early eugenicists as misguided humanitarians does not account for the economic expediency of eugenicism in educational policies then and now and in the systemic maintenance of cultural inequities and class inequalities. We are faced with the bittersweet realization that eugenicism is neither the same as, nor separate from, humanitarianism. The co-inherence of eugenicism and humanitarianism maps onto and illuminates the alliance between eugenics and education.

Eugenics, in its efforts to stamp out perceived social ills, eventually became a social ill to be stamped out. In the child welfare movement, the best intentions of the 'child-savers' and child-saving agencies further abused and abandoned the children they were trying to save. Industrial schools established in the name of 'progressive reform' were operated more as prisons than schools and were eventually shut down. Instilling discipline too easily turned into the infliction of child abuse, and the classification of feeble-mindedness easily became abusive and feeble-mind. In a culture of denial and blame, the denial of our own actions is the essence from which blaming others is constructed.

Constructing the Natural Child

If education represents opportunity and the pursuit of knowledge, eugenicism reproduces inequality through the suppression of knowledge. This suppression comprises a technology of domination based on racial and ethnic differences (Collins, 1990, p. 5) and permeates adult–child relations. We culturally construct what we perceive to be natural in children (because the natural alone cannot be known) through a socialization process that begins in infancy. Yet most critical theorists do not include children and age-status in their political analyses of oppression.

We *naturalize* children by inventing, constructing, and then perceiving them as purely natural beings; and we *socialize* children to conform to our constructions of the natural. Through naturalization, we have historically constructed children as pure or evil, innocent or willful, tender or terrible. We tend to see children as asocial, asexual, apolitical, and ahistorical beings, even while suffusing the natural with shifting moral assumptions (Jordanova, 1989, p. 4). We discipline children for failure to conform to the natural, and use violence if necessary to enforce conformity. We deny that this violence is child abuse and judge the consequences by blaming the victim.

The natural child is a cultural construction. Avoiding the extremes of natural or cultural determinism — or even economic determinism, where children are perceived as either assets or liabilities 'to be used in family survival strategies' — requires 'examin[ing] the place of children in a given society as a whole, without exempting them from the larger multi-faceted changes all societies have undergone' (Jordanova, 1989, p. 12). This is a risky proposal because eugenics–education policies did, indeed, focus on children. But they did not recognize children as the complex political actors Barrie Thorne has observed (1987). If we can understand that children's agency interacted with adult violence and that adult violence acted to suppress children's agency, then we can also change cultural notions of the natural, consider the implications for social policy and challenge that which is too horrible and too familiar.

Social Policy

The 'purification' of Canada proposed by the eugenics movement was aimed at subordinating new immigrants whose cheap labour and lower-class status systemically supported the middle and upper classes. This project depended upon a discourse that collapsed hereditary, evolutionary, and environmental factors to claim that 'since the struggle for survival no longer took place the feeble-minded flourished, were extraordinarily fertile, and spawned vice, crime, illegitimacy, and disease that burdened the community with crippling taxes' (McLaren, 1990, pp. 122–3). In making such claims, hereditarians sometimes switched to environmental arguments to support their policies. For example, if the 'unfit' gave birth to 'normal' children, eugenicists believed these children would still be damaged by poor parenting (McLaren, 1990, pp. 97–8). Poor immigrant parents and their children, the 'future unfit', were scapegoats for the social problems that plagued modern society and informed social policy.

Indeed, 'the history of children and childhood is inescapably inseparable from the history of social policy' (Hendrick, 1994, p. xii). In the eugenics–education alliance, symbolic violence manifested as actual violence inflicted by adults upon the minds and bodies of disadvantaged children. Social policy played a role in the construction of childhood and in the constitution of child abuse. Hendrick asserts that children have historically been perceived as bodies without minds, and '[m]uch of the history of social policy . . . is in fact the history of the imposition of adult will upon children's bodies', including medical inspections and treatments and 'the infliction of physical pain in elementary and industrial schools, reformatories, orphanages and [other] institutions' (Hendrick, 1994, p. 2).

The Educational State

The introduction and gradual consolidation of compulsory schooling confirmed the trend towards the creation of the child as a distinctive being characterised by ignorance, incapacity and innocence. This understanding of the 'nature' of childhood was then subjected to scientific scrutiny and elaborated upon through further description and explanation . . . Consequently, reformers also knew what they expected of children in terms of behavior, performance and development. (Hendrick, 1994, p. 37)

The eugenics movement and the educational state each perceived themselves as the moral guardians of Canada, but deconstruction of their imposition of morality reveals an immoral essence of violence. Compulsory schooling provided the moral regulation of the immigrant masses, but contained in education's promise of equality was the reproduction of inequality and the maintenance of ethnic struggles, class conflicts, and gender wars (Curtis, 1988, pp. 12–15). Indeed, schools were, and are, state-sanctioned sites for the reproduction of inequity and inequality (Foley, 1991, p. 539).

Building the educational state and enforcing compulsory education included idiosyncratic notions of teaching and learning, discipline and reward, obedience and punishment. Adult–child relations in the educational system involved the dynamics of power, control, resistance, and reproduction. Many children were subjected to physical, emotional, verbal, and even sexual abuse by their teachers. Ridicule, humiliation, and corporal punishment were typical 'disciplines' imposed in the commitment to teaching, learning, and moral development. A moral education was an 'efficient education' that required puritanism and punishment in the reproduction of children's subordination, the repression of sexual expression, and the suppression of critical thought (Curtis, 1988, pp. 103–4). The policies and practices of the educational state fortified the eugenics movement.

Although corporal punishment was theoretically abolished in schools as early as the mid-nineteenth century — in the belief that education could and should be a pleasurable experience — it has a long association with compulsory education. As recently as 1975, 93 per cent of a survey sample of men and women in the USA approved of corporal punishment as an acceptable form of discipline; today it is still a significant 65 per cent (Strauss, 1995).[9] In British Columbia's public schools, corporal punishment was allowed as a last resort until 1972. The pedagogical policy of moral discipline frequently manifested in the practice of corporal punishment. However, the sporadic elimination of corporal punishment did nothing to diminish the emotional humiliation children endured, an indignity no less brutal than physical violence (Curtis, 1988, p. 320). In any case, if corporal punishment was 'abolished', it was also 'indispensable' because violence against students was 'inherent to the system of public education', and its very regulation suggested its regularity (Curtis, 1988, pp. 330–1).

The hope and promise that education could be both gentle and pleasurable necessitated at least the threat of violence: 'Gentle means at school were preferable, but violent means would be employed where necessary. . . . [G]entle means were possible because they were known to be sustained ultimately by violent means' (Curtis, 1988, p. 338). Moral discipline could not be separated from discipline by violent means. In our state military society (all of our social institutions embody the military in their systems and structures) it is the normalization of violence that breeds violence. Even family violence is normalized in the traditional authoritarian family, an institution that literally teaches violence to children (Hendrick, 1994, p. 257). In capitalist societies, social relations are permeated with force and the potential for violence; political power depends upon a 'monopoly of violence' and property power saturates society with 'relations of force' (Curtis, 1988, pp. 368–9).

The normalization of violence and the naturalization of private property informs attitudes towards children (and women) as objects of possession. Perceiving children as property has historically legitimated violence against children. Property rights invest *parental power* with the familial right to violate children when children are constructed as private property (McGillivray, 1992, pp. 217–18), and grant *public power* over the children of disadvantaged and disenfranchised others. Through families and schools the structures of military violence and private property are brought to bear on children. These authoritarian structures interact with the public policies and social controls of the educational state.

The educational mandate of social control as moral development was an essential component of the social construction of the educational state during Canada's turbulent shift from an agricultural to an industrial economy. This mandate of morality informed the reconstruction of childhood:

> State schooling became a place for the systematic administration and reproduction of 'childhood', and of the social institutions needed to sustain

it, like the 'family'. . . . The 'schoolchild' is, by definition, a flawed entity in need of discipline and training, an incomplete social subject which must submit to the process of schooling for its 'own' good. This . . . is an accomplishment of the Educational State and not a fact of nature. (Curtis, 1988, pp. 16–7)

Middle-class childhood (and middle-class motherhood) was prolonged along the lines of industrialization and compulsory education. Although most middle-class children mostly benefited from the building of the educational state, working-class children were thrust into chaos and shifted back and forth from farm to factory to school. With agricultural livelihoods severely undermined, poor children were vulnerable to industrialization, compulsory education, and the looming eugenics–education alliance. The dangerous liaison between eugenics and education deprived already deprived children of an appropriate education and labeled uneducated and immigrant children feeble-minded in the state maintenance of ethnic inequity and socioeconomic inequality.

Constructing Children's Work

If the classrooms of compulsory education provided the laboratories for the eugenicists' examinations of children, they also offered a sanctuary of sorts to those working-class children who had toiled under untold hardships in agricultural and industrial settings. Most Canadians understandably cringe at the mere mention of 'child labor' because of the atrocities and exploitation of child labor during early industrialization (Parr, 1980; 1982). However, child labor has a more varied history. For example, the 'misery version' of child labor (early industrialization) can be discerned as a moralizing tale that views the past as primitive and the present as the culmination of 'constant progress' (Schrumpf, 1993, p. 222). By banishing 'child labor', we have ceased to recognize and acknowledge children's work. Jordanova (1989) reclaims school attendance as children's work:

When we state that children no longer 'work' we mean that they no longer endure long hours of labour daily, under the control of an employer, for which they may or may not have received wages. Yet children are not now free to do as they please, and, although they do not receive payment for attending school, it certainly counts as 'work'. (p. 19)

In today's world of global consumer capitalism, we 'often assume that adults work and children "play", a conceptual separation that tends to bracket children's activity from "serious" life . . . [but] young children do not experience a play/work dichotomy; they work while playing and play while working' (Thorne, 1987, p. 100).[10] But it is more than this. Children have worked in hunting and gathering, fishing and agricultural, industrial and technological societies. Today, many children work at home, at school, and in the marketplace. Like the social dimensions of earlier *apprenticeships*, the curricular and extracurricular activities of boys and girls are designed to turn them into contributing members of society.

Historically, children have been treated in at least two opposing ways: the first is *integrating* them into the social and economic world of adults; the second is *segregating* them in nurseries and schools and censoring certain issues and topics (Berggreen, 1988, pp. 832–3). The integration model can be under-protective; the segregation model is over-protective. The extreme states of integration and segregation are often the sites of child abuse and neglect.

Under-protected children are 'children without childhoods' facing inappropriate experiences and responsibilities. Over-protected children are 'greenhouse children', who do not mature to cope well with adult responsibilities;[11] they are separated from adult cultures and occupational spheres and perceived as innocent and childish, which reinforces the notion that they are socially ignorant and culturally incompetent. Berggreen calls this a self-fulfilling 'circle of ignorance' (1988, p. 833). This circle of ignorance resonates with the prophecies of the eugenics–education alliance and the social fear of, search for, and classification of, alleged feeble-mindedness in pre-selected children.

The dilemma of too much or too little integration or segregation is partially illuminated by examining not only what it is that we reproduce, but what we *desire* to reproduce. Rethinking our notions of the natural and our ideologies of childhood is a collective responsibility. Nurturing the innate and diverse capacities of children and youth can contribute to their development as responsible individuals. This means respecting, revisioning, and revaluating all children, not as possessions or commodities or consumers or objects for classification, but as productive, participating, and contributing members of society (Martineau, 1996). Such a perspective challenges the recurring alliance between education and eugenics and its investment in maintaining inequality based on the socioeconomic constitution of cultural inequalities.

Social Structures

The re/constitution of society is dynamic and organic:

> For history to become organic to theory, social structure must be seen as constantly *constituted* rather than constantly reproduced. And that makes sense only if theory acknowledges the constant possibility that structure will be constituted in a different way. (Connell, 1987, p. 44)

This *constant constitution* of social structure in the social world is mirrored in the tension between social actors and social institutions, and 'the reality of social institutions in structuring and limiting the choices of actors' (Hartsock, 1985, p. 104). Connell (1987) identifies constant constitution as the dynamic interaction between the reproduction and production of social structures and our social practices within those social structures.

In the same vein, Connell (1987) states that '[s]ymbolically, "nature" may be opposed to "culture" . . .' (p. 87), but in practical and historical reality nature is no more separate from culture than nature and culture are separate from history. Connell delightfully claims that biological reductionism (the engine of eugenicism) 'in essence, is two or three million years out of date' (1987, p. 72). If education is the socialization of children to fit the needs of capitalist industry, then we must consider the *structural* ways that children and education are reproduced and 'distorted to fit the needs of capitalism' (1987, p. 43).

Dangerous Liaison: Past and Present

The eugenics–education alliance is not simply a dangerous liaison confined to a naive past. It ruined the lives of those it targeted — people still living today — and it is resurfacing in Canada and the United States. Perceiving the present as progress blinds us to the social world around us, so that we see only through hindsight. In the areas of medicine, education, psychology, social services, and many others, Canada is influenced by American policies and politics. This raises many questions in the Canadian context related to American resources and influences.

For example, has incarcerating children as feeble-minded been replaced by today's labeling of ESL students as at-risk for dropping-out of school? (Dryfoos, 1990). On the other hand, why are *all* adolescents being pathologized along a continuum of risk developed by psychologists and social workers? And if all adolescents are at risk, why do social service intervention programs only target immigrant children and youth in 'inner-city' schools? (Dryfoos, 1990; Kagan, 1996; Luthar, 1995). The best of intentions notwithstanding, are yesterday's industrial reform schools resurfacing as today's full-service schools, which combine education, health, and social services in inner-cities? (Dryfoos, 1994).

And, why are millions of children — hyped up on the age of television and technology — being tranquilized for hyperactivity and attention-deficit disorder? (Associated Press, 1996; Begley, 1996; Hancock *et al.*, 1996; Stossel, 1995). Are the global politics of reproductive technologies vastly different from the involuntary sterilizations of the feeble-minded? (Ginsburg and Rapp, 1995). Why is the American rhetoric of a 'nation at risk' (National Commission, 1983) influencing educational policy and 'effective schooling' in Canada?

I raise these questions in the midst of two *unbelievable* phenomena: the continuing rape, torture, and slaughter of humans while the world watches, and our inability to collectively nurture our children. First, how is it conceivable that the 'final solution' of the Nazi Holocaust can recur in the 'ethnic cleansing' of Rwanda, Cambodia, and the 'ground zero' of the Croatian and Bosnian Serb death camps? (Maass, 1996). Second, how is it possible that just as corporal punishment is being banished and sexual abuse is being punished, so the loving, touching and healthy caressing of our children is generating fear and suspicion around and among parents, teachers, coaches, and caretakers? (Oxenhandler, 1996).

The inability to safely cuddle and protect our children, and the inability of countless children to trust and connect with adults, creates new forms of child abuse, neglect, and alienation that are destined to feed future atrocities. In this light, the following is a brief introduction to three issues that link today with yesterday: *involuntary sterilization, attention-deficit disorder*, and *full-service schools*.

Involuntary Sterilization

Within the context of the times, many physicians, judges and government officials considered heredity to be the transmissible root of all evils. 'Abolish Birth of Idiots Appeal of Court Magistrate', a *Vancouver Sun* headline of Sept. 11, 1926, reads. After sentencing a two-year-old and a five-year-old to the provincial lunatic asylum, Judge Stuart Jamieson of Burnaby juvenile court had declared: 'Until we have abolished the birth of idiots and the weak-minded we have not begun to get at the solution of crime.' (Gregory, 1996, p. A19)

One of the legacies of the early eugenics–education alliance was the enforced sterilization of those identified as feeble-minded. The Province of British Columbia passed the Sexual Sterilization Act in 1933, 'the same year in which Nazi Berlin's Court of Eugenics ordered the first sterilizations there, to 264 mentally ill, feeble-minded and homosexual undesirables' (Gregory, 1996, p. A19). In Vancouver, juvenile delinquents were considered mentally defective, and trouble-making teens were too easily institutionalized; boys and girls incarcerated in reform schools and insane asylums were involuntarily sterilized on the recommendation of authorities who observed deficient and undesirable behavior (Gregory, 1996, p. A19). Eugenicists contended that 'sterilization of the mental defective, the criminal and the poor was a beneficial and scientifically acceptable method of population engineering' (Gregory, 1996, p. A19).

Just as eugenics is re-surfacing today in a new alliance with schools and schooling, adults who were involuntarily sterilized in the past are today suing governments for compensation. The one million dollars recently awarded to one such woman — a normal child who was placed in the Alberta Home for Mental Defectives when her alcoholic mother abandoned her and who was subsequently tested and treated as retarded — was 'a human rights victory and a call to [other] victims' (Gregory, 1996, p. A19). Involuntary sterilizations have not ceased; they merely went underground. They continue to be carried out on poor, marginalized, immigrant, and third-world women without their knowledge in prisons, asylums, and hospitals during natural and surgical childbirths, and other surgeries; and indirectly through economic access to such reproductive technologies as expensive fertility clinics or those targeted for free birth control experiments; and through the focus of professional counselling for, and the availability of, abortion and family planning services (Corea, 1985; Dreifus, 1978; Ginsburg and Rapp, 1995).

Attention-deficit Disorder

Hyperactivity in children has been recently reconstructed as attention-deficit disorder (ADD). In an era when children are remote-controlled by television and technology, they are also being increasingly diagnosed with ADD, treated with behavior-modification therapy, and tranquilized with Ritalin. ADD is touted as a chemical imbalance, a biological predisposition to misbehavior, and a 'complex neurological impairment' (Hancock *et al.*, 1996, p. 51). It is described as 'television with the channels constantly changing' (Taylor, 1996), as 'brains crackl[ing] with static interference, as if a dozen stations are coming in on one channel' (Hancock *et al.*, 1996, p. 52). ADD children are pathologized through the medical rhetoric of *risk behaviors* and *behavior disorders*. Many are being overmedicated in overcrowded classrooms in underfunded schools (Stossel, 1995). Doctors, teachers, and parents who favor Ritalin want *calm* children; its adversaries describe children on Ritalin as *robots* who have lost their creativity (Stossel, 1995). And, although ADD was originally 'designed for children', adults are now also claiming it for themselves and adding Ritalin to their chemical cocktails (Hacking, 1996).

In the United States today, ADD is the number one child 'psychiatric disorder'. Three million children have been diagnosed with ADD and one million are on Ritalin (Taylor, 1996). In Canada and the United States combined, over six million prescriptions for Ritalin (or generic versions) were filled in 1993 (Associated Press, 1996, p. A11). In Alberta, prescriptions for Ritalin increased by almost 1,000 per cent (from 2,614 to 22,995) between 1986 and 1993; in Ontario, 125,000 prescriptions for Ritalin were dispensed from retail pharmacies in 1994, a 45 per cent increase over the previous year. While about 5–6 per cent of children have been diagnosed with ADD, doctors are estimating that up to 20 per cent of North Americans have 'inherited' the disorder (Associated Press, 1996, p. A11). A more realistic view is that ADD is a rare and extreme condition comprising hereditarian and environmental factors, and perhaps 1 per cent of children have a serious attention-deficit problem requiring treatment and intervention.

ADD children and adolescents are described as inattentive, impulsive, and hyperactive (Hancock *et al.*, 1996). Three-quarters of these children are boys who 'act out' under distress; whereas, ADD girls have trouble focusing and go through school 'in a daze' (Taylor, 1996). The boys are 'at-risk' for school failure, criminal behavior, and alcohol abuse (Taylor, 1996). This discourse is remarkably similar to the classification, of ESL students in inner-city schools who are earmarked as at-risk for crime, sexual promiscuity, drug and alcohol abuse, and dropping out of school. And it is remarkably similar to the language of deviancy and delinquency the eugenicists used to identify feeble-mindedness, populate reform schools, and impose involuntary sterilization. ADD is not a neutral *disorder*. Although the diagnosis cuts across socioeconomic class, it is deeply gendered and culturally constructed around its medical category as an essentially hereditary, biological condition. Yet class cuts through ADD with interesting consequences: middle- and upper-class families accept the diagnosis of ADD and can buy the drugs prescribed by doctors and urged by nurses, teachers, and counsellors; in contrast, working-class families cannot afford the drugs that tranquilize active children. These children will be increasingly labeled with escalating conduct disorders, and will likely become 'at-risk' for dropping out of school and engage in 'risk bebaviours' such as alcohol and drug abuse. And we can only imagine the addictions and afflictions that await children who have grown up on tranquilizers. It is not outrageous to wonder if particular ADD-diagnosed children will eventually be sterilized through experimental community drug treatment programs.

Full-service Schools

As already mentioned, *all* adolescents in the United States are being located along a continuum of risk — from low-risk behaviors to high-risk activities — requiring professional interventions by psychologists and social workers (Dryfoos, 1990). However, it is poor and immigrant children and youth who are targeted for social programming through the development of full-service schools in inner-city districts (Dryfoos, 1994). The pursuit of effective schooling (academic achievement) through full-service schools emerges from two decades of social and economic concerns over allegedly decreasing academic test scores and weakening global competitiveness of secondary school students in the USA (Ball, 1990; Lee, Bryk, and Smith, 1993; National Commission, 1983; Rutter *et al.*, 1979). This literature is influencing educators and educational policy in Canada and, in particular, Vancouver (Vancouver School Board, 1986).

Full-service schools are supported by educators and social service professionals in response to the needs of high-risk children and their families and in pursuit of:

> . . . *equalizing access to future opportunities* [italics added]. Schools are increasingly being called on to be those 'surrogate parents' that can increase the 'teachability' of children who arrive on their doorsteps in poor shape. Today's schools feel pressured to feed children; provide psychological support services; offer health screening; establish referral networks related to substance abuse, child welfare, and sexual abuse; cooperate with the local police and probation officers; add curricula for prevention of substance abuse, teen pregnancy, suicide, and violence (the new morbidities); and actively promote social skills, good nutrition, safety, and general health. (Dryfoos, 1994, p. 5)

By their very nature, full-service schools conform to the symbolic power, social control, and surveillance strategies that maintain systemic inequalities and that are masked by the ideology of 'equalizing access to future opportunities'. Implicit in the above description are claims that poor and immigrant parents are inadequate parents and that poor parents are responsible for their own poverty. The term 'surrogate parents' means *professionalized parenting* by middle-class social workers and educational psychologists working in inner-city schools.

To this point, '[p]rofessionalization is the proliferation of professions to treat and manage the citizenry' (Scheurich, 1994, p. 307). Targeting, naming, studying, and labeling by social service professionals creates a social grid that:

> constitutes both who the problem group is and how the group is seen or known as a problem. . . . The social order produces in complex ways both the failure in school of [particular] children . . . and the identification of this group as a problem group. The labelling of the targeted group as a social problem is critical to the maintenance of the social order. (Scheurich, 1994, p. 308)

Once the problem group is identified, the good intentions of the 'doctors of social diseases, professionals of all sorts including educators, social workers, health workers and psychologists' (Scheurich, 1994, p. 309) are marshalled to treat the targeted group with policy interventions. The emerging policies of 'linked school services' (education, health, and social services) in inner-city schools deserves our utmost scrutiny.

Our culture of denial and blame is inscribed in the full-service school movement, which both informs and is informed by public policy. 'We need to begin unpacking the multiple and insidious ways in which public policy has served to construct and maintain poverty, while simultaneously making its victims bear responsibility for such state-constructed poverty' (Polakow, 1995, p. 264). The rhetoric around 'youth at risk' is a ritualistic chant of failure and salvation that shapes the discourse into what Michelle Fine calls 'the perversion of possibility' (1995, p. 77):

> Perhaps no field surpasses public education as the space into which public anxieties, terrors, and 'pathologics' are so routinely shoved, only to be transformed into public policies of what must be done to save 'us' from 'them'. (Fine, 1995, p. 77)

Our society uses a *'language of pathology'* to label persons based on their race, first language, class, family structure, geographic location, and gender as "at risk for failure"' (Polakow, 1995, p. 263). How long will it take before full-service schools (*albeit*, initiated with the best of intentions) are entrenched in inner-cities? How long before the influx of child-service professionals in these schools dramatically increases the culturally based and culturally biased classifications of children, diagnosing new diseases, disorders, dysfunctions, disabilities, and deviant and delinquent behaviors, and prescribing ever-new medications, treatments, and interventions? Who will benefit?

The Politics of Childhood as Praxis

The politics of childhood as praxis disrupts the *disordering* of disadvantaged children and youth, and advocates the age-appropriate participation of young people in policy, planning, and decision-making processes in families, schools, and communities across class and culture. Such advocacy interrupts our adult-centered images of human agency, which have conveyed a 'preoccupation with the reproduction of adult social order' and have failed to account for the complexity of children's agency and children's lives (Thorne, 1987, pp. 94–5).

Over the past 200 years, children in Britain, the United States, and Canada have been viewed either as threats to society or as victims of society (Hendrick, 1994; Thorne, 1987). At one time or another, emphasis has been either on protecting adults from juvenile crimes or on protecting children from adult abuses. Classifying children as deviant threats or innocent victims is misleading and short-sighted because it fails to nurture their abilities to act in the world. The politics of childhood acknowledges that children have the capacity to increasingly influence, participate in, and contribute to the larger social world.

It is not my intention to project present analyses of children and childhood onto the past but, rather, to explicate the past in order to illuminate the present. Children are socialized (and naturalized) by the recurring alliance between eugenics and education — an alliance that confuses nature and culture in order to rationalize the superiority of the economic elite and the inferiority of the economic poor. Our social policies co-inhere with our culture of denial and blame and our failure to nurture collective responsibilities that both recognize and transcend differences. The recurrence of the eugenics–education alliance should direct our attention both to the praxis of systemic reforms in educational instruction and to the discrepancies between our policies and practices in educational institutions (Cohen, 1995).

The compelling insight that the 'experiences of children may be illuminated by, and in turn may challenge, our frameworks for understanding not only families and schools but also politics, work, poverty, social class, organizations, bureaucracy, urban life, social stratification, and social change' (Thorne, 1987, p. 99) urges our collective pursuit of, and investment in, the politics of childhood. The recurrence of the eugenics–education alliance remains a dangerous liaison that is both too horrible and too familiar.

Notes

1   The 'war' between Catholicism and Protestantism was as much a class and cultural conflict as a religious antagonism. In *The Protestant Ethic and the Spirit of Capitalism*, Max Weber describes Calvinism as 'the most absolutely unbearable form of ecclesiastical control of the individual which could possibly exist' (1958, p. 37). The lingering 'rule of Calvinism' and the 'tyranny of Puritanism' informed the English Protestantism of colonized Canada (and the United States) and the social control of the immigrant working classes, who were mostly European Catholics. See Linda Gordon's (1988) excellent analysis of the conflicts between middle-class Protestant women and working-class Catholic women in the context of social welfare in Boston, 1880–1960.

2   Citing Robert Coles (1971) *Migrants, Sharecroppers, Mountaineers*, Boston, Little, Brown; Robert Coles (1986) *The Political Life of Children*, Boston, Atlantic Monthly Press; Douglas Maynard (1985) 'On the functions of social conflict among children', *American Sociological Review*, **50**, pp. 207–23.

3 Drawing on the work of Pierre Bourdieu and Jean Claude Passeron (1977) *Reproduction in Education, Society, and Culture*, Beverley Hills, CA, Sage.
4 Citing W.I. Lochhead (1919, July) 'Genetics — The science of breeding', *Canadian Bookman*, p. 66.
5 See Stephen Jay Gould's (1981) excellent social history of 'scientific racism', hereditarianism, and the fallacy of IQ theories in *The Mismeasure of Man*, New York, W. W. Norton.
6 What makes Wolff's psychoanalytic archaeology so fascinating is that his study is located in 'Freud's Vienna', during the time that Freud was living in Vienna and developing the myth of the Oedipus complex. Wolff concludes his book: 'At the same time that children dream of the deaths of their parents, anyone who read the newspapers [in Vienna] knew that parents both tortured and murdered their children. But the latter was an even more painful discovery, more monstrous, more unbelievable. So child abuse was brought to light in Freud's Vienna for just a month, an "unprecedented" phenomenon; it played a part in the rich and tangled complications of Viennese culture and society, and then was buried again' (1988, p. 242).
7 MacMurchy also focused on infant and maternal mortality (McLaren, 1990, p. 30).
8 In addition to relentless news coverage of the economic problems of single parenthood, teenage motherhood, welfare dependency, and massive immigration — blown out of proportion and scapegoated for the financial deficit — I am specifically referring to four recent books: 1) Richard J. Herrnstein and Charles Murray (1944) *The Bell Curve: Intelligence and Class Structure in American Life*, New York, The Free Press; 2) J. Philippe Rushton (1994) *Race, Evolution, and Behavior: A Life History Perspective*, New Brunswick, NJ, Transaction Publishers; 3) Seymour W. Itzkoff (1994) *The Decline of Intelligence in America: A Strategy for National Renewal*, Westport, Connecticut, Praeger; 4) William A. Henry III (1994) *In Defense of Elitism*, New York, Doubleday. Each of these books develops a political economy of intelligence based on genetics in relation to immigration policies and multicultural populations. Each author conflates nature with culture, separates hereditarian factors from environmental factors, and perpetuates the culture of denial and blame. It is heartening that eugenics is less acceptable today, in large part due to the Feminist, Black Civil Rights, and Aboriginal Peoples' Movements; yet eugenicism recurs.
9 Strauss referred to an uncited American study, with no breakdown of subjects by sex, age, ethnicity, or socioeconomic status. He was the keynote speaker at a public forum on the 'neglected issues' of family violence, which include women's violence, sibling abuse, and corporal punishment.
10 Citing Valerie Polakow Suransky (1982) *The Erosion of Childhood*, Chicago, University of Chicago Press.
11 A friend introduced me to the Taiwanese concept of the 'greenhouse syndrome', which describes coddled children who do not learn how to survive outside of their overly protective environments.

References

ASSOCIATED PRESS (1996) 'Ritalin link to cancer in mice "not a signal" to halt its use', *Vancouver Sun*, p. 11, January 13.
BALL, S.J. (1990) 'Management as moral technology: A Luddite analysis', in BALL, S.J.

(ed.) *Foucault and Education: Disciplines and Knowledge*, New York, Routledge, pp. 153–66.

BEGLEY, S. (1996) 'Chemicals: The great impostors', *Newsweek*, 48, March 18.

BEHLMER, G.K. (1982) *Child Abuse and Moral Reform in England, 1870–1908*, Stanford, CA, Stanford University Press.

BERGGREEN, B. (1988) 'Infantilization of children as an historical process', in EKBERG, K. and MJAAVATN, P.E. (eds) *Growing into a Modern World: An International Interdisciplinary Conference on the Life and Development of Children in Modern Society*, Proceedings of the Norwegian Centre for Child Research, (Vol. 1), Trondheim, Norway, pp. 829–42.

COHEN, D.K. (1995) 'What is the system in systemic reform?' *Educational Researcher*, **24**, 9, pp. 11–17, 31.

COLLINS, P. HILL (1990) *Black Feminist Thought: Knowledge, Consciousness, and the Politics of Empowerment*, New York, Routledge.

CONNELL, R.W. (1987) 'Part I: Theorizing gender', *Gender and Power: Society, the Person and Sexual Politics*, Stanford, CA, Stanford, pp. 23–88.

COREA, G. (1985) 'The reproductive brothel', in COREA, G. *et al.* (eds) *Man-made Women: How New Reproductive Technologies Affect Women*, London, Hutchinson, pp. 38–51.

CURTIS, B. (1988) *Building the Educational State: Canada West, 1836–1871*, London, ON, Althouse.

DAVIES, B. (1993) 'Poststructuralist theory and the study of gendered childhoods', *Shards of Glass: Children Reading and Writing Beyond Gendered Identities*, New Jersey, Hampton Press, pp. 1–15.

DEMAUSE, L. (ed.) (1974) 'The evolution of childhood', *The History of Childhood*, New York, Harper & Row, pp. 1–73.

DREIFUS, C. (ed.) (1978) 'Sterilizing the poor', *Seizing our Bodies: The Politics of Women's Health Care*, New York, Vintage Books, pp. 105–20.

DRYFOOS, J.G. (1990) *Adolescents at Risk: Prevalence and Prevention*, New York, Oxford.

DRYFOOS, J.G. (1994) *Full-service Schools: A Revolution in Health and Social Services for Children, Youth, and Families*, San Francisco, Jossey-Bass.

FINE, M. (1995) 'The politics of who's "at risk"', in SWADENER, B.B. and LUBECK, S. (eds) *Children and Families 'at Promise': Deconstructing the Discourse of Risk*, New York, State University of New York Press, pp. 76–94.

FOLEY, D.E. (1991, August) 'Rethinking school ethnographies of colonial settings: A performance perspective of reproduction and resistance', *Comparative Education Review*, **35**, 3, pp. 532–51.

FUSS, D. (1989) *Essentially Speaking: Feminism, Nature and Difference*, New York, Routledge.

GINSBURG, F.D. and RAPP, R. (eds) (1995) *Conceiving the New World Order: The Global Politics of Reproduction*, Berkeley, CA, University of California Press.

GORDON, L. (1988) *Heroes of Their Own Lives: The Politics and History of Family Violence, Boston 1880–1960*, New York, Viking Books.

GREGORY, R. (1996) 'When B.C. sterilized children', *Vancouver Sun*, p. A19, March 9.

HACKING, I. (1991) 'The making and molding of child abuse', *Critical Inquiry*, **17**, pp. 253–88.

HACKING, I. (1996, March 4) Dissociative fugues: The body language of oppressed males. Presentation, Green College, University of British Columbia.

HANCOCK, L. with WINGERT, P., HAGER, M., KALB, C., SPRINGEN, K. and CHINNI, D. (1996) 'Mother's little helper', *Newsweek*, pp. 50–6, March 18.

HARKER, R. (1990) 'Bourdieu — education and reproduction', in HARKER, R.K., MAHAR, C.

and WILKES, C. (eds) *An Introduction to the Work of Pierre Bourdieu*, London, Macmillan, pp. 86–108.

HARTSOCK, N.C.M. (1985) 'The market as epistemology: The exchange abstraction in theories of power and domination', *Money, Sex, and Power: Toward a Feminist Historical Materialism*, Boston, Northeastern, pp. 95–114.

HENDRICK, H. (1994) *Child Welfare: England 1872–1989*, New York, Routledge.

HERMAN, J.L. (1992) *Trauma and Recovery*, New York, Basic Books.

HOSKIN, K. (1990) 'Foucault under examination: The crypto-educationalist unmasked', in BALL, S.J. (ed.) *Foucault and Education: Disciplines and Knowledge*, New York, Routledge, pp. 29–53.

JORDANOVA, L. (1989) 'Children in history: Concepts of nature and society', in SCARRE, G. (ed.) *Children, Parents and Politics*, New York, Cambridge, pp. 3–24.

KAGAN, J. (1996) 'Point of view: The misleading abstractions of social scientists', *Chronicle of Higher Education*, p. 52, January 12.

LEE, V.E., BRYK, A.S. and SMITH, J.B. (1993) 'The organization of effective secondary schools', *Review of Research in Education*, **19**, pp. 171–267.

LUTHAR, S.S. (1995) 'Social competence in the school setting: Prospective cross-domain associations among inner-city teens', *Child Development*, **66**, pp. 416–29.

MAASS, P. (1996) 'Bosnia's ground zero [Review of *Love Thy Neighbour*]', *Vanity Fair*, pp. 145–51, 199–203, March.

MARTINEAU, S. (1993) *Mainstream madness: Child abuse as gender socialization in the middle class*. Unpublished paper, University of Toronto.

MARTINEAU, S. (1996) 'Reconstructing childhood: Toward a praxis of inclusion', in FREEMAN, M. and McGILLIVRAY, A. (eds) *Governing Childhood*, Issues in Law and Society Series, Hampshire, England, Dartmouth.

McGILLIVRAY, A. (1992) 'Reconstructing child abuse: Western definition and non-western experience', in FREEMAN, M. and VEERMAN, P. (eds) *The Ideologies of Children's Rights*, Boston, Martinus Nijhoff, pp. 213–326.

McLAREN, A. (1990) *Our Own Master Race: Eugenics in Canada, 1885–1945*, Toronto, McClelland & Stewart.

MILLER, A. (1983) *For Your Own Good: Hidden Cruelty in Child-rearing and the Roots of Violence* (H. and H. Hannum, Trans.), New York, Farrar, Straus, Giroux.

MILLER, A. (1986) *Thou Shalt Not Be Aware: Society's Betrayal of the Child* (H. and H. Hannum, Trans.), New York, Meridian. (Original work published 1984)

NATIONAL COMMISSION ON EXCELLENCE IN EDUCATION (1983, April) *A Nation at Risk: The Imperative for Educational Reform. A Report to the Nation and the Secretary of Education, United States Department of Education*, Washington, DC, US Government Printing Office.

OXENHANDLER, N. (1996) 'The eros of parenthood: Not touching children can also be a crime', *New Yorker*, pp. 47–9, February 19.

PARR, J. (1980) *Labouring Children: British Immigrant Apprentices to Canada, 1869–1924*, London, England, Croom Helm.

PARR, J. (ed.) (1982) *Childhood and Family in Canadian History*, Toronto, McClelland & Stewart.

POLAKOW, V. (1995) 'Naming and blaming: Beyond a pedagogy of the poor', in SWADENER, B.B. and LUBECK, S. (eds) *Children and Families 'at Promise': Deconstructing the Discourse of Risk*, New York, State University of New York Press, pp. 263–70.

POLLOCK, L.A. (1983) *Forgotten Children: Parent–Child Relations from 1500 to 1900*, Cambridge, Cambridge University Press.

RUTTER, M., MAUGHAN, B., MORTIMORE, P., OUSTON, J., (with) SMITH, A. (1979) *Fifteen Thousand Hours: Secondary Schools and their Effects on Children*, Cambridge, MA, Harvard University Press.

SARAN, R. (1985) 'The use of archives and interviews in research on educational policy', in BURGESS, R.G. (ed.) *Strategies of Educational Research: Qualitative Methods*, London, Falmer Press, pp. 207–41.

SCHEURICH, J.J. (1994) 'Policy Archaeology: A New Policy Studies Methodology', *Journal of Educational Policy*, 9, 4, pp. 297–316.

SCHRUMPF, E. (1993) 'Attitudes towards child work in industry: An argument against the history of misery', *Norwegian Journal of History*, 2 (abstract).

SHAHAR, S. (1990) *Childhood in the Middle Ages*, New York, Routledge.

SKOLNICK, A. (1980) 'Children's rights, children's development', in EMPEY, L.T. (ed.) *Children's Rights and Juvenile Justice*, Charlottesville, University of Virginia Press, pp. 138–74.

SOMERS, M.R. (1992, winter) 'Narrativity, narrative identity, and social action: Rethinking English working-class formation', *Social Science History*, 16, 4, pp. 591–630.

STOSSEL, J. (1995) Reporter 'Attention Deficit Disorder'. *20/20*. ABC. KOMO-TV, Seattle, Washington, December 8.

STRAUSS, M. (1995) *Violence and abuse within the family: The neglected issues*. Keynote Address, Public Forum, Senate of Canada. Toronto, Ontario, June 9.

TAYLOR, K. (1996) Commentator 'Attention Deficit Hyperactivity Disorder'. *Real Life*. NBC. KING-TV, Seattle, Washington, March 15.

THORNE, B. (1987) 'Re-visioning women and social change: Where are the children?' *Gender & Society*, 1, 1, pp. 85–109.

VANCOUVER SCHOOL BOARD (1986) The school makes the difference: Vancouver public schools, no better place to learn. Unpublished report.

WEBER, M. (1958) *The Protestant Ethic and the Spirit of Capitalism* (T. Parsons, Trans.), New York, Charles Scribner's Sons.

WOLFF, L. (1988) *Postcards From the End of the World: Child Abuse in Freud's Vienna*, New York, Atheneum.

YOUNG, I.M. (1990) 'The ideal of community and the politics of difference', in NICHOLSON, L.J. (ed.) *Feminism/Postmodernism*, New York, Routledge, pp. 300–23.

3   Child Abuse and Teachers' Work: The Voice of Frustration*

Rosonna Tite

For a child's view of reporting abuse, see Leroy's analysis in Chapter 7 of this volume.

The teacher's role in detecting and reporting child abuse is often considered a simple procedural matter located more or less peripherally to the normal work of the school, instead of a complex systemic issue related to the perpetuation of violence. The reporting role not only prevents teachers from full professional involvement in the development and education of abused children; it also serves to mask the full extent of the problem. In this chapter, the focus is on the role of the teacher in reporting child abuse.

It is difficult to listen to teachers' talk about the cases of child abuse they have encountered. The problem is not the sadness of their descriptions, although that is an aspect of it, it is the predictable familiarity of the cases. In a typical scenario, the teacher comes across a case perhaps through a sudden disclosure or another similarly shocking incident, or by way of a nagging suspicion that develops over time. There is usually a period of doubt, often self-doubt, when the teacher carefully considers and reconsiders the case. She scrutinizes the child; she checks on the policies and regulations; she wonders how the principal will handle it; she worries about what will happen to the family if she reports the case and what will happen to the child if she does not. She considers her own life, her childhood, her own children, her job security, her legal liability and her position in the community. Finally, she goes forward (most do) and reports her case, usually to the principal, occasionally directly to child welfare. Sometimes she is told to forget about it, that she is overreacting, that she is overwrought and nervous. Occasionally she is applauded for her sensitivity and steadfastness. Usually, she is thanked for the information and then, in one way or another, dismissed. The case may proceed to an investigation, help may be channeled to the victim, and the offender might be charged and punished. Whatever steps are taken at this stage, however, often remain a mystery to the teacher; she is left to wonder and worry on her own.

* This research is funded by the Social Sciences and Research Council of Canada (File # 410-93-0970). I also wish to acknowledge the Department of Education and Training, Newfoundland and Labrador for their assistance with the mailing list, Cynthia Hicks and Maria Soldan for their assistance with interviewing and transcribing, and Sylvia Hopkins for her help with documents and for her helpful comments on an earlier draft of this paper.

The connection between the reporting of child abuse and systemic violence has long been ignored. Teachers' initial reactions are shaped, in large measure, by an institutional context that attends primarily to children's intellectual development and need for discipline. This creates group conditions that obscure all but the most obvious cases of abuse (Tite, 1986). Then, when teachers do confront a suspicious incident or a range of disturbing observations, they typically enter into a process which is largely guided by child abuse legislation, and reinforced by the reactions of principals and agents from the police and child welfare offices. When I asked one bewildered teacher about the results of her child abuse report, she said, 'Well, I think, between the jigs and reels, that it finally went to court'. It is the jigs and reels part that I find difficult because the institutional processes giving rise to the teachers' sense of uncertainty seem so obscure.

The dance metaphor is appropriate. There is a choreographic quality to 'coordinated action', the term generally applied to the school's child abuse reporting role. Coordinated action implies a well-rehearsed rhythm, with partners timing their steps to achieve an acceptable performance. Teachers play their part by observing children in the classroom setting and reporting their cases only after they have developed a well-founded suspicion. Then child welfare agents and a variety of medical, mental health and legal professionals step in and take their turns, processing the case and directing help for the abused child. Presumably, the main advantage of this co-ordination is that it draws on each group's professional strengths and institutional opportunities, while providing a strong multi-vocal message that child abuse is not acceptable. What troubles me is teachers' profound dissatisfaction with their part of the dance. Their continuing uncertainty, fears and personal frustration are so intense and widespread that we must recognize the reporting role as a systemic, as well as a procedural, issue.

Much of the research on coordinated action has been aimed at uncovering the legal and administrative difficulties associated with reporting (Brosig and Kalichman, 1992; Foster, 1991; McEvoy, 1990). Other topics emphasized are the teachers' lack of knowledge about abuse (Abrahams, Casey, and Daro, 1992; Baxter and Beer, 1990; Beck, Ogloff and Corbishley, 1994; McIntyre, 1987), their general wariness about becoming involved (Maher, 1987) and the conflicts that arise in dealing with agents from outside the school (Haase and Kempe, 1990; Zellman and Antler, 1990; Zellman, 1990). Often missing from this work is an understanding of the social and professional context in which reporting decisions are made. An analysis of that context and the links between systemic violence and teachers' experience of cases is the goal of my research.

By focusing in this chapter only on teachers who have made child abuse reports I hope to develop our understanding of this connection in particular ways. First, I will emphasize teachers' voices, providing their thinking and experiences at the reporting stage as a point of departure for understanding a wide range of problems. Then I will focus on teachers' normal work, taking the classroom, professional, policy and procedural difficulties associated with reporting as key to understanding the institutional context which gives shape to their experience. Finally, I will consider the extent to which coordinated action may be interpreted as a systemic effort to resist full school involvement in the education and development of abused children.

The Teachers

The information that follows comes from a larger study. Besides conducting an analysis of education and social services documents, I collected information from teachers in two stages. Surveys were sent to a stratified random sample of 1,000 teachers, of whom 35 per cent responded (Tite, in press). Teachers were asked to respond to a set of vignettes describing hypothetical cases, and to describe real cases they may have encountered. Teachers who had made formal reports were invited to participate in a telephone interview to provide details of those cases.

Of the 143 teachers who stated that they had made reports, 33 (less than one-quarter) indicated their willingness to be interviewed. This number is small but the teachers' wariness is understandable, given the sensitivity of the issue in general, and the more specific difficulties confronted by teachers who live and work in small communities. Almost every teacher began the discussion with a serious caution about the confidentiality of the case and the importance of remaining anonymous and unidentifiable in any written reports.

The teachers who were interviewed were broadly representative of the wider sample of reporters identified from the survey. Thirty of the thirty-three teachers (twenty-two women and eleven men) were employed as full-time classroom teachers (two were principals, and one was a guidance counselor). The teachers were fairly evenly scattered across regions, religious denomination, and grade levels (fifteen in primary/elementary, six in junior and senior high, and eight in all-grade schools). About half taught all subjects in contained classes, while the rest taught a range of subject specialties. All but three had made child abuse reports in the last five years. Also, in keeping with the characteristics of reporters identified in the larger sample, approximately 70 per cent of the teachers interviewed indicated that they were aware of their school board's child abuse reporting policy and had attended at least one child abuse inservice session.

The abuse victims reported by these teachers ranged in age from 5 to 16, evenly divided by gender. Parents or guardians were named as the abusers in eighteen of the thirty-three cases. Fourteen cases involved sexual abuse, ten involved physical abuse, and the rest involved neglect or some combination of physical, emotional abuse, and neglect. In nineteen cases the offender was male; usually he was the child's father, occasionally he was a brother, uncle or other adult male unrelated to the victim. In eight cases the mother was named as the abuser. The remaining six cases involved both male and female offenders.

Teachers' Voices I: Frustration

Even before I began a systematic analysis of the interview transcripts, I was struck by the teachers' frustration:

> I just feel very sorry for that child, or children in that situation . . . and I just think that this won't end, this won't be the end of that problem . . . If teachers aren't reporting it, I think it's because they feel burnout, and feel concern about stirring up things when they know nothing is going to change for that child. (Interviewee 41)

> From knowing the child and being here with the child all year, [you know] there is certainly a problem, a serious one, and it's going to get worse. And that's the frustrating thing about it, the system can't do much about it. (Interviewee 84)

> Things like that make me so mad. I was so angry last year, and you just feel like [saying] 'Oh, shit!'. (Interviewee 87)

At one level, the frustration appears as a simple expression of disappointment about the lack of available services. There was widespread concern about 'budget cuts', complaints about 'long waiting periods' and 'huge caseloads', and an overriding sense that, in spite of their best intentions, child welfare workers were simply unable to keep up with the reports coming from teachers and other sources. Several teachers suggested that their main reason for participating in the study was to raise awareness of the need for more services and facilities at the child welfare level. 'We need those facilities and those services that we don't have right now . . . and if this [interview] can bring it about, that's the reason I decided to answer these questions' (Interviewee 233).

While most of the teachers agreed that the initial contact between teachers and child welfare was positive, they worried about the lack of follow-up:

> I felt there was something else going on with the child that hadn't been uncovered because the caseworker was too overworked . . . I found this all very frustrating and disturbing because the child was emotionally distraught 90 per cent of the time and there was very little being done. Where do we turn to for help in situations like this? I just don't know. (Interviewee 197)

> They [the social workers] say they are going to do things, but they usually don't . . . I think that a lot of people just kind of give up after a while. Like you just don't feel that the system is going to be able to do anything. (Interviewee 136)

This frustration is often expressed as resignation. When teachers were asked if they would do anything differently if they were to come across another case, a frequent response was a long sigh, followed by a discussion of the legal obligation to report in spite of the less than satisfactory outcomes:

> In a way, I think the child would have been better off had it not been reported [but] I would report it again because I know that's my duty. I feel that where it broke down was with social services. (Interviewee 41)

Not surprisingly, perhaps, cynicism is another expression:

> This case really opened my eyes to the fact that there isn't much out there really for the children who are abused . . . it's almost like social services is a facade and they're just doing band-aid work. (Interviewee 149)

At another level, the teachers seemed frustrated with the practical difficulties and philosophical conflicts involved in dealing with school offices and agents from child protection services. One problem had to do with disagreements about the severity of the abuse, particularly evident in cases of neglect:

> They just go ahead and investigate and that's about it . . . unless it's physical or sexual abuse, with marks and witnesses. They really don't prioritize emotional abuse. (Interviewee 180)

> Social services doesn't want to apprehend children unless there is a kind of proven risk, but my concern is that neglect and emotional abuse isn't taken nearly as seriously as . . . physical abuse and sexual abuse. To me, neglect and emotional abuse are just as serious, and perhaps, in the long run, more so. (Interviewee 257)

Related to this was the frustration encountered by teachers who felt unheard or misunderstood by outside investigators when they believed that they had clear, ongoing classroom evidence of abuse or neglect:

> One day he came to school with his mouth all beat up . . . and we took him off to the hospital, and the doctor put it down to an isolated incident . . . he thought it wasn't worth reporting because it happened before and would wait to see if it happens again . . . but it's been going on for years. (Interviewee 87)

> They [Social Services] can do their monitoring, but not to the same frequency that we can do it at the school, because we see the children every day . . . This case is still ongoing, this is probably the fifth, sixth or seventh or tenth time I've called them regarding this. (Interviewee 257)

> They took the child to the hospital and all they could verify was the bruise, but they didn't think it had been made by a rod . . . But to me, the child is abused . . . because I have the child in my classroom and she came to school dirty at times, her clothes were filthy, and other times, she came to school with no lunch. So I believe what she told me that day. (Interviewee 331)

Possibly because of their own experience of child welfare's reluctance to intervene in 'non-urgent' cases, many principals seem reticent about encouraging their teachers to go forward with a report until they have carefully documented a number of incidents. This is another source of frustration:

> Like I said to him [the principal] the last time, I can document until hell freezes over, but that's not going to save the child if this bruising gets worse. I could send this child home . . . and he might not come back tomorrow. (Interviewee 280)

Another problem concerns questions about the appropriate division of responsibilities between the school, the police and agents from child welfare.

> I've been told by the Child Protection Worker to butt out, that Victim Services will assess the situation . . . I think this child is going to be victimized again. Nothing is really going to be done until it comes to court again, and I'm very disillusioned actually. (Interviewee 279)

A prevailing theme throughout the interviews was the use of such metaphors as 'stepping on toes', and 'overstepping boundaries'. Many teachers had been warned, for instance, about the difficulties associated with discussing the case with the child:

> What I did learn from that one is to be extremely careful . . . the worst thing to do is to sit down and question the student, because basically you screw up the investigation . . . this comes from long conversations with the RCMP who investigated the case. (Interviewee 108)

Similarly, teachers have been cautioned that it is not their role to deal with parents, or to follow up with the police or caseworkers from social services. In some cases, the guidance counsellor is expected to handle the teachers' suspicions and teachers are thus discouraged from making even the initial contact:

> I did go to the guidance counsellor . . . and said, 'You have to see her before the day is out . . . you're the expert and you have to see her.' And just to make sure, I said I was going to contact social services. He wasn't too pleased that I would do that . . . it was his area, and you certainly don't want to step on people's toes. (Interviewee 256)

The frustration of being compelled to stand silently on the sidelines after a child has made a disclosure is compounded in cases where the teachers perceive that the police and child welfare agents seem unsympathetic or threatening in their investigative role:

> The youngster was 15 or 16 years old. She was sitting across the table from a police officer . . . and to that youngster, that's an authority figure, and she's frightened . . . frightened the child half to death. (Interviewee 182)

Clearly, teachers hold a different kind of relationship with children than either the police or the caseworkers assigned to handle their cases, and this is at the centre of their frustration. They feel quite helpless in confronting the issue of how to deal effectively with a child in the midst of a disclosure, during the course of the ensuing investigation, and after the case has been taken up by the authorities outside the school:

> I think that, as a teacher, I should be informed [of the outcome of the investigation]. Maybe other people have greater wisdom than I at this, and maybe they're right, but . . . I mean I'm working with that kid eight hours a day, five days a week. (Interviewee 153)

Some of the teachers' frustration was obviously personal. There was a kind of collective sadness throughout the interview material which defied a more systematic analysis, but which nevertheless revealed itself in the consistent use of such words as guilt, regret and personal torment. In part, the distress seemed to stem from the emotional bond that teachers had developed with their students. 'Well, I was upset because to think that somebody in my class had gone through that . . . you don't like to think that it really happened to them' (Interviewee 30). 'It was very emotional . . . emotionally, it hurt me because the two children are lovable children' (Interviewee 295). Not surprisingly, this was compounded in cases where the teachers felt that they might have prevented the abuse if only they had been more astute or more careful in their judgments or observations:

> I got this call, summoned to the office by Child Welfare. They had documented that several of the children in my class were sexually abused by the bus driver. I was devastated. I kept saying, 'Why didn't I pick it up?' But he was like a grandfather and he was so good and he took us on our outings free of charge, and I just kept thinking this is a person who really cares. (Interviewee 280)

The personal issues became even more complicated for teachers who lived in their school communities:

> In a small community like ours, one of the things that I think teachers have a bit of a problem with is it could be a next door neighbour, people that you've known your whole lifetime, people you went to school with, and all of a sudden, you've got to report them for sexual assault. (Interviewee 84)

As another interviewee noted: 'If it's a close personal friend, for instance, or someone influential in the community . . . it's uncomfortable because you know you have to live here forever' (Interviewee 328). For some teachers, the personal torment is rooted in their own history of abuse. One reported 'I felt . . . stomach sick. When you've been there yourself, you don't think justice ever gets done' (Interviewee 65). Another reported:

I've seen a lot of abuse in my own family, and when dealing with this, I guess I was shocked to find out that there was still . . . I do know that I was definitely not prepared for this. (Interviewee 295)

Teachers' Voices II: Uncertainty

A second theme evident in the interview material was uncertainty:

What upsets me is that should another case come to my attention, I'm not sure what I will do. I'm concerned about doing the right thing and I'm not sure I would be doing the right thing. (Interviewee 197)

You wonder, and you look for her first thing in the morning and think to yourself: My God, if anything happens to her tonight, what didn't I do? Or even if nothing happens and she mentions it at home and all hell breaks loose, did I go too far? It's something that really torments you. (Interviewee 256)

The teachers' pervasive sense of uncertainty and self-doubt appears to arise out of the increased demand to be more responsive to abused children, and a lack of confidence in their ability to do so:

I'm nearing the end of my career and I just don't know what is expected of us because . . . there are so many needs and there's so much lack of training. It's an area I don't feel competent in. I've been looking for answers in the past fifteen years. First year, I started out thinking I knew how to teach, and now it seems that there are so many needs, you hardly know what is correct. (Interviewee 75)

Much of the uncertainty seems centered in teachers' perception that, in dealing with child abuse, they are taking on a role which is outside their normal teaching duties: 'You're accountable for the academics, but also the social part of the child as well, and I don't feel qualified to deal with things like that' (Interviewee 233).

For others, the uncertainty lies in determining whether the parents are intentionally or unintentionally abusive:

It's not quite as cut and dried as that, because in this case, this particular mother, I feel, does care about the child and her other children, but she has many problems herself, and she's not really able to deal with the children as she should. But, it's not on purpose, I don't believe. (Interviewee 257)

There wasn't any neglect, I'd say intentionally. I think the mother was probably doing her best. I don't think it was deliberate, not caring about them. I think she probably did care . . . but I still felt that the boy was suffering. (Interviewee 278)

Another expression of the teachers' uncertainty appears in a lack of consensus about how to balance their concerns for children's safety against the need to maintain the child's family as a unit. 'I don't like to see the child taken away from the home. I think the child should be with the parents . . . but I still fear for that child' (Interviewee 331).

> The principal's biggest concern was that the child would be removed from the home, and he figured he had enough against him as it was. I said that it wasn't my intent that that should happen, but if it meant that the child was going to be safe, then I didn't care whose home was cracked. (Interviewee 279)

Some teachers are quite clear about their interest in keeping families intact:

> Social services walked in after we reported it, and took the child away from the parents, took him out of our school and moved him to another community. I thought that was very detrimental to the child . . . they didn't do what was best for the child, as far as I'm concerned, as an educator. (Interviewee 295)

Others were equally adamant about the need to place abused children in foster care:

> When he was taken away from his parents, he was a very happy child . . . but we seem to be getting that same old rhetoric about how it's much better to try and change the family situation from within and we don't take kids out of homes anymore. (Interviewee 41)

> I asked [the social worker], 'What has to happen to take a child from the parents?' and she said, 'That's the very last thing they will do', and I found that very frustrating. (Interviewee 330)

For others still, there is the question of whether it is worth disrupting families in the face of child welfare's inability to provide much in the way of long-term solutions for the children:

> Sometimes, even when justice is done, you start wondering whether it was in the best interests of the child . . . basically, the kid is left hanging. They come and disclose, they go through hell in terms of being in court, it becomes public knowledge, and so on. Sometimes the perpetrator doesn't even get any jail time, and basically, what you do is you wreck a family. (Interviewee 108)

Adding to their confusion about what type of intervention is best is the fact that few teachers ever found out about the full outcome of their cases:

I don't know what happened there. I really don't, not for sure. I don't know if anyone pressed charges, or how far the case was investigated . . . I was sort of left out in the cold . . . and we at the school said, 'Well, I guess it's not for us to push this issue now.' (Interviewee 153)

Teachers' Voices III: Concerns about Consequences

Closely connected to the uncertainty about what could happen as the result of their reports was the teachers' fear that reporting abuse could sometimes make the situation worse. This was frequently expressed as some apprehension about traumatizing the child at the early stages of disclosure:

I was a little apprehensive about the reaction, in terms of contacting the RCMP (police), having them drive up to the school. I was worried about what that might do to the girls. Everybody is going on the bus this afternoon, and they don't go home. And the RCMP is going to be showing up at the school in a squad car. (Interviewee 108)

For some teachers, there was also concern about traumatizing the other children:

I think next time I wouldn't let the child talk . . . within the whole class. I think maybe I would stop her and take her outside and talk to her . . . but where they're feeling comfortable in that situation, you don't know whether to let them go on and expose the other children to it, or whether it's better for other children [not] to hear about it. (Interviewee 30)

He was arrested here at school. When the girls didn't show up on the bus, he came to school looking for them, which was another problem, to have the arrest made here on the premises. It was uncomfortable for everyone. (Interviewee 108)

There is clearly the risk, as well, that parents may react to the report by becoming even more abusive:

It was obvious what had happened to the child and he was taken out of home at that point and he was living at his grandparents' across the street. Now, his whole family kind of turned against him. His brothers weren't allowed to cross the street to play with him. (Interviewee 169)

The younger daughter took a lot of heat. She was basically black-listed by the family for disclosing, and that bothered me. (Interviewee 108)

He has a frightened way of interacting . . . he's too frightened to say anything anymore to anyone. He knows better than to talk about it. I think he's been warned not to say anything more. (Interviewee 41)

Another risk involved the difficulties associated with trying to maintain good home–school relationships after the report. Some teachers were faced with a good deal of anger on the part of parents: 'The mother got pretty irate about the fact that we took him to the hospital' (Interviewee 87). Apart from outright anger, however, there is also the problem of trying to deal with such ordinary school matters as report cards and homework:

[The parents] refuse to have any contact because these cases have been reported through the school. I guess they feel a fair bit of animosity. They will not come in for anything, they don't even come in for report cards. (Interviewee 41)

Clearly, teachers depend on parents to help with their children's schooling in a variety of ways, and, in reporting abuse, they run the risk of alienating them:

We had one case of a family that moved . . . to our community. And those people were very good. They approached the school right away to offer help, to put on shows, to raise money for the school. But, then one of the teachers had to have social services in to check on some bruises on one of the youngsters. It just turned everything around. The people never forgave, never forgave the school. (Interviewee 165)

Even when there is no explicit anger or animosity, there is often still a great deal of discomfort and apprehension about dealing with families after a report:

The mother is still living with the guy after he got out of jail. Instead of being concerned with the daughter, she spent her time up in jail visiting this guy until his trial. And that bothers me . . . I didn't have any dealings with them after this . . . it made me feel really uncomfortable, uncomfortable with the mother's attitude. (Interviewee 108)

The discomfort extended in many cases to the teachers' relationship with the children:

I never really talked to him about that because I felt somewhat uncomfortable after, because I know the kid didn't want it to be reported. There is some kind of trust relationship between the student and the teacher, I hope there is anyway, and in some ways, it sort of seemed like maybe I broke the trust with this young man. (Interviewee 153)

Finally, it is clear as well that some teachers feel that reporting puts them at some personal risk:

In a small town, everybody knows everybody else, so I have to be careful about this. I have to have proof before I can report it. I have to know that it's true. If it's not true, I may lose my job. (Interviewee 329)

My name will need to be kept out of [this report] because we're in a very small town and if my name goes into the study it becomes very obvious who we are talking about, which could lead to some uncomfortable situations for me. (Interviewee 108)

I'm a bit scared, even about calling social services, because I know the situation in that family, and you don't know what retaliation these people will take . . . There should be more guidance provided . . . to let us know what we can and can't do, because everybody is frightened, frightened to death. That's the way it seems. (Interviewee 330)

Systemic Links: Child Abuse and Teachers' Work

Perhaps the most unfortunate aspect of the teachers' descriptions of their experiences of coordinated action was what they did not say. Their voices ring out the alarm for those who would assess the efficiency of coordinated action, but the teachers are oddly silent on where their dilemmas originate. They provide some clues, of course, perhaps most notably in their descriptions of the lack of resources for teacher training and for caseworkers at the investigative and child welfare level. But, their silence on issues related to their own work as teachers is disturbing.

I think there are at least two aspects to this. One is that child abuse appears as such an extraordinary event in the day-to-day life of the school. Unlike dealing with a child who is hurt on the playground, a youngster who has forgotten homework, or a student who is questioning exam results, coping with a suspicion or disclosure of abuse obviously requires an extraordinary effort, and there is a kind of flurry of activity which seems at once both unusual and confusing. This situation is deeply perplexing given the conventional wisdom that teachers are particularly well-placed for identifying victims and given the high level of child abuse incidence rates among school-aged children. It is estimated, for instance, that as many as one in two girls and one in three boys suffer from sexual abuse, that over 8,000 cases of physical abuse are reported in Canada each year, that the incidence of neglect and emotional abuse is higher than all other abuses, and that as many as 50 to 60 per cent of child abuse victims are of school age (Health and Welfare Canada, 1989). More than half of the teachers I surveyed in two provinces indicated that they had come across at least one case in the past five years (Tite, in press). Suspicion rates stand at anywhere from 50 to 75 per cent. If there are so many cases of child abuse, why is the reporting of it such an extraordinary event?

Beyond its extraordinary quality, dealing with child abuse seems also to be disruptive. A public disclosure can disrupt a class, a report can destroy a child's confidence in the teacher, dealing with the police or caseworkers can alter an otherwise routine day, and working with parents after a report can lead to a range of unforeseen difficulties. The disruptive nature of child abuse for the normal work of the school is troubling given that schools are the main social institutions concerned with children, and especially in light of the fact that teachers may be the only trusted adults in a position to help.

To the extent that a suspicion or disclosure of abuse appears as an 'event', because it seems both extraordinary and disruptive, it raises questions about the school's inability or unwillingness to deal with child abuse. It suggests, in fact, that coordinated action, as it appears in the voices of the teachers who have described their experiences of it, may be more appropriately understood as a systemic effort to deflect the school's responsibility for child abuse (and perhaps societal violence more generally), while maintaining the appearance of providing a principled effort to deal with the problem. To make this connection, we need to begin with an understanding of teachers' normal work and the systemic resistance to change.

Teaching is at the heart of teachers' normal work. But successful teaching requires careful planning, a knowledge of curriculum, pedagogy, and learner characteristics, and an ability to manage groups of learners through the time and space of a day's work. Also involved is a set of understandings about how to evaluate the outcomes of teaching and learning and how to communicate the results to students, parents, administrators, guidance counsellors and other resource personnel in ways that promote further learning (see also Tite, 1986). This must be understood before considering where, and to what extent, an attention to child abuse might be appropriately integrated, given a full educational commitment to the problem.

First, consider the knowledge that teachers bring to their normal work, at its most fundamental level, knowledge of curriculum, pedagogy and learner characteristics. Presumably an attention to child abuse could involve teacher knowledge at several levels: an awareness that child abuse is a pervasive social problem, an understanding of the signs and symptoms of abuse, an awareness of the learning needs and characteristics of abused children, the ability to both develop and deliver child abuse prevention curriculum, and insight in to the hidden curriculum in terms of messages about violence. The silence of the teachers in this sample indicated only a very weak knowledge base in these terms. The uncertainty, which they expressed quite clearly, and the fact that less than half of the teachers in the wider sample have had any child abuse training at all, indicated an overall systemically weak commitment to teachers' knowledge of abuse.

Next consider the work normally involved in planning, classroom management, evaluation and communication. If we assume that a fully responsive approach to child abuse would draw on teachers' expertise in these areas, we might expect fewer problems with respect to public disclosures in the classroom. We could hope as well for less difficulty in dealing with parents, and a more routine approach to communicating with the principal, guidance counsellors, caseworkers and the police. While the teachers in this sample have expressed a great deal of frustration and uncertainty about all of these issues, what they have said, perhaps more importantly, is that they take much of their direction from caseworkers and from the police. Questions about how to handle the information provided by the abused child, how to help the child cope with the trauma while maintaining the child's trust in the teacher, how to deal with other students, and how to communicate with parents are clearly not seen as part of teachers' normal work. This became even more evident in the teachers' silence on the educational implications of the abuse.

If teaching is at the center of teachers' normal work, we might expect teachers' responsiveness to abused children to be at its most obvious in the classroom. In order to consider this aspect of teachers' normal work, we asked the teachers if they had experienced or made any changes in their teaching after they became aware that a child in their class had been abused. Their responses were quite telling. Of the thirty-three teachers interviewed, twenty-two indicated that the abuse had no influence on their teaching, in a few cases because the child left the school after the report, but in most cases because the teachers felt that they were already doing everything they could. One teacher suggested that it might be harmful to the abused child to make any changes:

> No, no, not for the child, no . . . I didn't change my attitude towards him or my teaching techniques with him or anything like that, no. And we just carried on as natural, I hope, as it was before. (Interviewee 153)

Another teacher appeared a little resentful about the question, evidently seeing in it, and perhaps resisting, its implication that there might be a need for change:

> On the basis of what I saw, he seemed to be okay, and there was really no need to change anything . . . I didn't see any need to change and had I seen a need, I didn't know to what extent I could have changed and still maintained any semblance of what you would think a classroom should be. (Interviewee 75)

The changes made by the teachers who indicated that they had made some kind of change in their teaching seemed quite modest overall. Two indicated that they had brought in a child abuse prevention curriculum kit. Four others indicated that they had become personally more sensitive to the child's needs and had become more aware of the issue in general. Five teachers told us that they began offering something more in the way of individual attention, such as after-school counselling, extra help with homework or study skills, and peer teaching.

These descriptions need to be understood in the context of the teachers' frustration, uncertainty, and concerns about the consequences of reporting. Teachers, seem individually, very anxious about doing the right thing, while systemically, they are unable to respond to the problem as educators. They do not have a store of pedagogical knowledge that could be applied to the problem of child abuse. They are unable to call on their skills in managing children and their expertise in dealing with parents, administrators, colleagues, and professionals outside of the school. And they are unlikely to change their approach to teaching in the face of the problem.

The resistance to change is systemic, maintained in large measure by the reporting policy and the school's role in coordinated action. Although the reporting policy calls on teachers to recognize that child abuse is a social problem, it casts teachers into a surveillance rather than response role. Encouraging teachers to identify abuse and hand their cases over to experts outside the school, confirms them in the role of reporter and reminds them that teachers are not normally in the business of dealing with abuse. As such, it effectively removes from schools, not only the responsibility for developing a full educational response to the problem, but also the opportunity for creating new visions of teachers' normal work.

The systemic unwillingness to change teachers' normal work to reflect a commitment to abused children is evident in most policy documents. Although I plan a full analysis of the documents for the next phase of this research, two points are worth noting at this stage. The first is to be found within the child abuse policy documents and concerns the continuing effort to define the teachers' role in terms of reporting. Although most documents provide some background about child abuse and some general statements about the need for schools to develop counselling or other services for abused children, the overwhelming emphasis is on the importance of developing teachers' knowledge of their reporting role, i.e., the legal obligation to report and the procedures outlining under what circumstances a report should be made, to whom, and how the paperwork should be handled (Government of Newfoundland and Labrador, 1993).

The second issue has to do with an increased emphasis on coordination with outside agencies. This emphasis also shows up in education documents of a more general nature, often appearing as a concern about teachers' frustration with the increasing numbers of children with special problems and special needs. Although these documents frequently identify child abuse as a growing concern for teachers, they do so in ways that clearly underscore the reporting role, while redirecting the ultimate responsibility for social problems to outside agencies. For example:

> An over-reliance on the province's schools to address medical, social and judicial problems has resulted in confusion, frustration, classroom disruptions, burgeoning demands on teachers and lost instructional time . . . To remove some of these pressures from the schools and thereby enhance the quality of education all children receive, there is a critical need for better co-ordination of physical and mental health services, social services, juvenile justice, and youth employment services, in addition to the changes required in the school system itself. (Government of Newfoundland and Labrador, 1992, p. 365)

This situation raises serious questions about teachers' work and the extent to which we may expect the school to become fully involved in the development and education of abused children. It also compels us to reflect on coordinated action in ways that go beyond the procedural difficulties associated with the teachers' reporting role, and which would instead draw us into the debate about how social problems get systemically defined and acted on. We should begin by listening to teachers when they voice their concerns about the children they are trying their best to protect.

References

ABRAHAMS, N., CASEY, K. and DARO, D. (1992) 'Teachers' knowledge, attitudes, and beliefs about child abuse and its prevention', *Child Abuse and Neglect*, **16**, pp. 229–38.

BAXTER, G. and BEER, J. (1990) 'Educational needs of school personnel regarding child abuse and/or neglect', *Psychological Reports*, **67**, pp. 75–80.

BECK, K., OGLOFF, J. and CORBISHLEY, A. (1994) 'Knowledge, compliance, and attitudes of teachers toward mandatory child abuse reporting in British Columbia', *Canadian Journal of Education*, **19**, 1, pp. 15–29.

BROSIG, C.L. and KALICHMAN, S.C. (1992) 'Child abuse reporting decisions: Effects of statutory wording of reporting requirements', *Professional Psychology: Research and Practice*, **23**, pp. 486–92.

FOSTER, W.F. (1991) 'Child abuse in schools: The statutory and common law obligations of educators', *Education and Law Journal*, **4**, pp. 1–59.

GOVERNMENT OF NEWFOUNDLAND AND LABRADOR (1992) *Our Children, Our Future*, report of the Royal Commission of Inquiry, St. John's, Newfoundland, Government of Newfoundland and Labrador.

GOVERNMENT OF NEWFOUNDLAND AND LABRADOR (1993) *Provincial Child Abuse Policy and Guidelines*, St. John's, Department of Education, Division of Student Support Service.

HAASE, C. and KEMPE, R.S. (1990) 'The school and protective services', *Education and Urban Society*, **22**, pp. 258–69.

HEALTH AND WELFARE CANADA (1989) *Family Violence: A Review of the Theoretical and Clinical Literature*, Ottawa, Health and Welfare Canada.

MAHER, P. (1987) *Child Abuse: The Educational Perspective*, Oxford, Basil Blackwell.

McEVOY, A. (1990) 'Child abuse law and school policy', *Education and Urban Society*, **22**, 3, pp. 247–57.

McINTYRE, T. (1987) 'Teacher awareness of child abuse and neglect', *Child Abuse and Neglect*, **11**, pp. 133–5.

TITE, R. (1986) 'Sex-role learning and the woman teacher: A feminist perspective', *Feminist Perspectives*, **7**, Ottawa, CRIAW.

TITE, R. (1994) 'Muddling through: The procedural marginalization of child abuse', *Interchange*, **25**, 1, pp. 87–108.

TITE, R. (in press) 'Who knows? Who cares? Schools and coordinated action on child abuse', in EPP, J.R. and WATKINSON, A.M. (eds) *Systemic Violence in Education: Promise Broken*, Syracuse, NY, SUNY Press, pp. 37–54.

ZELLMAN, G. (1990) 'Linking schools and social services: The case of child abuse reporting', *Educational Evaluation and Policy Analysis*, **12**, 1, pp. 41–5.

ZELLMAN, G. and ANTLER, S. (1990) 'Mandated reporters and CPS: A study in frustration', *Public Welfare*, **48**, 1, pp. 30–7.

4 Systemic Barriers between Home and School

Sharon M. Abbey

> Schooling takes children from the mothers and gives them to the fathers. It provides a passage from domestic and maternal nurturance to public institutions and patriarchal identifications . . . It is the female elementary school teacher who is charged with the responsibility to lead this great escape . . . Mothers relinquish their children to her, and she hands them over to men who respect the gift but not the giver. (Grumet, 1988)

When I first read these words in Madelaine Grumet's book *Bitter Milk* my reaction was intense. Her accusations forced me to re-examine my dual role as teacher and mother and threw me into a disturbing chasm of self-doubt and uncertainty. A sequence of snap-shot images flashed through my mind, which I describe here to introduce issues related to home–school barriers as a form of anti-domestic systemic violence.

Image 1 — I see myself as a child playing with dolls. Sometimes I am their 'mommy' and I rock them to sleep. I am kind and loving. Other times I sit my dolls in neat rows in front of a little blackboard. I am now their 'teacher' and they are some other mothers' children. They dare not move or make a sound for I am stern and strict and I often scold them. My own mother is standing nearby, amused by my imagination. Neither of us identify the contradictions I am replicating in my childhood play as I separate the two worlds of 'home' and 'school'. Nor do we consider the realities for women who choose to undertake both of these roles at the same time.

Image 2 — I am a first-year kindergarten teacher desperately pulling weeping children from their mothers' arms and shutting the classroom door to prevent their escape. If they try to bolt for the door I tighten my grasp on their tiny wrists. The windows are covered with paper so that the mothers cannot see inside. These children are mine now and I view their mothers as a distraction and a nuisance. It is time for them to separate and sever emotional ties with home.

Image 3 — I am a single mother with two teenage children and I am entering the principal's office for the first time as the newly appointed vice-principal. I feel the knot in my stomach tighten as he warns me never to let my home responsibilities interfere with my duties at school. I am determined to live up to his expectations. I view my motherhood responsibilities as a disadvantage to my career aspirations.

Although I relate to many children in my office, classroom or playground every day, I am not consciously aware of how my experiences at home influence and enrich me as a caring, compassionate, teacher.

Image 4 — As a pre-service instructor in a Faculty of Education I am criticized by some of my students for discussing my daughter's life-threatening illness during social studies classes. These students are not able to connect the social theories we are studying to my personal struggles to cope. They have already internalized the hidden curricula about keeping private lives separate from public duties.

Grumet's conclusions challenged me to reclaim these fragments and re-story myself into a whole being (Bateson, 1994). How do women bridge the two worlds of home and school and deal with systemic disadvantage, discrimination or denial? In a three-year qualitative study, which involved ongoing conversations with ten women teachers who were also mothers, I attempted to define maternal pedagogy. Throughout the discussions, there was a disturbing sense of bitterness about the compromises women felt forced to make between the two incongruous worlds of mother and teacher. No one had ever asked them to talk about their experiences before. They expressed surprise at my interest; initially they were doubtful about having much to say that would be interesting or worthwhile. I was especially struck by their overtone of resignation — *things are the way they are, no-one talks about the dissonance or alienation, and, furthermore, no one cares!* This was perhaps why they welcomed the opportunity to dialogue. There was a resilience, optimism and energy woven into their conversations and a sense of pride in their domestic expertise, insights as caregivers, and ability to cope with multiple demands, interruptions, and responsibilities. This was their opportunity to talk about skills and wisdoms that were not regularly acknowledged or valued in schools. In this chapter, I will be examining the dual roles of women who are both mothers and teachers. To distinguish the roles, I will refer to teacher-mothers, that is women performing the teacher role who are also mothers, and mother-teachers, women performing the mothering role who are also teachers.

Teacher-Mothers

The women who participated in this study were between 35 and 55. Some had only a few years of teaching experience while others were preparing to retire. The age of their children ranged from pre-school to adult. One woman was pregnant with her second child, two others were single parents, while another was widowed and became a grandmother during the time of the study. Most of these women were the eldest in their families and had often been expected to look after younger siblings. Most did not feel particularly close to their own mothers, were critical about the way they had been raised, and were determined to handle motherhood and careers differently than had their mothers.

In most cases, these women were teachers before they became wives and mothers, so each was forced to decide whether or not to return to teaching after having children. Some had children soon after marriage, while others deliberately chose to delay motherhood. In a few cases, pregnancy was resented as an unexpected intrusion. Two women remained out of the workforce for twelve years after their children were born. Two others resigned from teaching with great reluctance and resentment. The others relied on baby-sitters or day-care facilities in order to return to teaching as soon as possible. Prominent in their dialogue was an intense resentment about losing seniority due to maternity leaves. Each had struggled to find a satisfactory balance between career and mothering obligations and identities. These women often felt controlled or overwhelmed by the needs or expectations of others and struggled to cope with guilt, regret or disappointment with their life choices. The women seldom spoke of husbands or partners willing to take over domestic responsibilities, nor did they mention any flexible arrangements or accommodations made on their behalf by school boards.

Denial of the Domestic

Our education system teaches, reflects and is sustained by androcentrism that imposes a male-oriented cultural filter and elevates male experience and values to universal status (Acker, 1994; Biklen, 1993; Eisler, 1987; Gilligan, 1982; Grumet, 1988; Robertson, 1994; Spender, 1982). As a result, there is an overreliance on analytical rationality, cause and effect, instrumental predictability, hierarchical power dominance and competitiveness. Jane Roland Martin (1992) points out that 'warfare' or 'factory' metaphors abound in terms such as quality control, standardized testing, regimentation, and student compliance. The role of the school is reduced to that of preparing children to carry out economic and political tasks and of transforming inhabitants of private space into inhabitants of public space (Grumet, 1988). This process of education which 'prepares children for the self-alienation of civilized adulthood' (Bateson, 1994, p. 23) is seldom questioned.

The same patriarchal mind-set has traditionally assigned the domestic arena to women and all matters associated with it to the mundane, commonplace and trivial. The social significance of the home's contribution to education is discounted and silenced. Emotional, relational and care-taking skills are assumed to be inadequate or insignificant pedagogies which fail to prepare children for the competitive world. Domestic images and 'soft' qualities, such as affection, intimacy, connection, harmony, kindness, and sympathy, are considered less worthy of attention in schools (Bateson, 1994; Martin, 1992). The traditional patriarchal viewpoint, perpetuated in school curricula, not only reinforces barriers between home and school but also discounts half of western heritage (Martin, 1992). Martin argues that caring ethics and education for citizenship are especially crucial during this 'second transformation of the American home' when more mothers have joined fathers in the workforce away from home and more children have been left without parental guidance for longer periods of time. The hidden curriculum of anti-domesticity in both education and society cannot be addressed without making it a topic of study in the curriculum proper. Schools are forced to adapt to and compensate for changing family structures — or are they?

The Juggling Act

Sources of stress that women face as they struggle to fulfill commitments and expectations in the dual role of teaching and mothering are: societal expectations; lack of support; the trauma associated with impersonal resignation processes; fatigue and guilt resulting from multiple demands; decisions over child care; and the relentless pressure of time constraints. Women's stories of moving between the worlds of home and school are filled with tensions based on the conflicting societal expectations in each domain. Mothering — that is bringing up well-behaved children — is viewed as a primary source of female identity. Society is critical of women who take on additional jobs and responsibilities outside the home. Some women who stay at home with their children enjoy being removed from the workplace. Others are less contented but may discount their own feelings of being isolated, trapped, and disadvantaged without sources of diversion and income. As one respondent who gave up teaching noted:

> You can't have it all. I never was very good at dividing myself. I only have so much to give and I really want to give it to my own kids. When I get home from school there is no elastic left. I usually yell and get really grumpy . . .

The same respondent noted the friction between mothers who stay in the workforce and those who choose to remain at home:

> I find there is a lot of friction between mothers who stay at home and mothers who don't. Several women told me I was crazy to resign. I was in tears a lot. My sister-in-law assumes that I must be intellectually inferior because I stay home . . . My neighbor is a teacher and she dumps her kids on me. She has missed their entire childhood and they are all walking wrecks. She values a new sofa more than her child. I feel sorry for her. I wish I had known how hard this all was before I got into it!

Mothers who return to work may feel guilt, stress, or fatigue. Their commitments to their families are often interpreted as lack of interest in their teaching careers and vice versa:

> In a job interview I remember being asked how many more children I planned to have . . . If worse came to worse, I would lie and phone in sick. I'm sure they knew it was really my daughter and not me who was sick. (Anna)

The mother/martyr archetype exerts a powerful and persuasive force. This ideology assumes that a mother can only pursue her own self-actualization at the expense of others. Leaving the children to continue a career outside the home implies self-ishness or irresponsibility. In what Caplan (1989) calls 'mother blaming', mothers are held responsible for any maladjustments, failures or problems their children experience.

Discounting personal needs in order to preserve relationships and nurture others sets up an internal conflict for many women. The fusion of identity and intimacy in the lifecycle of women makes choices between home and work espe-cially difficult for mothers (Gilligan, 1992). Although independence and separation are highly regarded for others in our society, it is not easy or desirable for mothers to pursue it. The need for affiliation and attachment is viewed as immature and child-like, and is not rewarded or recognized. Little wonder women feel inferior and uncomfortable about their choices.

Choice for women is nothing new. Historically, women have always been expected to modify their values and behaviors in response to societal development and economic circumstance (Jones, Marsden, and Tepperman, 1990). Women have been influenced by the experts and gatekeepers of each generation who tell them when to breast-feed, when to stay home or pursue careers, and when day-care is appropriate or detrimental. The choices women are encouraged to make are directly linked to current societal needs. As a result, the lives of women have lacked unity and integrity. In comparison to the lives of men, they may appear to be more com-pliant, flexible and adaptable. In describing the lives of women who move in and out of the workforce, Bateson (1984) points out that 'these are not lives without commitment, but rather lives in which commitments are continually refocused and redefined' (pp. 9–10). Women's lives are interrupted and continually in transition which could be viewed as rich and fulfilling rather than inferior and limiting (Bateson, 1984).

Deciding to resign or take a leave of absence can be very difficult as women try to take into account their own need for fulfillment and the expectations of their families. Support and reassurance during such transition periods is seldom avail-able. Since pregnancy is usually the reason for leaving work, they are forced to adjust to major changes within their bodies at the same time as they are making complex, crucial choices. As a result, they tend to seek change on a personal level rather than encouraging procedural modifications at the workplace.

When mothers make the decision to return to teaching, they often feel com-pelled to prove that they can handle the added load. Typically, they complain about never finding time for themselves and never feeling that their work is finished. Consequently, they take time from other places — time with their families, time from their own leisure, and time from their sleep. The majority of the household tasks still fall to the mothers. Consistent with Dinnerstein's (1992) findings, the women I talked to utilized three strategies to deal with the responsibilities at home to husbands and children. As 'accommodators', some women simply did all the work themselves rather than face resistance from their family. These women tried to keep everything the way it used to be when they were at home full-time. Other women tried to be 'negotiators' and either give up tasks, delegated some to others, or paid for outside services. They took shortcuts, reduced their expectations, found support and/or adopted guilt-reducing strategies. Only one woman managed to become an 'equalizer' by making egalitarian arrangements for housework, cooking and child care with her husband. In this situation, they each took responsibility for one child including sick days and appointments.

Leaving young children in the hands of a substitute caregiver is always a stressful experience. Taking babies from their warm beds very early in the morning, feeding them, dressing them, packing them up and then leaving them somewhere else all day seems jarring and unnatural. Children often cry when parents leave them behind. Parents worry about early separation and adjustments or resign themselves to limited involvement in their child's development:

> I remember feeling so guilty when I had to peel my baby off me to get out the door. There were so many kids. I worried about him getting enough attention. I cried all the way to work and went directly to the bathroom to get myself together so that I could come out and be the cheery teacher. Then I came home to the formula, the diapers, the endless stream of things. (Keri)

Older children can be more vocal in making mothers feel guilty: one mother reported her own children saying: 'Gee, I wish you had a different job', or 'Mom's students are more important than us' (Sue).

In whatever context, time was a problem, be it flexible time, down time, quality time, interrupted time, personal time, saved time — there was never enough of it, no matter how these women tried to organize it or control it. They found ingenious shortcuts to accomplish routine and mundane chores. They bought more socks, froze lunches, threw away their plants, cooked simple dinners, and stopped ironing sheets. They learned to reduce their expectations and mastered the art of doing many things at once. Even with their demanding schedules, they found creative ways to build in personal time, especially significant interactions with their own children:

> If I'm standing there with a dish rag in my hand and a discussion comes up, I have to be flexible enough to put the dish rag down. Because you are so busy, it's snatches of time here and there that count. (Cathy)

These women often described doing many things at once and feeling out of sync with linear timetables and schedules in schools. Hall (1983) refers to these temporal orientations as polychronic and monochronic uses of time. Polychronic time values relationships and connects people and networks as opposed to tasks, schedules and procedures. It gives a higher priority to humanity than to organizations and is seldom experienced as wasted or controlled. It is also associated with informal, creative or leisure activities which take place at home. 'The time system of the dominant

Sharon M. Abbey

culture adds another source of trauma and alienation to the already overburdened psyches of many women' (Hall, 1983, p. 53).

Living in Both Worlds

Women who undertake the roles of mother and teacher have the unique advantage of viewing each role as both an insider and an outsider. Many teachers maintain a largely negative, mistrustful attitude toward the parenting practices in their school communities (Shepard and Rose, 1994). Teachers may blame families for not providing the skills, resources, and stimulation necessary to prepare children for school (Smith, 1990). They feel inclined to protect children from mothers who are apathetic and show little interest in school. Deeply embedded stereotypical images of mothers, as either over-demanding or *laissez-faire*, are used to justify teachers' decisions to keep mothers systematically excluded from schools.

Teachers expect mothers to send their children to school well disciplined, full of curiosity, and eager to learn and may blame parents for children's difficulties in school. As Dorothy Smith (1990) points out, 'The extent to which the teacher can institute types of learning activities producing middle-class levels of achievement depends greatly upon much of the prior and supplementary work of mothers' (p. 236). These attitudes negate any sense of mutuality that might bring about collaborative, cooperative acts between home and school.

In this study, both sides of mother-blaming surfaced in a single interview. Stella began by stating: 'When children have definite behavioral problems, I sometimes wonder what the family life is like.' A few moments later, she expressed resentment toward mothers who were too involved: 'There are mothers who are in and out of the school all the time. I think they feel that if they are not there the job will not be done as well. I kind of resent that. They would be better off if they went out and got jobs. Let us do our work!'

Although they shared many of the same goals as the mothers of their students, these women often assumed that parents lacked the expertise of educators and admitted resenting the intrusion of over-demanding parents in the school. Ironically, in their own maternal roles, these same women recalled times when they were too outspoken and domineering as well as too busy or overwhelmed with work to spend adequate time with their own children. On other occasions they described feelings of guilt for becoming too involved in their children's school work and perhaps not allowing the necessary space for them to develop autonomy and independence. As teachers, these women encouraged parents to participate in school programs, yet they did not have the time to do that themselves. Their own children's school events were not considered legitimate reasons to be absent from their classroom duties.

In their relationships with their students, teacher-mothers seemed particularly committed to fostering self-esteem. They attempted to respect the children's autonomy and were more willing to negotiate, compromise, and accommodate themselves to meet the needs of children. For these women, the affective domain took precedence over academic subjects or mandated curricula lessons. They often spoke of the pressure they felt from these conflicting agendas. They all stressed that learning cannot be achieved if personhood and self-worth are ignored.

> Since I've had my own kids, I respect them differently. As a teacher, you haven't a clue what these kids have gone through when they come to you in kindergarten. They have already had five years of experience at home. My 3-year-old knows what she wants, so don't confront her. Give her choices and options and she will make her decisions and come around. Just don't push her. It's more important that a child feels good about what she is doing. (Bev)

Teacher-mothers also had a heightened awarenes of the needs of parents and respected the knowledge parents had about their own children. They described empathy, trust and tolerance for the parents in their community, because they shared many of the same maternal and domestic experiences. As a result, they stressed how important it was to actively listen to parents during interviews and to be open and receptive to what parents had to say about their own children:

> Going back teaching after having children made me more sympathetic to the needs of children. I was much more aware that this was someone's baby. I was much more open to parents. I was speaking to them as a mother first. It changed the tone of the interview when I was able to say that I could relate to their concerns. (Stella)

Since becoming parents themselves, these women admit that they had changed their approach to parent interviews. They knew how it felt to sit on the other side of the conference table. As teacher-mothers, they viewed parents as valued partners and sources of information in the educational enterprise, and saw children as belonging to interconnected, concentric contexts and in which it was to everyone's advantage if the teachers could 'play off of' the strengths of these environments.

> The whole idea of what was important was so different before I became a parent. I worried about whether children could spell and add. Now I also worry about whether they function as a happy human being first. (Keri)

Mother-Teachers

Schools are the first socializing agency in which a child's status must be earned by academic merit. Mothers often view teachers as gatekeepers of their children's future economic opportunities and social mobility, and may feel intimidated or marginalized by schools. Mothers often feel lonely, uncertain, or left out, as well as resentful, or fearful of the perceived takeover of their responsibilities by teachers. They may resist attempts by teachers to become surrogate mothers or to influence their children's values and emotions:

> I want teachers to be teachers. I don't want them to be friends or substitute
> mothers or social workers. I want my kids to respect the role of the teacher
> and know that they won't always be coddled or necessarily happy. (Stella)

With a foot in both worlds, the women I talked with were able to consider the
tenuous relationships between families and schools and the dynamic process of
negotiation and interaction involved. These women favored teachers who were
sensitive to their children's personal needs and who took a holistic interest in their
children as complex emotional, thinking, and acting beings: 'First of all, a teacher
needs to know what makes a kid tick, what hurts him, what makes him happy, his
sensitivities, what bothers him, what he is afraid of' (Keri).

These women all expressed a reluctance to interfere with the teacher's domain
or to confront their own children's school problems directly. They emphasized the
importance of being tactful and empathetic and worried that their intrusion, as a
fellow teacher, might have a negative effect on the relationship between the teacher
and the child. They were also aware that children often resent parental involvement.
However, lack of involvement should not be mistaken for a lack of interest. 'Because I am a teacher I keep my distance. I don't want my children's teachers to
think that I am sort of checking up on them or judging them' (Stella).

Teacher-mothers were willing to admit that other teachers were sometimes the
worst parents to deal with. But as mother-teachers they recalled times when they
tried to manipulate teachers when they felt their child's best interests were at stake:

> When my daughter had bad teachers I deliberately told them how marvelous
> they were and how confident I was that they could identify her weaknesses
> and bring them to my attention. I've done all these dishonest things be-
> cause I wanted the best for my child. (Anna)

These women's involvement in their children's schooling changed with age
and grade level. The mothers of younger children were more concerned about their
children's successful adjustment and smooth transition from a private, nurturing
home environment to the impartial public context of school:

> Alex is a really quiet kid and sometimes I don't think teachers know what
> a wonderful kid he is . . . One teacher knows who he is. He spends a lot
> of time in her class and I'm sure she spends more time talking to him than
> the other teachers do. She looks after him at school. (Elaine)

Although the fostering of self-esteem and emotional security are still important for mothers of older children, they value teachers who also inspire and motivate
intellectual growth and independent learning. They hoped that curricula expectations and the meeting of standards would not interfere with their child's integrity
as a person. Although these women all seemed to respect the territorial boundaries
between home and school, and refrained from intruding into the domain of the
other, the mothers of younger children seemed more optimistic about the quality of

schooling they imagined their children will receive. The mothers of older children were far more cynical and critical of their children's schooling.

Mothering and Teaching: Diffuse or Specific?

Although the acts of teaching and mothering inform and support each other, Sara Lightfoot (1978) has identified several distinctions based on the type of relationship each role assumes as well as its purposes, expectations, status, and socialization function: the intimate and all-encompassing interactions in families focuses on present and past heritage and are 'functionally diffuse'; the prescribed, time-measured relationships in schools focus on comparing the competence and status of the participants and are 'functionally specific'. As a result, mothers develop 'particularistic' expectations of their children as unique individuals. Teachers hold a more 'universalistic' view of children as 'members of categories which focus on achievement and reflect the preparatory, transitional and sorting functions of schools in this society' (Lightfoot, 1978, p. 24). Women who undertake both roles blend the distinctions and functions as they struggle to find common ground between the two domains.

The women I talked with emphasized the creative elements involved in both roles that allowed them to share their personalities, talents, and values with children. They felt a pride and ownership in teaching and parenting, related to personal bonding and shaping the minds and bodies of young children. There was a sense of identity, satisfaction and purposefulness associated with each role, especially when the accomplishments of the children they interacted with reflected their care, influence and dedication. Regardless of conflicting agendas, they appreciated the strong connections between teaching and parenting. They emphasized how their dual roles as teachers and mothers closely paralleled, complemented, and influenced each other, and how they used their experiences in each domain to enrich, strengthen and influence the other.

The stories shared by the women in this study also revealed diffuse/specific distinctions between the two domains, especially with respect to the energy, devotion, and focus each job required, the length of bonding time and the number of children they were expected to interact with in each role. At home, these women spoke of an intense attachment that develops with a few children based on love and nurturance and which evolved over a lifetime:

> There is a different type of caring at home. You are not accountable to a public body at home. There is more of an investment in my own kids and I will never stop caring about them. There is a different motivation because they are a reflection on me. (Cathy)

In contrast, they described a positive, respectful attachment to twenty-five or thirty children at school, a relationship from which they usually disengaged after ten months. The stronger emotional investment in their role as mother, was balanced by a greater sense of accountability and personal satisfaction in their role as teacher.

The issue of power and authority represented another contrast between home and school. It was easier to assume a position of authority with students at school than it was with their children at home. They explained that there was a broader range of diffuse tasks at home where they were caretakers rather than disciplinarians: 'I'm harder on the kids at school than I am on my own kids as far as expectations. I'm much stricter at school than at home. There are more important things around the house' (Emma).

Grumet (1987) points out that the tensions for women teachers are compounded by the fact that they are involved in an alien task of socializing children to conform to the dominant group's ideals, whose values and goals they do not determine, do not relate to, and may not even agree with. She argues that women learn to tolerate such contradictions by blurring the distinctions between the two roles. The women in this study consciously resisted the universalistic expectations of school systems by trying to humanize the curriculum. They viewed their ability to adapt to and operate from multiple perspectives as a technique which would inform and enrich education. As pointed out in Chapter 1 of this volume, the education system might do well to address the stress between contradictory and incompatible realms. As one respondent suggested:

> The eight years I spent teaching was to some extent parenting. I'm just confirming what I already knew. (Bev)

Valuing Teacher-Mothers

Although the family and the school are the two critical institutions that contribute significantly to the education of children, they operate from an incompatible set of expectations and value systems which often collide or exclude each other. They blame each other for perceived shortcomings of children and set up social barriers that keep home and school divided. Educational institutions and legal systems expect parents to break their strong ties with young children. Parents face public scrutiny when their child enters school for the first time and often feel threatened, excluded or maginalized. As a result, they are reluctant to voice opinions or interfere with school systems for fear of the consequences that this might have for their children. On the other hand, these same systems encourage elementary teachers to prepare and deliver children to a society struggling to compete in an unpredictable global economy (Grumet, 1987). Teachers, feeling the pressure of accountability, resist and resent parents who challenge their authority, question their professionalism or intrude on their turf.

The current atmosphere of dissonance, resentment and mistrust creates an unexamined form of systemic violence for women who undertake responsibilities in both domains and for the children torn between the two influences. Children and parents, especially mother-teachers, find themselves caught in the complex intersection of these two spheres of influence — one that nurtures and accepts children unconditionally, and the other that categorizes and evaluates them according to prescribed standards. Rather than seek out connections that could result from their common interests in the well-being of children, mothers and teachers often separate and isolate themselves from each other or struggle for power and status in the eyes of the child (Lightfoot, 1978). In fact, mothers and elementary teachers often lack confidence in, and feel a great hostility or jealousy toward, one another (Biklen, 1993). The anxieties and tensions that grow out of the ambiguities about who has the right to govern certain areas of a child's life and the struggle for clarity of these boundary lines makes it difficult to clarify responsibilities and competencies in a multi-layered, interdependent system.

When domestic experience is held up to the light and examined through the dual lens of women who are both teachers and mothers, we begin to see subtle forms of systemic violence woven into the fabric of schools and schooling comes into focus. A diverse range of affective and relational orientations emerge that could significantly contribute to humanizing education; but attitudes and patterns that continue to block, ignore, and trivialize these same qualities and characteristics also emerge. Our educational system was designed to serve the needs and work patterns of men and unmarried women. Although married women and mothers have long since joined the teaching ranks, these women are still forced to fit into existing structures, cope with unrealistic expectations, and keep their domestic wisdom carefully separated from their professional knowledge. Those who cannot ignore feelings of alienation, inadequacy, or guilt, resign.

Other possibilities and options could be made available in order to support mothers who want to teach and to tap into their experiential wisdom and talents. Efforts to eliminate the contradictions and conflicts between home and school might include exempting all parents from work for one day per month in order for them to attend school with their children. Such a level of commitment and support by institutions would enhance the value of home–school connections and provide time for deeper partnerships to develop between parents and teachers. These home–school interactions might serve to counteract the sense of reluctance, insecurity, or resentment that currently seems to be an issue when territory boundaries are crossed.

There are also many possibilities for restructuring schools, administrative practices, and pedagogy to accommodate the diverse needs of teachers with domestic responsibilities. For example, flexible working hours, job sharing, and on-site child-care facilities might reduce the burden of parents with dual roles. An idea as simple as installing telephones in classrooms would also facilitate communication between home and school. Provision for absence from work to care for sick children, attend to their appointments or take part in their school projects would support domestic commitments.

A central issue is the assumption that when a teacher takes a maternity leave she is interrupting her career. Her seniority should not be lost nor should her maternity absence be viewed as a lack of commitment to her career. In fact, women should be compensated for maternity leaves and these should be recognized by school boards as an alternative form of valuable professional development.

Sara Lightfoot (1978) states that 'In order for parents and teachers to relate productively they must be able to see the significance of the other's relationship to the child, and each of them must be aware of the universal "other" within themselves' (p. 220). Expanding the role of parents in schools beyond expectations for attendance at interviews and concerts might help dismantle the barriers between home and school as well as encourage more interactive dialogue between the significant adults in children's lives (Shields, 1994). Teachers should study parental involvement in schools and be trained in the skills necessary to develop partnerships with parents (Pipho, 1995).

There are ways to promote opportunities for parents and teachers to come together for meaningful dialogue and authentic interactions which are relaxed, ongoing and positive. Support groups, retreat centers and programs to encourage dialogue, networking and information sharing would be useful. Centers could be created to allow teachers and women in the community to work together and be available to counsel young people, particularly girls who have difficulty adjusting to the transition of female adolescence. Collaborations such as these might be facilitated if schools remain small in order to accommodate the local culture and to allow people to control their environment. An intimate, informal atmosphere provides familiarity of a family where there is a collective sense of knowing all the children and a feeling of responsibility for their well-being (Lightfoot, 1978).

McCartney and Phillips (1988) propose several ways to relieve mothers of some of the conflict when leaving children with caregivers. It would require action from many people. Of course, fathers should be encouraged to participate equally in child rearing. Teachers need to offer the same sort of open communication as child-care workers give to the mothers. Family and friends need to be accepting of different choices of child care. Women need to unite on this issue and realize there is not one 'right way'. Also, principals and administrators must appreciate the stressful schedule of mothers of young children and be willing to accommodate them with respect to school duties and meetings.

Judith Kaufman (1994) reminds us that there is more than one way to construe the world and that we construct our own understanding of the world with both thought and feeling. By valuing maternal pedagogy in our schools, we might begin to look beyond a linear, monochronic mind-set and honour diversity, uniqueness and multiple commitments for the new levels of productivity and possibilities for learning that these perspectives open up. We might also be inclined to question our institutional model of schooling that rewards objective compliance and teaches children to stop touching, feeling and being for the sake of standardized thinking. Further, we could even endorse alternatives to competition that might encourage students to collaborate, to care more about each other and to learn for self-growth and fulfillment rather than for marks or praise. A maternal pedagogy might even cross boundaries and move beyond the subordinated position of 'women's work' where it could be embraced, celebrated and valued by everyone.

References

ACKER, S. (1994) *Gendered Education*, Toronto, OISE Press.
BATESON, M.C. (1984) *Composing a Life*, New York, Penguin.

BATESON, M.C. (1994) *Peripheral Visions: Learning Along the Way*, New York, Harper Collins.

BIKLEN, S. (1993) 'Mother's gaze from teachers' eyes', in BIKLEN, S. and POLLARD, D. (eds) *Gender and Education: Ninety-second Yearbook for the National Society for the Study of Education* (Part 1), Chicago, University of Chicago, pp. 15–173.

CAPLAN, P. (1989) *Don't Blame Mother: Mending the Mother–Daughter Relationship*, New York, Harper and Row.

DINNERSTEIN, M. (1992) *Women between Two Worlds: Midlife Reflections on Work and Family*, Philadelphia, PA, Temple University Press.

EISLER, R. (1987) *The Chalice and the Blade*, Toronto, Harper & Row.

GILLIGAN, C. (1982) *In a Different Voice: Psychological Theory and Women's Development*, Cambridge, MA, Harvard University Press.

GRUMET, M. (1987) 'The politics of personal knowledge', *Curriculum Inquiry*, **17**, 3, pp. 319–29.

GRUMET, M. (1988) *Bitter Milk: Women and Teaching*, Amherst, MA, University of Massachusetts Press.

HALL, E. (1983) *The Dance of Life: The Other Dimension of Time*, New York, Doubleday.

JONES, C., MARSDEN, L. and TEPPERMAN, L. (1990) *Lives of Our Own: The Individualization of Women's Lives*, Toronto, Oxford University Press.

KAUFMAN, J. (1994) 'The wedge between emotion and cognition: Feminism, knowledge and power', *Holistic Education Review*, **7**, 4, pp. 43–9.

LIGHTFOOT, S. (1978) *Worlds Apart*, New York, Basic Books.

MARTIN, J.R. (1992) *The School-Home: Rethinking Schools for Changing Families*, Cambridge, MA, Harvard University Press.

McCARTNEY, K. and PHILLIPS, D. (1988) 'Motherhood and child care', in BIRNS, B. and HAY, D. (eds) *The Different Faces of Motherhood*, Albany, NY, SUNY Press, pp. 157–84.

PIPHO, C. (1995) 'Parental support for education', *Phi Delta Kappan*, **76**, 4, pp. 270–1.

ROBERTSON, H.J. (1992) *The Better Idea Book: A Resource Book on Gender, Culture, Science and Schools*, Ottawa, The Canadian Teachers' Federation.

SHEPARD, R. and ROSE, H. (1994) 'The power of parents: An empowerment model for increasing parental involvement', *Education*, **115**, 3, pp. 373–7.

SHIELDS, C. (1994) 'Students and parents: Missing links in restructuring schools', *School Executive*, **14**, 3/4, pp. 15–20.

SMITH, D. (1990) 'Women's work as mothers: A new look at the relation of class, family and school achievement', in FORMAN, F., O'BRIAN, M., HADDAD, J., HAMILTON, D. and MATER, P. (eds) *Feminism and Education: A Canadian Perspective*, Toronto, OISE Press.

SPENDER, D. (1982) *Invisible Woman: The Schooling Scandal*, London, Women's Press.

Part 2

Schools and Violence

5   Expanding the Lens: Student Perceptions of School Violence

Irene M. MacDonald

> We think too small, like a frog at the bottom of the well. He thinks the sky is only as big as the top of the well. If he surfaces, he would have an entirely different view. (Mao Tse Tung)

As an issue of law enforcement, school violence is synonymous with criminal activities that occur at school: gang wars, illicit drug use, vandalism, weapon possession, and personal assault. From an educator's perspective, school violence encompasses those behaviors that seriously disrupt the safe learning environment of a classroom or school. For students, 'school violence is anything that makes us afraid to come to and stay at school' (Grade 7 female).

School violence, as recognized by students, is not limited to schools in large urban centers. Surreptitious and often subtle forms of violence such as intimidation, harassment, and discrimination can occur in any school: urban, rural, public, separate, suburban or inner-city. Although officials in many schools believe it to be a minor issue, probably because it has not come to their attention, it is not a low-key problem for students. In many schools, young people are accepting physical or psychological conflicts as a natural part of adolescence. Students tolerate conflicts and behaviors because they feel powerless to do anything about it. Adults would not have to endure such conditions. Adults, for example, would not be subjected to racial taunting in the workplace, or be expected to endure insults directed at body size, clothing or accent. It would be rare, in the adult world, for an individual to be shoved up against a wall, knocked to the ground, spat upon, groped, attacked by a group of colleagues for coffee money, or denied access to the bathroom until they forfeited their ballcaps. Adults would be in a position to ameliorate such conditions. But this is reality for an increasing number of students in our schools.

Victimization at school is often suffered in silence with long lasting and traumatic effects. A recent article in the *British Journal of Medicine* (Dawkins, 1995) urged doctors to recognize that bullying was essentially a form of child abuse that could lead to high levels of distress, school absenteeism, and even suicide. Physical and non-physical acts of violence are committed by students on a regular basis. In one study, 29 per cent of Grades 6 to 9 students had been threatened, 31 per cent had been bullied, and 16 per cent had been beaten-up while at school (Ryan, Mathews, and Banner, 1993).

Violent behaviors have always existed in our schools. A generation ago, the schoolyard bully was typically a physically intimidating individual whom everyone knew should not be agitated. Today, that bully may still be the 'big kid', but he or she is just as likely to be a 'little kid' with a big knife. The use of weapons in settling disputes is reported to be increasing (Walker, 1994; Smith, Bertrand, Arnold, and Hornick, 1995), with knives as the preferred weapon — used by perpetrators but also by victims for protection. Walker's (1994) study on weapons use in Canadian schools found that 42 per cent of police agencies polled reported seizing knives from youths aged 12 to 17 years within schools and on school property. This figure increased from 35 per cent reported the previous year. The consensus in Canada amongst educators (Ontario Safe School Task Force, 1994; Alberta Education, 1993; British Columbia Teacher's Federation, 1994) researchers (Smith *et al.*, 1995; Ryan, Mathews, and Banner, 1993), and the public, is that school violence is an escalating problem both in its nature and extent. What is not as readily agreed upon are the root causes of this violence and who should be responsible for managing and reducing it in schools.

Exploring Student Perceptions

In 1995, data were collected from 231 students from five junior high schools, regarding the nature and frequency of school violence and their perceptions of the school authorities' awareness of and responses to violent behaviors. Similar questionnaires were completed by school administrators. The student questionnaire solicited data regarding the students' grade and sex, and violent behaviors the student had experienced and/or observed at school. Students were requested to provide their perceptions of the seriousness of specified violent behaviors, and comment on the principals' and teachers' awareness of school violence. Students were asked how they dealt with specified conflict and under what conditions they would be prompted to inform a teacher or principal.

The schools' administrators were asked to report their perceptions of the seriousness of specified violent behaviors, the types of violent behaviors they had encountered, and the extent to which they were considered a problem. They were also asked about their perceptions of students' satisfaction with the way victims and perpetrators of violence were dealt with, and how confident they were that students were informing staff about violent behaviors.

That school violence was an important, and perhaps divisive, issue became apparent in the difference in the way students and administrators responded to being asked to participate in the study. The enthusiastic response of the students pointed to their genuine interest in the topic. Several students expressed appreciation for having had their opinions solicited. One student wrote on the survey: 'Getting our input and our ideas and opinions was really a good idea. Not many people want our opinion. Thanks.' Administrators expressed a different form of interest. Some espoused support for the study but concern about the research design; they worried that students would exaggerate.

You know how teens at this age are, always challenging, pushing our buttons . . . it would not surprise me if some of them blew things out of proportion on their surveys. They may paint a worse situation than actually exists, which is too bad. They would not know how knowledgeable staff actually were. Kids may think we [the staff] don't know what's going on, but we have a pretty sharp eye on things. We know pretty well everything that they're up to, even when they think otherwise. You can ask them, but in the end I can tell you all you need to know.

Some principals did not think there was a problem but agreed to participate anyway. As one principal said: 'I'll be very interested to see what my kids say. We have the odd problem, nothing serious . . . school violence isn't a problem here.' Others refused to participate at all. After receiving a copy of the student questionnaire one principal indicated that neither he nor the school staff would be interested in having the researcher 'come into the school and have students answer those types of questions'. He said: 'I find the whole matter of even suggesting that we have violence in our school to be rather offensive.'

Feeling Safe

Students were asked to classify behaviors as minor or serious. Over 50 per cent of students considered fights, verbal threats, bullying, teasing and name-calling to be minor infractions. Over 60 per cent considered weapons threats, damaged or stolen property, and ethnic conflict as serious. More than 70 per cent of students, slightly more female students than male students, ranked sexual harassment as a serious behavior. Students were most undecided about how to categorize the seriousness of ethnic conflict (13 per cent undecided) and bullying (10 per cent undecided).

Approximately 75 per cent of the students indicated that they felt safe at school 'most of the time', or 'always', yet over half of the male students stated that they had experienced physical forms of violence such as fights, bullying, punching, hitting or grabbing, verbal threats, theft or damage to property. Approximately 35 per cent of female students said they had experienced fights, bullying, punching, hitting, grabbing, theft, or damage to property. Verbal threats were experienced by 60 per cent of the females. One in five male students indicated that they had been threatened with a weapon at school, and ethnic conflict affected one-third of male respondents. Only 4 per cent of students responded that they never felt safe at school, yet 20 per cent had observed weapons at school and over 50 per cent considered bullying to be a 'very big' or 'big' problem. Sexual harassment was experienced by over 25 per cent of female students. Forty-five per cent of the students wrote comments indicating that they were concerned:

Elementary school I feel is pretty safe but junior high seems to be a big step and is much more dangerous. If junior high is this dangerous what is high school going to be like? (Grade 8 male)

> I think school violence sucks because it makes people afraid to come to school. It makes people more self-conscious. You coordinate your wardrobe or do your hair differently just so you don't become a victim for being the way you are. (Grade 9 female)

> I think that school violence should try to be stopped, because some people are afraid to even come to school, because they think they'll be beaten up. (Grade 8 female)

When asked whether or not they knew how to deal effectively with conflict, a number of strategies for coping were presented. Many suggested carrying knives to protect themselves. Some avoided conflict:

> Sometimes in the morning coming to school or passing a different school I feel insecure. I try to walk by quickly or get to class. When someone tells me someone is out to get me, I get scared. I look around before I go outside and look inside the bathroom before I go. (Grade 8 male)

> Violence stops us from talking to people cause the more people you know the more likely you are to get in a fight. (Grade 8 female)

Others felt it was best to retaliate:

> If someone is beating you up you have the right to beat them up. (Grade 9 female)

> Nothing will happen to you if you have back-up like tough friends or older brothers. If someone does something get your back-up or connections and get him beaten up even if hospitalized. (Grade 7 male)

Many were resigned to violence as something they could do nothing about:

> They punch you for no reason and attack you on a field for no reason. I can't defend myself or he'll get more of his friends that are tougher than mine. (Grade 9 male)

> When one of my friends have been beaten up I'm afraid to come to school the next week or so . . . I was so f___ing scared that I'd be next and it would be my ass they were kicking. (Grade 8 female)

Many equated schoolyard fights with school violence and suggested that they were normal, a means for settling disputes and even a form of entertainment:

> I think that school violence is everywhere and there's so much of it that it's normal to watch a fight . . . it's everyone's source of entertainment. (Grade 8 female)

There are some fights at lunch or after school and people get hurt, but I think the fights are funny and fun to watch. (Grade 8 male)

There also seemed to be a perception that adults should just stay out of it:

People shouldn't fight for no reason but fighting does solve problems for us so adults should just stay out of it; we can handle it ourselves. (Grade 9 female)

Would You Tell?

Students did not perceive that their teachers and administrators were always aware of violent behaviors at school. Students suggested that things were 'not noticed by teachers and principals' (Grade 9 male) and that 'teachers should be more alert and aware of some of the categories so they could help solve it' (Grade 9 male). One student felt that 'teachers could do more and not sit in the staff room [and] eat donuts and drink coffee, they should look for more violence' (Grade 7 male). Teachers were accused of responding only to the most severe forms of violence:

Some things are so common that they are ignored . . . teachers don't care enough about name-calling, ethnic fights, teasing and stealing. They only care if blood is spilled so they can't be charged. Name-calling can be hurtful but nobody cares. (Grade 8 female)

Others suggested that certain people could get away with violence while others could not:

Sometimes the principal never does anything. I was threatened by a lot of popular people, that is why I never want to be popular. (Grade 8 female)

Students were asked to indicate under what circumstances they would inform a principal or teacher about witnessing or experiencing school violence. Decisions to report school violence were linked to relationships. Reporting depended on the relationship between the victim and the perpetrator, the victim and the witness and the witness and the perpetrator. A full 35 per cent of students responded that they would 'never' tell if they witnessed violent behaviors. When those who would report 'sometimes' were included, this number increased to 70 per cent. The most influential factors affecting students' decisions to report victimization were: (a) friendship with the perpetrator; (b) the popularity of the perpetrator; (c) whether the perpetrator was physically smaller; and (d) the absence of other witnesses to the incident. Witnesses, especially females, were willing to report observed violence in those cases where the victim was a friend, younger, or unpopular. Age, physical size and popularity of the perpetrator were the greatest determinants of witness reporting.

But reporting would depend on the crime. If the crime was sexual harassment or a threat with a weapon, approximately 40 per cent of students would 'always' tell, whether they were victims or witnesses, and 30 per cent would report if it was ethnic conflict. One of the most common themes expressed in making the decision to report related to fear of retribution, a finding consistent with other studies (Ryan, Mathews, and Banner, 1993; Kasian, 1992):

> Kids are scared to rat on other kids because they will get the shit kicked out of them. This is wrong. I wish that things would change. (Grade 9 male)

> I have seen the victims and witnesses who had told on the person making the fight, who have been beaten up for it. (Grade 7 female)

> Fights are really brutal and nobody tells because then they'll get beaten up. (Grade 9 female)

Only 60 per cent of students considered theft or vandalism of property to be a serious offense, yet, witnesses and victims were more willing to report property 'violence' than bullying, verbal threats, ethnic conflict or fights.

Students were asked to indicate their level of satisfaction with the treatment of victims and perpetrators of violence in their school. Over half of the students were dissatisfied with the way victims of school violence were treated. Students wanted more protection:

> If you can help get school violence like bullying out it will feel safer except that often you will tell on someone they will want to fight . . . so you have to protect the victims. (Grade 8 male)

They were even less satisfied with the way the perpetrators were handled. A number of students advocated changes to the legislation governing young offenders. They wanted more severe punishments for perpetrators and even called for a focus on societal violence:

> The teachers need to be more strict with worse punishments. I know my brother causes some trouble and he does it because he can get away with it. (Grade 8 female)

> I think that the kids should be punished more because of their bad behaviors . . . I think that the law should get involved in certain situations, because when bad stuff happens to you, it doesn't just blow over, it's with you forever. (Grade 8 female)

> If you want to help us out you should focus on violence at home and what kind of parents you get. Because if a kid is messed up in the head he doesn't care what the punishment is going to be. (Grade 9 male)

Not all students recommended increased intervention on the part of school staff. Several students suggested that teachers 'mind their own business' and leave students to cope with violence on their own terms. They saw it as a step toward adulthood, an initiation into the violence that they expect will continue throughout their lives. For some of these young people, violence had become normalized and was considered a natural part of growing up:

I don't really want anything done about school violence. I think this is the way that people learn how to stick up for themselves in real life. Violence itself is a part of this world, and most people have come to accept that and deal with it. (Grade 8 female)

Administrative Response

Administrators in these schools perceived school violence to be less of a problem than the students did and believed that teachers were more aware of school violence than the students felt they were. Administrators also perceived students to be more satisfied with the treatment of victims and perpetrators than the students did and were more confident that students would inform school staff about witnessing or being a victim than student responses indicated they would.

Administrative responses to student violence included the following: 19 per cent suggested a community-based resolution; 26 per cent felt there was a need for a greater awareness of school violence; 31 per cent advocated greater consequences for offenders; 23 per cent sought a move towards zero tolerance of school violence; and 42 per cent felt solutions lay in more student rules and clearer behavior expectations.

Although administrators considered their own schools to be relatively violence free, they were taking the topic of school violence seriously. One administrator summed up the official response:

If we do not take immediate and severe action, then we are giving a message that it [school violence] is not serious. By our response we demonstrate the degree of acceptability . . . school violence does affect learning and should not be tolerated. Bullying and threats elevate to violence of the highest order. Take a stand that students who seriously contravene the law and school regulations will lose their right to a public education. The safety of the majority far outweighs the rights of the serious violators.

Violence and Pedagogy

Violence is a part of this world and most people have come to accept that and deal with it by taking self-defense courses and carrying weapons. I'd like to see how you try and change the way people in the world today think. (Grade 8 female)

Although there have been several recent studies on school violence, the data has been gathered largely from police, teachers, administrators, but not extensively from students themselves. If practices and policies that currently exist in our schools are developed on the basis of administrator or teacher perceptions of student needs and concerns, how effective can these practices be?

Teachers and administrators are faced with a seemingly impossible task. The public expect educators to maintain violence-free schools, but any initiative taken by the schools to reduce violence is often perceived as a failure of administrators to have 'maintained order and discipline'. Why would a school implement an anti-violence program if their school was at the optimum in terms of student safety? Such pressure to maintain a positive image constrains administrators' motivation to request resources for school violence reduction.

There is a marked difference in students' and administrators' perceptions of the magnitude and nature of violence in schools. If these differing views are generated by an under-reporting of school-based violence, who is not reporting what, and why not? Several possible explanations can be offered.

Very often students indicated that they were reluctant to report incidents of violence out of a real fear of reprisal. Perceptions of ineffective consequences or the perceived lack of teacher awareness and concern were additional factors that exerted pressure on students to accept victimization and to develop alternate coping strategies such as taking matters into their own hands. Students also indicated that they were often undecided as to whether to classify a behavior as a major offense and were not sure what they should be reporting. These children had never discussed these issues in the school context as a part of their school day. Although school violence was a part of their everyday fears, which for some governed their physical movements, daily habits and appearance, it had not been talked about in the classroom. The subject was taboo and students felt they could only talk about it if they had something to report to a teacher.

Garofalo, Siegel and Laub (1987) found that some children may feel that adults are inept or disinterested in protecting them, particularly from bullies. Children consciously choose to keep their victimization to themselves. For children whose only opportunity to talk about violence is in the reporting of it, the way the report is treated becomes of paramount importance. Students expressed feelings of frustration related to a belief that little could be done to positively change the anxieties and fears that accompanied actual or anticipated victimization. Unfortunately, ignoring victims in order to concentrate on policies and practices that provide consequences for perpetrators compounds the number of incidents.

Smith *et al.* (1995) found a positive correlation between students who experience high levels of victimization and later demonstrated their own delinquency. A number of students in this study expressed a preference for taking matters into their own hands. Lack of awareness amongst staff, together with students' reluctance to report episodes of violence, seems to be a 'recipe' for the kind of 'code of silence' that Mathews (1994) speaks of as so often distorting knowledge about the nature and extent of school violence. Is it possible to break this 'code of silence' and work toward solutions? What if we were to talk about school violence as a part of the curriculum, if we were to address issues of violence in the larger context of world history and human relationships? At the very least, we could acknowledge that school violence does exist and that often its nature and management is perceived quite differently by students and administrators.

In response to the open-ended question in this study that asked students what they felt could be done about school violence, numerous suggestions were provided. One comment in particular served to emphasize the urgency for increased attention to the study of and response to school violence:

> Us students have seen a lot of bad stuff. But everything goes when you adults turn your back on us. We don't want you to watch us all the time, but just experience how much we've seen through our years of schooling. But we live with it. We don't let [it] show that it bothers us. (Grade 8 student)

Our youth are growing up to accept physical or psychological conflicts as part of the everyday school milieu. When school violence is ignored, it spreads. It could be argued that school is simply a reflection of the violence that is seen and experienced in society. However, Smith *et al.* (1995) found that victimization rates were higher at school (81 per cent at school and 69 per cent elsewhere), thereby challenging the view that youth violence is a problem more prevalent in the larger community than in schools. Some educators view their role in addressing youth violence as the imposition of yet another responsibility that more rightfully lies in the hands of others, be they parents, police or the larger community. They do not seem to recognize the opportunity to focus their pedagogical work in a realistic way that would affect positive change in all aspects of their students' lives.

Undoubtedly, for the 4 per cent of students who indicated that they 'never' felt safe at school, there is a serious need for schools to identify and deal with the problems. The more important challenge for educators is to recognize that school violence may affect far more students than they realize. Unless educators understand how student victims, perpetrators and observers respond to school-based violence they are unlikely to be able to determine appropriate strategies and programs for intervention. What better way to get to the root of the problem than to talk to the students in the classroom context? Ask them to be the problem-solvers. What could intelligent, thoughtful people, forced to live together on a daily basis do to make that interaction better for all?

Programs which focus on prevention, intervention and response must be ongoing; they must become a daily part of the curriculum; they must work towards facilitating a more peaceful and safe learning environment. Just as the reporting of child abuse must be moved from the peripheries of daily school interactions, as advocated by Tite in Chapter 3 of this volume, so must the treatment of violence become central to what is learned in school. Pedagogy that separates the cognitive from the affective assumes that these issues are someone else's problem. Awareness of and strategies for dealing with daily acts of injustice and brutality must become part of a pedagogy dedicated to bettering everyone's lives.

Irene M. MacDonald

References

ALBERTA EDUCATION (1993) *Proceedings: An Invitational Forum on Student Conduct and Violence in Schools*, Edmonton, AB, Alberta Education.

BRITISH COLUMBIA TEACHER'S FEDERATION (1994) *Task Force on Violence in Schools: Final Report*, Vancouver, BC, British Columbia Teacher's Federation.

CAMPBELL, S. (1993, November) 'Media violence and children', *The Bulletin*, pp. 12–16.

DAWKINS, J. (1995) 'Bullying in schools: Doctors' responsibilities', *British Medical Journal*, **310**, 4, pp. 275–6.

GAROFALO, J., SIEGEL, L. and LAUB, M. (1987) 'School related victimization among adolescents: An analysis of national crime survey narratives', *Journal of Quantitative Criminology*, **3**, pp. 321–37.

JOHNSON, N. A. (1987) 'Perspectives: The pervasive, persuasive power of perceptions', *Alberta Journal of Educational Research*, **33**, 3, pp. 206–28.

KASIAN, M. (1992) *Report and Recommendations: Safe School Survey*, Ottawa, Ottawa Roman Catholic Separate School Board.

MATHEWS, F. (1994) 'Drawing lines and circles', *ORBIT*, **25**, 3, pp. 38–41.

ONTARIO SAFE SCHOOL TASK FORCE (1994) *Safe Schools: A Survey of Ontario School Employees*, Toronto, Ontario Safe School Task Force.

RYAN, C., MATHEWS, F. and BANNER, J. (1993) *Student Perceptions of Violence*, Toronto, Central Toronto Youth Services.

SMITH, R., BERTRAND, L., ARNOLD, B. and HORNICK, S. (1995) *A Study of the Level and Nature of Youth Crime and Violence in Calgary*, Ottawa, Office of the Solicitor General.

WALKER, S. (1994) *Weapons Use in Canadian Schools*, Ottawa, Office of the Solicitor General.

6   Voices from the Shadows

Linda Wason-Ellam

Canada has an ethnically diverse population that is often described using a patch-work quilt metaphor. Teachers are being encouraged to make schooling inclusive for all learners so that they can value the variety that is their heritage, and cherish their racial, ethnic, and cultural differences in the belief that when children learn about each other, socially and academically, they begin to appreciate variety within the global community (Ravitch, 1983) and learn to live and work in harmony.

The reality is that classroom cohesion can become a thorny issue when schools embark on 'culturally sensitive curriculum'. In many cases, integrating cultures has led to the dominance of 'naive multiculturalism' instead of transforming the status quo by focusing on social issues. As a result, many schools serve the interests of some groups better than others, creating a power imbalance among children that can lead to bullying. This is a social and covert form of systemic violence.

Outside the Classroom Community

Creating a multi-ethnic community is not an easy task. Learning together, including others in cooperative learning groups and setting a cooperative classroom envir-onment actively promotes mutual care and respect for others. In this way, positive peer relationships are built, other ways to communicate ideas develop and, most importantly, the perspectives of others are more easily understood. But not all class-mates are willing to view others as equals with a right to share in the democratic process. To illustrate this point, I draw on data collected during a full year spent as a researcher of the social lives of literacy learners in an urban, ethnically mixed elementary school in Canada (67 per cent of the school population were from the 'plural' cultures).

During this ethnographic project, located within a working-class community, I joined the social milieu of a Grade 2 classroom where teachers were attempting to be attentive to the social and cultural background of the learners. My goal was to understand how literacy developed in a culturally diverse context. An analysis of the dynamics of classroom life revealed an intricate mesh of power relation-ships that threaded gender, race, and systemic bullying throughout daily literacy interactions.

In this study, I gained access without intrusion to the crucial site of everyday school life by observing situations of time, place and action where literacy learning was most likely to occur (Erickson, 1982). I observed, participated in events, and audio-taped discussions, that focused on gender, race, and power in reading and writing engagements. I was an honorary classmate, taking part in all classroom activities. Instead of relying on querying children, I chose to be more conversational in my interactions. It is through conversations — as talkers, questioners, arguers, gossips, chatterboxes — that these children do much of their most important social learning. And it is within these same interactions that tensions often sprout.

Schools have never been immune to squabbles between children. However, in this particular school I witnessed numerous instances of physical violence where students, especially young boys, brought knives and other weapons to school to threaten or act out aggression on playgrounds, in washrooms and gyms. When asked why the weapons were needed, the response was 'to keep *enemies* from fighting first'. Not surprisingly, the school was taking preventive measures, but there were other pervasive acts of violence enmeshed in the social interactions that were not specifically addressed. Bullying, a negative action repeated over time (Olweus, 1993), was covert and prevalent. It was acted out in the nooks and crannies of the classroom, well hidden from teacher scrutiny and buried in that curriculum organized by the children themselves — 'the school culture'.

Although racial bullying as a form of violence is difficult to document (Besag, 1989), my vantage point as a participant observer in a classroom gave me access to the inner worlds of classroom life where I witnessed the moment-to-moment happenings as they unfolded. I found myself zeroing in on observing six girls of color who were cultural outsiders and conforming into the mainstream Anglo culture of without integrating. During the year, I recorded thirty-seven instances of bullying and aggression in interactions among these girls. The instances occurred in co-operative social activities such as writer's workshop, reading partners, class meetings, and book-making activities. Patterns began to emerge.

The bullying demonstrated to me that the polarization of classrooms continues to be a critical issue in achieving a multi-ethnic balance. Particularly vulnerable are relationships among girls. One of these children was Surinder, a Canadian-born girl who did not speak English when she started school, nor was she fluent in her home language which was Punjabi. An excerpt from my fieldnotes describes my first encounter in early September:

> I watch a girl, whom I call Surinder, standing alone on the playground. Never a part of the class or an ethnic cluster, she is at the periphery of the class activity. As other children scamper across the playing field in a frenzied game of freeze tag, Surinder is quickly eliminated with an aggressive *whack* not a tag to her shoulder. She stands frozen waiting for a friendly tag or an invitation to re-enter the class game. She stands and waits. Others run past her or call out to classmates, 'Tag me, tag me.' Silently, she remains like a thin shadow in the distant grass; a solitary reminder that she is a child of color as no one calls to her, bothers to invite her to join a group, or includes her as a participant in the game. Patiently she stands, rebuffed and alone. From time to time she cracks a thin smile as she

intently watches or listens to others darting past. Time passes and the game continues without her. Finally, our eyes meet. I move closer. Wistfully, she looks at me. I tag her and release her from the frozen stance. I check my watch — 37 minutes have elapsed. It's time to go back in the classroom. Surinder runs back into the sunshine and disappears into the throng rushing to the school entrance but looks back at me and we exchange smiles.

Questions began to float through my head about racial mixing. Do children reflect the patchwork patterns of our country's quilt or do they all weave their own tapestries? Is color or being a girl a barrier as children learn the ways and the language of school?

Like Schofield (1984) who described black and white interactions, my fieldnotes recorded many instances where race as well as gender were barriers to the development of friendship or inclusion in literacy engagements. Gender grouping was particularly problematic for girls like Surinder who strictly adhered to ethnic dress codes, diet and hair style, and were frequent victims of bullying. When other girls altered a religious dress code by cutting their hair, wore western dress, used diminutives of ethnic names (e.g., Sari), or brought pizza slices or western foods in their lunch kits, their presence was more acceptable to the classroom culture.

Surinder was still struggling with English when I became her chum as she was unbefriended by classmates. Since peers did not value Surinder's conversational accounts told at the coathooks or the work table, she chose every opportunity to work alone in the carpeted corner on the floor or with me. I was a willing listener and directed my observations to the dilemma of other girls of color — Bandhana, Nisar, Amandeep, Pham, and Rajinder. I hoped that from the contextual understanding of ethnography would emerge some reasons for their ostracism and their lack of cohesive involvement in the classroom.

Conversational Outsiders

Literacy is learned and constructed within social contexts. To accommodate the diversity within the classroom, the teacher seated children in small working groups appropriate for easing interactions. Striving to overcome the scenario that Maria Campbell recounts about her schooling in *Half Breed* (1973), 'the whites on one side of the room and the half-breeds on the other', the teacher orchestrated a variety of social contexts. Learning configurations included interpersonal and intrapersonal opportunities for seeking, accessing and evaluating knowledge — partner reading, writers' workshop, author's chair and collaborative projects. Small, multi-racial groups worked together on mutual tasks, then discussed, adjusted, and adapted decisions. It was thought that hearing differing points of views, exchanging ideas, and listing problems and their solutions, would contribute to respect and a deeper level of understanding of others. But collaboration seemed to work better for the boys in the classroom. Surinder and the other girls of color did not intermingle well with mainstream girls in these natural communicative settings. Quickly, I began to realize that peer conversations were not egalitarian, especially those involving girls of color who were *marked* by those in power as an 'out-group' because of their ethnicity.

Thorne (1994) documented that in conversational interactions asymmetrical relations with the sexes are a continual strife. Although there has been research in playground language and comparisons between boys' and girls' talk (Swann, 1992; Delamont, 1990; Sadker and Sadker, 1994) there has been little research that illuminates the classroom conversations between and among young girls. Unlike boys, who use physical force to gain power, I found that girls use alienation from the group as their bullying technique with putdowns, jeers, ridicule, slander or spiteful slurs. In this classroom, interactions of girls were characterized by clustering into pairs of best friends in shifting alliances within a complex network of 'likes' or 'being mean to'. Relationships were often broken off and the girls hedged bets by maneuvering networks of potential friends. 'You can be my best friend if you . . .' was the going bid in a triangle of tensions (Toth, 1978).

Within the conversational exchanges of mainstream girls and girls of color there was constant strife in what Shuman (1986) calls 'negotiations of identities and social relationships'. The social order was hierarchical. Girls were either in a one-up or one-down rank, a pecking order based on color. A typical barb would be: 'Your writing is not as nice as mine. I am going to write about my friends. Nobody will read yours 'cos it is not interesting.' Both groups of girls — white and colored — were jockeying for a position from differing situated vantage points; the former maintaining the status quo and the latter wanting to gain entrance. There seemed to be an oppositional climate, a sense of 'us versus them', an attempt not to let ethnic girls join in. On several occasions in group work, Surinder was edged out of the group discussion with a putdown: 'Go away, we don't want you in the group.' Surinder's response would be: 'You are not doing what you are supposed to; the teacher says we're supposed to be working at groups.'

One girl who seemed to feel that Surinder was appropriating her space was Elise who frequently verbalized the most overt racial slurs. She would voice negative remarks such as, 'I'm going to Renee's house after school to play with make-up, because we are best friends. And I am not going to invite *you*, 'cos your clothes are funny and you're a paki dot.' At other times, she would play upon her privileged status within the community, bragging about her after-school lessons or social network that played Barbies. Not wanting to be seen as outside this circle of after-school activities, Surinder's usual response was to offer a match to establish some association such as: 'I know Barbies, too. Barbies are fun. I like them very much', or 'I like to comb Barbie's hair.' In a way, she was exhibiting a sense of doubleness — letting the mainstream girls know that she too knew about Barbies when, in reality, she was not allowed to own one because of her religious orientation.

Surinder was outside the mainstream sphere; thus, she did not have access to peers in talking about most topics. Although, her conversations were a continual play on connections, mentioning everything that others do to establish an intertextual link, she always failed to be let in. On many occasions, Surinder grabbed her pen and paper and took off in stress to a solitary corner to be away from the continual taunting and teasing. When chided by the teacher about disruptions at the work table, Elise and her friends would just shrug their shoulders. They regarded their own teasing and taunting as nothing serious, 'We're just messing around.' Children who bully, like Elise, may have real difficulty in understanding the views of others and being able to empathize with the distress of peers.

Racial slurs were an effective way of diminishing an ethnic classmate and excluding her from the group. Sometimes racial slurs were accompanied by hitting and punching. Racial bullying was systemic and pervasive. It was a discrete and continual form of social harassment. Unfortunately, teachers may see it as only isolated incidents in the bustle of the school day rather than as an ongoing process (Besag, 1989). Thus, bullying may be overlooked and not addressed.

Learning Gender

Gender plays a role in the racial bullying and in the forms it takes, and children's toys reinforce racial and gendered stereotypes. Video-game playing was the game of choice in this community, consuming much of the after-school playtime. Stereotyped images of girls were pervasive as transmitted through games such as Ninja Turtles, and companion cartoons. Usually, girls are presented as secondary characters or victims, appearing as white, attractive and submissive — never as the initiators of actions. This fact has important consequences for young girls who learn to construct models of gender from observation and participation within a social milieu. The videos and cartoons not only socialize girls to be dependent, but also condition males to assume dominant gender roles (Provenzo, 1991).

Additionally, the popular Barbie doll represented a white, middle-class paradigm of gender. After a quarter century of popularity, Barbie appears mainstream, attractive, and seductive, which leads to a powerful form of cultural conditioning. We know that images formed from mediated percepts become a part of a young girl's conception of herself. In gestures of intimacy, Elise and her troupe of friends shared lip gloss, pierced earrings, and hair ornaments — mimicking Barbie's fashion world of preening and grooming which traditionally is a way of distinguishing gender. Barbie helps girls like Elise try on 'in their fantasy play the life-style that their society encourages them to hope for in their future' (Nodelman, 1992, p. 46). In much the same way, the subliminal image of mainstream 'beauty' permeated Surinder's image of self. As I sift through my reflective notes, I come upon such an entry:

> I inadvertently address Surinder as 'princess' as she arrives in school in a fancy dress. Soulfully, she looks up at me and says, 'I can't be a princess because I don't look like a princess, Linda.' I assured her that as a girl, she could be anything she wanted to. I knew I might be on slippery ground with this statement as other cultures might socialize girls differently.

And being a feminist, it surprised me that the word princess had slipped out. I worried that I might be perpetuating the Cinderella myth that had trapped so many girls before us. However, my agenda was really color and I wanted to help Surinder see her brown skin as valued. Together we walked to the library and I showed her *Mufaro's Beautiful Daughters, An African Tale* and other ethnic folk tales from India and the Middle East. Delighted with these stories, she lingered over the illustrations, responding, 'Those princesses have brown skin like me!'

Attention to race made me aware of the differing perspectives that young girls hold about skin color — perceptions of beautiful, attractive or ugly. Ironically, although Surinder's classmates did not appreciate brown skin as egalitarian, Elise and her friends valued 'tanning' during play in the sun and made deliberate attempts to sport scanty clothing on sunny days 'to get a dark tan', a demarcator of beauty like Barbie's. On several occasions, they rolled up their sleeves to compare how brown they were becoming.

Slowly, I was beginning to see why many of these children stayed so close to their homes and didn't forge intimate relationships with others in their neighborhood. Was it any wonder? Those of us who are in the privilege of the mainstream culture may never experience this kind of exclusion. One of the girls, Bandhana, talked about racial bullying in this way: 'My mom got used to it when she was a little girl. Kids were mean in her school.' A child such as Surinder may be reluctant to admit to difficulties encountered in the classroom for fear of reprisal. Socially isolated children may endure loneliness and ostracism without being able to verbalize the confused emotions they experience.

Creating a School Persona

Racial bullying is not new. It is a diminishment, a quiet erosion of identity and self-esteem. Surinder was never chosen willingly as a partner nor did she belong to the gender cliques. The two other Punjabi girls in the classroom did not follow the strict dress codes, diet or hair restrictions practiced by Surinder's kinship. Surinder never visited classmates after school nor ever attended the important Grade 2 social occasion — the birthday party. She watched telephone numbers exchanged, valentines distributed and party invitations handed out, but none had her name on it. Incidentally, it was only I, an 'older friend' who was invited and attended her 8th birthday party among her extended family members. I am also an immigrant but there are few parallels between my story and Surinder's. I am white — my patch of fabric is neatly stitched in the cultural quilt.

To counter her classmates' hostility, Surinder learned to reveal little about herself in oral and written texts. Instead, she developed a social compass that kept her from crossing the line between her school self and her cultural self. Efforts in writer's workshop, a cooperative authoring activity, were closely guarded, too.

I lik stors [stars] on my hose [house]. Do you have stors on your hose. I
do to. My Dad likes stars. My mom like stors I like stors to. My babey
sastre [sister] like stors. Do you like stors. I do to. (December 13)

During the year, Surinder produced very little that was authentic writing (79
per cent of her stories began with an 'I like . . .' sentence frame). She relied on a
repetitive pattern that allowed her words to cover the page. Rarely, did she initiate risks or tap her own experiences. At one point, she had commented about the
quantity of a mainstream girl's writing: 'Linda, she must have a big brain because
her writing goes to the bottom of the page.' Not wanting to be left out of the writing
game, she set her standard and quickly remedied her approach by filling a page of
her writing journal each day with a longer repetitive pattern and using bigger print.
After all, isn't that what the writing workshop was about?

Surinder's de-personalizing texts reflect a lack of authentic voice since cultural
topics such as family times at the neighboring gurdwara (Sikh temple) were not for
class consumption. Underpinning her contrived, artificial texts are the suggestions
that writing is a self-conscious in-house activity with a 'careful eye on teachers'
expectations' (Protherough, 1983). Producing writing was for the reader-over-the-
shoulder (Barr, 1983) rather than for discovery; a journey that reminisces through
personal experiences.

The multi-ethnic children were living in the cold shadows, a world of 'dual
roles'. In *Voices of the Self*, Gilyard (1990) described how one self participated and
flourished in the mainstream school life and how the Afro-American self dwelt
within the ghetto community. Similarly, by assuming mainstream names such as
Michael for Minh Tan, Jeff for Duc Lan or Jessie for Rajinder, Surinder's ethnic classmates were not allowing others to meet the real children — the children
from the plural fabric of society. Each of these children put 'someone else together'
for their classmates. They were wearing two pair of shoes — a mainstream and an
Afro-American pair — knowing when and how to wear each pair. They were keeping a part of themselves, the culturally situated self, safe from the social world of
the school. Surinder, and the other multi-ethnic children, had learned the strategy
of 'accommodation without assimilation' (Gibson, 1991). That is, while not giving
up language, cultural beliefs and practices, she was willing to play the classroom
game by the rules and try to overcome bullying despite frequent cultural clashes. For
her, schooling was done for teachers, a prospect 'to do well and please her parents'.

Why Do Girls Bully?

According to Schofield (1982), friendships between girls of different races are
rare with little crossing of borders. The boys in the class rarely made overtly racial
remarks. Perhaps, young boys have more opportunity than girls to form positive
racial images as they have superheroes of color. Sports heroes such as Shaquille
O'Neal serve young boys as the symbolic carriers of racial and cultural desires to
soar beyond limits and obstacles (Dyson, 1994). Girls have few models. Olympic

figure skater, Kristy Yamaguchi's fame was fleeting and no other non-mainstream idol replaced her.

Within the social interactions of the classroom or playground, young boys live their rough and tumble lives in competitive games (Thorne, 1994). However, young girls usually are in more shifting alliances (Thorne, 1994). They play more exclusionary and intimate activities with friends by swapping stories, sharing the world of pretend, 'best friends secrets', or forming their own cliques or 'clubs' that selectively screen members. In Surinder's classroom, friendship was according to skin privilege — whites with whites, browns with browns. On the playground, Surinder clustered ethnically, whenever possible, by seeking companionship from her kinship network, a cross-age grouping that gave her a 'sense of rootedness' (Banks and Banks, 1993).

A second reason why girls tend to befriend only members of their own race may be related to the political and economic climate of the city. Recessionary belt-tightening helped to foster a backlash against immigrants who were accused of overburdening the social system. With several plant closings and the laying-off of workers, the climate was ripe for hostility. There was a xenophobic notion that 'others' might be working for less and taking jobs away. Still holding to the nineteenth-century philosophy that becoming Canadian meant giving up what was in the past — language, values, attitudes — and assimilating into the society, newspapers headlines, editorials and letters to the editor kept these racial sparks fueled and ignited.

In addition, this school took a *laissez-faire* policy. The process of schooling was a form of social and cultural reproduction intertwined with other structures, mainly economic advancement (Apple, 1982). Schools maintained privilege by taking the form and content of the mainstream culture and defining it as legitimate knowledge. The teachers felt that it was their job to 'Canadianize' immigrant children as quickly as possible rather than cherishing and building on the language, values, beliefs and ways of learning that they were bringing to school. Although multi-ethnic literature had been added to the classroom library, books that were culturally conscious and could help learners understand authentic social issues were rare. The school had modified its curricula to recognize the increasingly culturally diverse population. 'Otherness' was a marker of comparison rather than something to celebrate. Instead of discussing critical issues such as attitudes toward ethnic groups, equal rights, discrimination, and societal change, multi-ethnic literature stimulated follow-up activities related to the tasting of new foods, making decorations or celebrating holidays. There was little to indicate an adjustment of instructional patterns to include patterns beyond those of the typical Eurocentric perspective. Curricula did not reflect the assumption that ethnic diversity would enrich a classroom community as children share ideals, values and spirit (Ravitch, 1983). Instead of utilizing multi-ethnic literature and constructivist models of instruction to allow learners to wrestle with issues such as justice and prejudice, instructional practices advocated a superficial understanding of self and others without sharpening thinking about social issues. Fueled by these narrow contexts, the seeds of hostility and prejudice ripened.

Negotiating a Culturally Sensitive Curriculum

As the school year progressed, I wanted my presence to be more transformative. I wanted to help the classroom teacher use alternative strategies, other than admonishment or rules, to attack some of the roots of the bullying behavior. It was apparent that for Elise and some of the others in the bullying circle a display of power over others was an acceptable measure of social success. The classroom teacher was alerted to inequities within the class and we initiated steps to intervene.

Intervention 1: The Book Circle

The teacher and I negotiated a literature circle focusing on culturally conscious literature that addressed sensitive issues. By using bullying as a topic for discussion, we were able to introduce the language of problem-solving and describe the emotions, issues, social difficulties, and consequences of working in a dis-harmonious classroom community. The teacher tackled issues of prejudice and bullying head-on within the circle of 'talk about books'.

Literature has the potential to help students reflect upon ways that they might carry inclusionary values forward in their own lives. At the heart of a lively discussion of Mary Hoffman's *Amazing Grace* (1991) was the hurtful discrimination targeted at Grace who couldn't play the lead character in the school play because she was black. In small groups, learners chatted about how racism oppressed others. Other books such as Peter Golenbock's (1990) *Teammates*, which recounted Jackie Robinson's harassment in the major leagues, or Shannon K. Jacobs's *Song of the Giraffe* (1991), in which Kisana feels ostracized because her skin color was different, helped the class lift their blinders to see what happens when negative attitudes exclude others. Over time, the tenor of these discussions became more critical, reflective, and evaluative as attitudes were broadened. As one classmate, Megan, explained, 'We don't say we don't like kittens because of the color of the fur; so we should not [not] like people 'cos their skin is different colors.' Collectively, young learners began to gain heightened sensitivity to the needs and problems of others and a respect for the pluralism flourishing in their own classroom community. By the children's consensus, it became clear that there would be zero tolerance for bullying within the class that was striving for cohesion and democratic values.

Intervention 2: The Power of Story

I knew that literacy needed to be more enabling so that Surinder could have the linguistic opportunities to be present and active in the struggle for claiming her voice, her history and her future. During my year in the classroom, I found that my role was continually changing from participant to mentor and critical friend. Anxious to mend the tattered scars from racial bullying and help build self-esteem,

I wanted to help Surinder tap into stories of herself to gain a sense of visibility. As I became Surinder's confidant, we shared stories together. We filled our conversations with relating to each other something of life's small moments. I told her and others stories I wove about Michael, the greedy Magpie, who always raided our frontyard bird feeder, gobbling all the best bits and pushed out the smaller birds. Sometimes, I narrated tales about Sebastian, my friend's Golden labrador.

Storytelling, the telling of children's personal stories, can add to the fabric of the classroom. It helps individuals to recognize the value of life experiences and builds in the class a sense of the worth of each person's story. I was a participant researcher in the classroom, not a teacher. It would be a challenge to build a storytelling culture in this classroom. These children were open to me talking about ethnicity and culture but reticent to reveal their inner feelings or display their curiosities, hopes or dreams to the classroom community.

Concerned about their restricting lifestyle, I began to take Surinder and the other five multi-ethnic girls outside the classroom in pairs or in threes and fours. I made an effort to extend their horizons and acquaint them with the mainstream culture. I thought these experiences would be the springboards for stories. Using public transit, I accompanied the children on excursions to the zoo, walks through the downtown, and tours of museums, parks and historical sites. New doors were opened and some became possibilities for writing.

Always taking a camera, we returned to the classroom with a treasure trove of snapshots as memories. We talked and talked about these memories and stories came spilling out about our adventures. These once silent children discovered and built stories together, which they shared with their classmates and each other. Through story, they found connection points. Language experience stories — group add-on stories, unexpected incidents, humorous incidents — were all swapped in the safety of small storytelling circles, a tapestry of stories — each tale embroidered with the strands of others. Their personal experiences became storyable as they made the ordinary interesting and the commonplace remarkable. What made the difference was that their stories mirrored the realities of their new experiences. From the shadows their voices rang out.

Once Surinder became accustomed to seeing ideas grow from these experiences, she began finding that almost everything in her life could become seeds of thought. In time, these seeds blossomed into stories. Each story incorporated different syntax, a unique rhythm and emotional shading. Every time she wrote, she taught me something anew about herself and others. Together we wove our patches of a story together. It added fibre to the classroom quilt.

Voices from the Shadows

Over time, by participating in everyday school events, I have come to appreciate a sense of membership in a peer culture embedded in and not easily separated from the social structures of school. In the unravelling, the threads became more apparent, each with its distinct color. As I unravelled, I also began to weave a story combining the voices from ethnically diverse children in the shadows of classroom life.

Through ethnography, I have learned to view children through strengths, a way of thinking that is important when considering multi-ethnic learners. Labels such as 'at-risk' or 'limited English proficiency' are terms that imply deficits. By learning to mistrust all labeling and rely on what I see, I can look beyond the labels. What I discovered is the whole child sitting beside me in the class, working and socializing.

A non-mainstream girl can be given voice and visibility in everyday school life. Recognizing the connectedness of gender, race, literacy, and systemic bullying in group engagements allows teachers to use literacy to uncover the issues and oracy to provide avenues to integration. With Surinder and with the others, I hope to snip and stitch new patterns into the quilt with threads of unity so that all voices are securely interwoven.

References

APPLE, M. (1982) *Education and Power*, London, Routledge.

BANKS, J.A. and BANKS, C.M. (1993) *Multi-cultural Education: Issues and Perspectives*, Toronto, ON, Allyn & Bacon.

BARR, M. (1983) 'The new orthodoxy about writing: Confusing process and pedagogy', *Language Arts*, **60**, 7, pp. 829–40.

BESAG, V.E. (1989) *Bullies and Victims in Schools*, Milton Keynes, Open University Press.

CAMPBELL, M. (1973) *Half-breed*, Toronto, McLelland & Stewart.

DELAMONT, S. (1990) *Sex Roles and the School*, London, Methuen.

DYSON, M.E. (1994) 'Be like Mike? Michael Jordan and the pedagogy of desire', in GIROUX, H.A. and MCLAREN, P. (eds) *Between Borders: Pedagogy and the Politics of Cultural Studies*, New York, NY, Routledge, pp. 119–26.

ERICKSON, F. (1982) 'Taught cognitive learning in its immediate environments: A neglected topic in the anthropology of education', *Anthropology of Education*, **13**, 2, pp. 140–80.

GIBSON, M.A. (1991) *Accommodation Without Assimilation: Sikh Immigrants in American High School*, Ithaca, NY, Cornell University Press.

GILYARD, K. (1991) *Voices of the Self*, Detroit, MI, Wayne State Press.

GOLENBOCK, P. (1990) *Teammates* (P. Bacon, Illus.), Orlando, FL., Harcourt Brace Jovanovich/Gulliver Books.

HOFFMAN, M. (1991) *Amazing Grace*, (C. Binch, Illus.), New York, Dial Books for Young Readers.

JACOBS, S.K. (1991) *Song of the Giraffe*, (P. Johnson, Illus.), New York, Little Brown/Springboard Books.

NODELMAN, P. (1992) *The Pleasures of Children's Literature*, NY, Longman.

OLWEUS, D. (1993) *Bullying at School: What We Know and What We Can Do*, Cambridge, MA, Basil Blackwell.

PROTHEROUGH, R. (1983) *Encouraging Writing*, London, Methuen.

PROVENZO, E.F. (1991) *Video Kids*, Cambridge, MA, Harvard University Press.

RAVITCH, D. (1983) 'A culture in common', *Educational Leadership*, **49**, 4, pp. 8–11.

SADKER, M. and SADKER, D. (1994) *Failing at Fairness: How America's Schools Cheat Girls*, New York, Charles Scribner's Sons.

SCHOFIELD, J. (1982) *Black and White in School*, New York, Praeger.

SHUMAN, A. (1986) *Storytelling Rights*, New York, Cambridge University Press.

SWANN, J. (1992) *Girls, Boys and Language*, Cambridge, MA, Basil Blackwell.

THORNE, B. (1994) *Gender Play: Girls and Boys at School*, New Brunswick, NJ, Rutgers.

TOTH, S.A. (1978) *Blooming: A Small Town Girl*, Boston, MA, Little Brown.

7 Disclosure and Resistance: Girls' Silence in an Inner-city Classroom

Carol Leroy

Without dialogue there is no communication, and without communication there can be no true education. (Freire, 1968, p. 81)

One part of a qualitative study I conducted on the reading and writing of children in a Grade 5 inner-city classroom involved an examination of girls 'continually reading the world' (Freire and Macedo, 1987, p. 35). I was startled by the extent to which features of the girls' social milieu constrained their ability to speak publicly about their experiences with social conflict and oppression. It has been argued by critical theorists (Freire, 1968; Giroux, 1992; McLaren, 1989) and by others in this book (Epp; Tite; MacDonald; Wason-Ellam) that there is a need for a pedagogy in which students can speak critically about their experiences and their relationships with others. This form of pedagogy is more difficult to arrange than one would expect.

The school in which this study took place had many of the features common to other 'urban poor schools' (Maynes, 1990, p. 5) including the following: a multi-ethnic population; a substantial number of children who were living in poverty and/or experiencing problems in the home; a high turnover rate among the students; and student violence which was reported by the staff to be more prevalent and problematic than they had encountered in other areas. Another feature of the school's inner-city status was the use of the playground by prostitutes and their customers after school hours, with the result that the caretaker had to clear the grounds of used condoms and needles every morning.

There were eighteen children in the regular Grade 5 program in this classroom. An additional six children attended the class in the mornings, but were withdrawn to a special needs class in the afternoons and, therefore, were not full participants in the study. There were five Euro-Canadian girls in the regular class, and four girls who identified themselves as Native. Two of the female special needs students were status Indians who came from Cree families with strong ties at particular reserves. The other two claimed Native status on an informal basis because they had a parent or stepparent who was Native, but these girls did not consistently maintain this ethnic identity in public and were not acknowledged to be Native by the Cree girls. In this classroom there were also three boys who were of Chinese or Vietnamese ancestry, and seven Euro-Canadian boys. Two of the latter had been formally identified as 'behavior disordered'.

When the study began in January, the children were seated in rows facing the front of the classroom, and many of their interactions were closely monitored by the teacher. In mid-April, the teacher rearranged the classroom so that the children were seated in groups of four, an arrangement she had used with every other class but had found caused troubles with this particular group so she had saved it for later in the year. Even before this new arrangement was in place, the children interacted a great deal. Some of this interaction was covert but much of it occurred when the children worked in groups in a number of different activities. The teacher designed these activities in the belief that learning is a creative process. In the content areas, these included hands-on exploratory activities in science, carrying out research projects in social studies, games and sports in physical education, and various projects in art. Language arts activities, which took place in the afternoon, were designed more for completion by children on an individual basis.

Over a six-month period, I visited the classroom two or three times weekly. I kept fieldnotes of my observations, and audiotaped a variety of classroom interactions. I also engaged the children and their teacher in extended private conversations, which took place outside the classroom and were audiotaped. The nature of the conversations varied from participant to participant. In some cases these conversations were restricted to the topics of reading and writing and revolved around questions that I posed, but in most cases the participants and I used the conversations to meander through a variety of topics, which included my life experiences as well as theirs. Many of the children came to see me not only as a confidante but also as a consultant on their personal affairs. When they asked me for information or advice I tried, as much as possible, to engage them in dialogue through which we could explore together the possibilities for meaning and decision making. With some of the children this became an important part of the research process.

Some Constraints on Girls' Talk

The realities of these girls' lives made it possible for the text of a conversation to have grave impact on them, in very real ways. These included the possibility of apprehension by social services, 'getting burned', and being betrayed. These terms took on new meaning when applied to their circumstances.

Apprehension

Apprehension: . . . to come to know . . . to anticipate with anxiety . . . to take (a person) in legal process. (W*ebster's Third New International Dictionary*, 1986, p. 106)

In the social context in which my study took place, the word 'apprehension' usually referred to the process by which a child was removed from his or her home by authorities, and placed in an alternate living arrangement. Although this was presumably for the child's protection, the prospect of apprehension for these girls was a threat that constrained the extent to which many of them were willing to disclose their experiences to adults.

One of the girls in this class was sexually assaulted in February. She reported this to her teacher, and the teacher reported it to the school counselor and authorities in child welfare. Earlier in the school year, this girl had witnessed a stabbing in her home and had had to testify against a relative in court. Prior to that, she had been apprehended because of neglect and because of a crime that had occurred in her home. She had then lived in several foster placements.

After the investigation began for the sexual assault, one of her parents went on a drinking binge, suffered a drug overdose, and ended up in the hospital. In the meantime, the girl ran away and joined what she called a 'street gang'. She returned to school a week later and wrote this to her teacher in her journal:

> Are you glad I'm back? Were you worried while I was gone? Well I missed all the classmates and you and Carol. Sometimes it's hard leaving someplace when you like the place.

This is what she wrote a month later. It was an extension of conversations she had been having with the teacher, school counselor and with me:

> Mrs T. also I need your advice, I guess I'm growing too fast. I feel 11 [years old] but on the other hand I feel 10 years old but I don't know how to act my age and I'm wondering what you did when you felt [this way] but I almost forgot. Did you feel this way? I don't know what's happening to my mind. It's concentrating and then not concentrating. Well I got nothing else to say, so I'll write and say [something later]. So I'll Let You Go.

Shortly after this, the girl left the class and community, sent by her parents to live in another place. She remained there until the court case, in which the man pleaded guilty, and then, right after the hearing, the family moved to a different town. The last we heard of her that year was that she and her parents went directly from the courthouse to the greyhound bus depot. Someone asked her where their suitcases were. The girl replied, 'We don't have suitcases. We only have bags.'

There was another girl in this class whose home was under investigation during the study. This time it was for suspicion of neglect, rather than abuse. Like the first girl, the second was very much on edge about the prospect of being placed in foster care. During this time she was often agitated, crying, and misbehaving in the classroom. This was happening at the same time that there was a widely publicized trial of a foster parent in whose care a young boy had been severely beaten and left dependent on life support systems. Although I thought it probable that the girl had heard of this case, she did not bring it up. When I asked her what scared her most about being placed in foster care, she said it was that her mother would kill herself if she lost custody of the children.

Life was not easy for these children. A third girl told me:

> My father, my real father, is dead . . . My mom moved out on him 'cause
> he was an alcoholic. And she didn't like him drinking around us and that.
> So we moved and he killed himself because he couldn't ever see us again
> . . . he stuck a drug needle in his arm and killed himself.

With these kinds of experiences in their background, it is no wonder that four of
the girls in this classroom told me that they would not tell anyone, including their
parents, if an adult abused or assaulted them. It was also a very difficult position
for an adult in a position of authority. One day, one of the girls approached me in
a very agitated way and said that she wanted to talk to me about something serious.
She hoped that, in contrast to her teacher and her school counselor, I would not
repeat anything she told me to the authorities. I had explained the boundaries of
my confidentiality to her earlier. When I reminded her that I was under the same
obligations as her teacher, she closed her eyes. Then she put her head down and
sobbed.

The problem of having to report accounts of violence against children is not,
of course, confined to researchers and teachers (see, Tite, Chapter 3 of this volume). It is a problem that is faced by anyone who works with children. Under law,
we must report to authorities any evidence that indicates a child's well-being is in
danger. When we do so, the child's care is placed in the hands of others. Police
and/or social workers are now making the decisions and once they are involved
it can be difficult for us to know what is going on, let alone play an active role.
Parents are also making decisions. In my experience in the inner-city, a common
consequence of allegations is that the child simply disappears. When she reappears
in a new location, you can be sure that she thinks twice about raising the topic of
violence with another adult.

Getting Burned

Burn: . . . to produce or undergo discomfort suggestive of pain accompanying a burn. (*Webster's Third New International Dictionary*, 1986,
p. 299)

In this classroom the children used the term 'burn' as a noun and as a verb. As
a verb it referred to the process by which one delivered an insult which rendered
another child speechless and/or caused the child to lose control and resort to crying,
yelling, lashing out physically, and so on. Among the children it was generally
agreed that the worst (or best, depending on one's stance) burns were those which
contained explicit detail about having sex with one's mother. These verbal burns
had non-verbal equivalents in the many physical gestures which were used by children to threaten each other and which resulted in silence. Burns often started out
in subtle ways but once the process began, it quickly escalated and spread among

the children. That was one reason why one of the girls referred to the classroom as an 'enemy warp'.

In this classroom, the Euro-Canadian boys dominated much of the action around burning. They were involved in seemingly constant chains of verbal and physical conflicts in which a boy would have to publicly demonstrate that he was smarter, stronger, and/or more in control than someone else was. Although this process was usually initiated and directed by relatively few Euro-Canadian males, the other children inevitably became swept up in it. An example of this was when there was much bickering back and forth among children who sat near each other while engaging in science experiments. One boy said loudly and disdainfully about one of the girls, 'She's a virgin.' The girl retorted angrily, 'Well you know all about it, 'cause you do it with Scott!' When a girl engaged in an exchange like this with boys, she was basically in a no-win position. If she did not reply to an insult, then the implication was that the insult was true and/or that she was too stupid to think of something to retort when under fire. On the other hand, if a girl topped a boy in this kind of competition, he lost a great deal of face and this required stronger retaliation from him and his friends than would have been necessary if he had lost in a conflict with a boy. (For a detailed discussion of the pressure on boys to maintain their position of masculinity see Frank's analysis in Chapter 8 of this volume.)

What made this process of one-upmanship particularly problematic for the girls was that they wanted to be popular. In order to be popular, they thought they needed, or would soon need as they grew older, a high-status boyfriend. Boys gained status and power by harassing other children. The boy whom most of the girls wanted to date was the one who bullied others the most. One girl said he did this because, 'Violence is his game.' One day, I overheard this boy telling a girl who had complained about his bossiness in a small group, 'If you want to be popular, you've got to learn to shut up.' She did.

Betrayal

Betray: . . . to lead astray . . . to disclose in violation of confidence . . . to deliver into the hands of the enemy by treachery or fraud in violation of trust. (*Webster's Third International Dictionary*, 1986, p. 209)

In this classroom there were two groups of girls. One of these groups consisted of the Euro-Canadian girls who played mainly with girls their own age. The other group included the four girls who were Native, or at least described themselves as such on occasions. The latter girls hung around with a larger group which included their older sisters and others who engaged in such activities as smoking, drinking, taking drugs, stealing, vandalism, and fighting. They placed a high value on being 'tough' and 'cool'. Although many of the youth in the larger group were not Native, the girls in my study who were in this group linked their toughness and coolness to their Native identity.

Among the girls in both groups, relationships were in a constant state of flux, due to the girls' engagement in round after round of conflict. One girl put it this way:

> Well, we get into a fight. Next minute we're friends again. Fight. Friends. Fight. Friends. And then friends and friends and friends. And then fight and fight and fight.

These fights started in a variety of ways: disputes over who was 'allowed' by one friend to be friends with another; arguing over belongings; and so on. Once a dispute started it would take on a life of its own, and quickly escalate to the point where girls would fling at each other the meanest things they could say. These insults involved deeply personal and hurtful matters that one girl would have confided to another at an earlier time when the two were friends. One example of this was the girl who yelled at another, 'Well at least my dad's not a drunkie!' — referring to a matter about which her friend was extremely sensitive and which often upset her. By bringing this up in public, the girl not only opened a sore wound but did so in such a way that it was exposed to subsequent picking at by the other children. One girl emphasized that this was far worse than the kinds of burns that the boys delivered.

One of the girls told me that this was one of the things girls feared about menstruation. If you told your best friend that you had started your periods, then as soon as she was mad at you she would tell the whole school. This was not your enemy, nor your acquaintance who would do this. It was your very best friend, or at least, as this girl pointed out, someone who appeared to be your friend at the time.

The problem of not trusting other girls (let alone boys), was deeper among those girls who hung around with the tougher crowd. This was because the older girls frequently intervened in the affairs of the younger girls and told them what to do in ways that extended and escalated their conflicts. An example of this was when 10-year-old Shannon approached me for advice one day. She had been set up by her older sister for a fight that was scheduled to take place after school and off school property (which was a common practice because then school authorities did not intervene). The fight had been set up because another girl had 'frenched' Shannon's boyfriend. Shannon had asked her sister to threaten to beat the other girl up, but the older sister had told the other girl that Shannon was going to beat her up. Shannon was scared. She was small and the other girl had big male friends from a local junior high school. If Shannon fought she would probably get hurt, but if she did not fight, everyone would know that she was a 'wimp'. She said this would result in the loss of her boyfriend. She specified that he would be embarrassed in front of his friends if she was unwilling and/or unable to fight another girl for him.

In this milieu, anything you said could later be held against you. In another example, Jolene and Elaine were quarreling on the playground. Elaine insulted Jolene. Several days later Jolene's older sister and her friends came to the school ground and said that they were going to beat up Elaine. They had beaten up kids before. They were belligerent toward the playground supervisor and then the principal. They refused to leave the playground, and the matter was transferred over to the police. Although in this instance Elaine was a potential victim of violence, she (like Shannon and some of the other girls) readily admitted to having been the aggressor in fights she had had with others.

One day the school counselor came into the classroom and asked if any of the children would be interested in joining a small discussion group on the topic of 'friendship'. All the children said they wanted to talk about friendship, but many of them said they were hesitant to do it in a group. 'What if your friend was in the same group?' asked one girl. The teacher and the counselor explained that this would probably be a good thing. If you and your friend were in a group together, you could get the support you needed to talk about your disagreements with each other. 'Yeah', said one girl, 'But what if you said something your friend didn't like? And then later she beat you up?'

For these children, sharing stories did not necessarily have positive results. In their experience, sharing stories with peers was likely to provide others with ammunition to use against them. Sharing stories with teachers could disrupt their lives. If the stories were particularly traumatic, they could result in apprehension or, if the parents suspected apprehension, the child could be moved to another place to start all over again. Open discourse was dangerous.

What to Do? Who's to Do It?

When I was carrying out this study, there were many times when the teacher, school counselor and I asked ourselves, 'What to do?' Many writers suggest that for students living in unjust social contexts it is essential for them to be able to engage in a kind of pedagogy in which they can speak openly about their lives and experiences. Yet even in university settings, where presumably most students do not threaten to beat each other up and the teacher presumably does not report their experiences to police and social workers, many educators are met with student resistance to what was intended to be a liberatory curriculum (Ellsworth, 1992; Lather, 1991; Ng, 1993; Orr, 1993). Giroux (1993) states that this is the problem 'faced most often by teachers experimenting with critical-democratic methods' (p. 28).

I raise two additional questions: 'Who should dialogue here? Who should act?' As Orner (1992) suggests, 'Calls for students to speak in the name of their own liberation and empowerment must be scrutinized' (p. 77). The girls in this class had the need and the right to be able to speak about their experiences. But their silence was, in part, due to the threat of 'social isolation or violence', which has been identified as being problematic for girls in other contexts (Brown and Gilligan, 1992, p. 3). To speak about their experiences, these girls needed privacy and support, which in some cases would involve adult intervention in the family context as well as on the street and in the classroom. For a critical pedagogy to be fruitful for them, it would need to be a community endeavor.

References

BROWN, L.M. and GILLIGAN, C. (1992) *Meeting at the Crossroads: Women's Psychology and Girls' Development*, Cambridge, MA, Harvard University Press.

ELLSWORTH, E. (1992) 'Why doesn't this feel empowering? Working through the repressive myths of critical pedagogy', in LUKE, C. and GORE, J. (eds) *Feminisms and Critical Pedagogy*, New York, Routledge, pp. 19–11.

FREIRE, P. (1968) *Pedagogy of the Oppressed*, New York, Seabury.

FREIRE, P. and MACEDO, D. (1987) *Literacy: Reading the Word and the World*, MA, Bergin and Garvey.

GIROUX, H. (1992) *Border Crossing: Cultural Workers and the Politics of Education*, London, Routledge.

GIROUX, H. (1993) 'Paulo Freire and the politics of postcolonialism', in MCLAREN, P. and LEONARD, P. (eds) *Paulo Freire: A Critical Encounter*, New York, Routledge, pp. 177–88.

LATHER, P. (1991) *Getting Smart: Feminist Pedagogy with/in the Postmodern*, London, Routledge.

MCLAREN, P. (1989) *Life in Schools: An Introduction to Critical Pedagogy in the Foundations of Education*, Toronto, Irwin Press.

MAYNES, W.G. (1990) The education of Edmonton's urban poor: A policy perspective. Unpublished doctoral dissertation, University of Alberta, Edmonton.

NG, R. (1993) '"A woman out of control": Deconstructing sexism and racism in the university', *Canadian Journal of Education*, **18**, pp. 189–252.

ORNER, M. (1992) 'Interrupting the calls for student voice in "liberatory" education: A feminist perspective', in LUKE, C. and GORE, J. (eds) *Feminisms and Critical Pedagogy*, New York, Routledge.

ORR, D.J. (1993) 'Toward a critical rethinking of feminist pedagogical praxis and resistant male students', *Canadian Journal of Education*, **18**, pp. 239–54.

WEBSTER'S THIRD NEW INTERNATIONAL DICTIONARY OF THE ENGLISH LANGUAGE (Unabridged) (1986) Springfield, MA, Merriam-Webster.

8   Masculinities and Schooling:
       The Making of Men

Blye W. Frank

> Some guys use cars, some guys use weights, some guys do it through what
> they eat, how they stand, the deep voice, some guys see how much alcohol
> they can drink, and some use girls. There are a lot of different ways to
> keep at the top. (Trent)

This chapter is part of a much larger project called 'Everyday Masculinities' (Frank,
1987; 1990; 1991; 1992; 1993; 1995), an examination of the ordinary, routine,
everyday/everynight activities of boys and men in the practice of masculinity in
schools. The analysis includes the messiness of the lives of men and boys, with all
the ambiguities, tensions, and contradictions, as well as the privilege and the pain
(Kaufman, 1993). My concern for doing this work arose out of my experience as
a teacher, where I saw and experienced the social terrorism of boys and men in
schools. Increasingly upset by the sexism, the homophobia and heterosexism, the
racism, the violence against property, self and others, I wanted to talk to men and
boys about what it means to be men and boys.
   Recent analyses in masculinity since the mid-1980s (Brittan, 1989; Brod, 1987;
Clatterbaugh, 1990; Connell, 1987; Kaufman, 1987; Kimmel, 1987; Kimmel and
Messner, 1992; Messner and Sabo, 1990) begin to make visible how past theorizing, particularly socialization theory with its reductionistic notions of how 'boys
become men', is inadequate in explaining the complexities of getting gendered.
No longer is there the 'possibility of a general or universal account of the nature
of human experience which ignores or limits both the social context and the status
of the knower' (Alcoff and Potter, 1993, p. 1). Rather, all theory and knowledge are
social products, contexted by and relative to specific circumstances and surround-
ings (Smith, 1990), but always informed by a larger set of social relations.
   'Everyday Masculinities' shares the individual and collective practice of
masculinity in the lives of young men and men teachers at a particular point in
the history of that practice, and in the larger configuration of all men's historical
practice of masculinity. It tells us that in the everyday lived terrain in the classrooms and the corridors, on the playing fields, in the staffrooms, and in the most
ordinary activities, there remains a great deal to be done if relations between the
sexes and within the single sex category of boys and men are to be without violence
and abuse.

The data for this chapter was gathered from several sources including in-school observation and ethnographic work and many in-depth interviews with young men in schools. In 1987 and 1988, I had two separate interviews with each of fourteen young men between the ages of 16 and 20 years. In 1992 and 1993, I interviewed twenty-four young men in three high schools, and in 1995 I interviewed twenty-three more: a total of sixty-one interviews with male students. In addition, I recently interviewed thirty-one men teachers, thirteen of whom identify themselves as gay.

In the first group of interviews, the fourteen boys were all from one school, all were in the academic stream, all were white and Anglophone, and most were from economically secure households. None was physically or mentally disabled. The second group were boys from three schools in very differing areas and reflected more diversity. The more recent student interviews were carried out in eight schools, some urban, some rural.

Postmodernism and Masculinities

> In the end, that's all men have is their masculinity. Money really doesn't do it. Women can leave you. If you are gay with lots of money, it might help, but you could still lose your job or get put out of your apartment. All you've got left is yourself, your masculinity, and so that's all you can count on and the best way to demonstrate it is through your body. (Sean)

Contemporary postmodern philosophers are not only upsetting the knowledge applecart, they are dismantling it by challenging and contesting the underpinnings and the resulting restrictions and limitations of modern thought and the processes that hold its production in place (Alcoff and Potter, 1993; Nicholson and Fraser, 1990; Sands and Nuccio, 1992). In the aerial views, and 'grand narratives' (Lyotard, 1984), the everyday practice of masculinity was most often seen as binary (self/social; heterosexual/homosexual; privilege/oppression; gender/sexuality). In the absence of 'situated knowledge' (Haraway, 1988, p. 595) arising from within the local narratives of men's and boys' lives, we received a 'man-made' theory-world of men that offered a fixity, a view that was linear, bounded, dichotomized, and disconnected from the everyday relations in which men exist and practice their masculinity.

Men's and boys' practice of masculinity is always local, temporal (Connell, 1987), ever shifting, intermeshed rather than sequential, with boundaries that materialize only in social interaction. By recognizing the seams and the ruptures of the *not*-so-rational self and of men's *not*-so-unified daily/nightly practice, and the diversity, multiplicity, and pluralism of both the self and the practice of masculinity, masculinity itself can be illuminated and clarified, but perhaps not classified. Once we begin to take apart the foundational blocks of masculinity (heterosexuality, rationality, privilege, and so on), with the cracks, crevices, and cross overs, we can no longer offer up explanations of the concrete stability that we once thought existed (Bernstein, 1983; Smith, 1987; Haraway, 1988; Harding, 1990, 1993). Dismantling the theoretical assumptions of masculinity 'allows us to demystify the resulting foundational realities that we have created' (Lather, 1992, p. 96), and the pillars of both the rational subject and the unified structure begin to crumble. Seeing how masculinity 'works' allows for different insights about how we might proceed to bring about change in schools, as well as in other institutional settings.

Grand narratives of men's lives have been used to reinforce a textual hegemony in the medical, legal, religious, and educational discourses about what constitutes the appropriate reality (Kinsman, 1987). This textual hegemony, with its power to both name and invent men's lives, is most often how we come to 'know' the world (Kinsman, 1987) and it continues to influence teacher education programs, curriculum change, hiring procedures; indeed, the very way teachers think about men and boys. The resulting partial and fragmented accounts elevate certain ways of seeing and understanding men and boys over others, in part by allowing some voices to go unheard or to be misrepresented by others (hooks, 1984). These 'silent' or 'distorted' voices may be physically present in a variety of textual forms, including in the lived text of our classrooms, but are in psychic exile due to a profound sense of alienation or fear. Cultural representations by oppressed groups (gay and bisexual men, men of color, physically and mentally challenged men, men who 'cross-dress') exist at the bottom of the constructs of image and text that we call culture, most often forming its least-funded, least-seen layer, especially in schools. Many men and boys find themselves screened out by these assumptions: 'on the outside looking in' (hooks, 1990, p. 25), both in theory and in all the ways in which we represent 'the' culture of men's lives, including the representation of self.

Historically the sources for understanding young men's lives and masculinity have largely been the writings of 'experts' (Kimmel, 1987). Little has been heard from young men themselves. In accounts of the lives of young men, history is made 'behind their backs'; young men do not make their own history. 'Oppositional' behavior has primarily been documented through psychological categories that have served to define such young men's behavior as deviant, as disruptive, and as inferior. This overly deterministic analysis has produced a view of young men as the passive receivers of a monolithic social system through a process which is mechanical and consensual (Connell, 1987). Masculinity was seen as a character trait that could be assessed, 'fitted' somewhat nicely to a curve and, if not adequate, 'restored' through a variety of methods, from shock re-socialization to therapy. Each man was thought to be endowed with a more or less fixed amount of 'maleness', usually called 'masculinity'. A few men were seen to be very masculine, many in the middle, and a few subnormal (homosexuals, transvestites, transsexuals, sissies, effeminates, and so on) (Connell, 1987).

The conversations of the young men interviewed for this research demonstrate that there was nothing 'fixed' about their masculinity. Rather, their masculinity was constituted and reconstituted over negotiated circumstances and time, consuming a great deal of thought and energy. As one student commented 'Well, it isn't like it just happens. It takes a lot of time to be sure that you're always doing it right' (Trent).

In Their Own Voice

> Most guys are so tied up in being men that they can't let on that they care
> about anything, even with their girlfriends. They tell them that they love
> them to their faces and curse them behind their backs. (Jack)

Here, young men speak for themselves about their lives. They are the 'experts' in
the description of what it means to be a young man. As much as possible, it is their
'talk' that I have attempted to capture. And through this talk, it is their practice,
which is their 'history in the making', that we hear. Understanding the diversity,
the plurality, and the similarity, as well as the accommodation and the resistance,
demands a careful 'reading' of their talk and, more generally, of the discourse
through which men and boys are both spoken and written into existence, but not
necessarily determined by it (Butler, 1990).

These young men experienced struggles and mediated lives full of tension and
contradiction concerning what it means to be a young man. Masculinity was not a
simple matter of learning a role and carrying it out to 'become a man'. Socialization
theories, which continue to be part of the grand narrative in much educational theory, work well in the abstract, but not so well in the lived terrain of daily life of
men and boys. If such were the case, schools, in their attempts to socialize their
clientele differently, would have been much more successful by now! The penalties
for non-conformity have always been severe. As one student said: 'Most of the time
you do it or you will suffer the consequences, which can be pretty bad, depending
on how far you stepped out of line. You can get called names, or isolated, but you
also take the chance of getting the shit beaten out of you' (Trent).

Bodies, Sports and Sexuality

> Men act in ways that produce masculinity. That's what sports is about.
> That's what fighting's about. That's what having a girlfriend or having a
> good body is about. Those are things that gain you authority and power
> ... over other men and women. Men's relationships are about competi-
> tion. You compete through women. You compete through sports. You
> compete through fighting. You compete through body size ... through
> various things. But all of it is about competition. (Evan)

The conversations of the boys ranged widely from family to the future, however,
within their talk three sites of the practice of masculinity stood out as important:
the body, sport, and sexuality. As Jim suggested: 'Sports, looks, and a woman,
that's what every guy needs to be masculine.' However, as we 'locate' masculinity
in three social sites, we must not oversimplify the issue of practice. It was not
necessary, for example, that each boy engage in sport, produce and maintain what
was considered an appropriate masculine body, or engage in heterosexual sexual
activity (Pronger, 1990). The actual activity was not the critical feature; rather, it

was the support of these three pillars that was central to the maintenance of masculinity (Bunch, 1975). Being 'one of the boys' means supporting these themes.

Power in and through the body has always been an important part of the production of masculinity (Messner, 1989). For these young men, power translated as violence, sexism, and heterosexism, expressed and practiced in and through the body (Kidd, 1987). Working through the often complex process of giving various meanings, and forming multiple emotional and physical links with their bodies and those of others, was never a simple or smooth procedure. Each boy found himself with multiple positions and struggled, in varying degrees over time and context, to both fit in to and challenge the dominant codes of masculinity in relation to what he did with his body. For some of them, their bodies became their suits of armor that carried them into the social world to offer them security, protection, and freedom from harassment (Messner, 1990a). Many of the young men were willing to put vast amounts of time, money, and energy into producing a body that helped gain them power, often at the expense of other things.

> The ultimate for a man is to be big. Big men are it. The big body-builder body is the pinnacle; it's the gladiator, it's the warrior. Underneath it's what most men would like to be because it's so safe. (Mike)

For others, their bodies offered them little protection against an often hostile social environment:

> I've been made fun of a lot by people who think that I'm not appropriately male. I've been harassed because of the way I choose to decorate my body. I can't even tell my father that I want to go to drama school next year and eventually be a dancer. He wouldn't be happy . . . his only son a dancer! I cope through violence, and sometimes when it becomes too much I just stay at home. (Trent)

The boys' relations in sport came with a history and most often revealed the broader ideological, psychological, social, and economic relations of gender and sexuality (Sabo, 1986). Tied as it is to the frequently brutal features of patriarchal culture, such as misogyny, violence, sexism, and heterosexism, sport for these boys was much more than an 'innocent' pastime played for fun. Their sport activities helped to maintain inequality between and among these young men along divisions of physical size and strength, class, and sexual orientation (Messner and Sabo, 1990). The accompanying violence — often accepted and celebrated by many staff and coaches within the school — created apprehension, fear, low self-esteem, and self-loathing for some of the boys. They never seemed to be able to measure up.

> It's a training. It's a mental training for people to get the right mentality for competition and all that in later life. Not just physically, but it's the idea of competition and success and domination. Sport, more than anything else, separates the men from the boys. (Thomas)

However, the problem is not simply schools and those who work in them. The values that sport embodies are tied to a much larger set of practices in the broader society: competition, the notion of winning at any cost, and the economics of profit (Messner and Sabo, 1990). For many of the boys, sport gave them a sense of self-worth, power, control, and manhood. In order to exhibit, enhance, and amplify their masculinity, they used sport to live up to the prescribed social norms. But the contradictions and the tensions always poked through, and some boys were clear that they did not value the very practices in which they engaged.

Listening to these voices, it was evident that sexuality was not simply individual, but was also a set of practices saturated with meanings which were often confusing and difficult (Steedman, 1987).

> Well, if you're labelled a fruit or a fag or so on socially, you might as well forget about it because you won't get a girlfriend, you won't get invited to any parties, you won't play any sports, you won't get invited to come over and jam on the drums. You have to sit at home or work at Towers. Being a heterosexual is definitely at the top. But at the same time, you're not allowed to hang out with girls or be too nice to them. That's a real no-no. (Derrick)

Sexuality contains within it social relations of power, much of which is manifested in socially regulated acts of violence toward women and other men. Harassment by some boys (and some girls) in the form of name-calling and physical bashing resulted in exclusion, silence, and emotional upset for many boys who did not meet the standard.

> There are guys that everyone considers losers. To be a loser is to not have asserted your heterosexuality in society yet. You're a wimp or a fag. If you don't participate in sports, then you're at the bottom and at the same time that you got a girlfriend, you can't be too nice to her. The guys, including my father, would say that she wears the pants if you let her make the decisions. (Jim)

We hear from these voices how sexuality is organized around activities permeated and interwoven with different amounts of power. Some activities result in rewards and encouragements, while others result in punishment, harassment, and a life of misery for some:

> Sex is all about image. I think that a lot of guys when they go out they put it on. It's like this hard shell. It's like a jacket. They put it on before they step out the door and they strut their stuff and then they take it off when they come home, or if they come home with the guys they leave it on. And a big part of that is making sure that others know you're not a queer. (Luke)

The lives of these students illustrated the extent to which doubt, choice, strategy, planning, transformation, and contradiction were central to the practice of masculinity. The boys developed strategies to allow themselves to avoid the harassment, while at the same time increasing the possibilities of power.

> I find it's easy getting along if you play your cards right. You have to make strategies. First of all, I got on a sports team to get accepted by the administration. If you're on a sports team, you're rewarded. You're let off things. I did that at the first of the year so I wouldn't be hassled as much throughout the year by both other students and the administration. I hang around with the bigger guys who also play sports, the more popular people. I have a girlfriend. Those things make life pretty safe. (Eric)

The practices of the boys show how their masculinity was historically specific, socially constructed and imposed, and personally embodied (Connell, 1987). Several boys reported that they purposely hid many things from other male friends, and sometimes from their fathers: the caring for houseplants, their interest in cooking, sewing, or cleaning the house, their desire to care for children, dreams of becoming a nurse. Their lives often demonstrated blocked paths, and school did little to open up the possibilities for them to break out of the prescribed gender and sexual roles and regulations (Connell, 1989b). Most of the time, there is little acknowledgment by those who work in schools of the institutional power invested in the production and maintenance of certain practices of masculinity.

The fact that the school reinforced and supported many of the strategies of dominant masculinity does not mean that the students were simply determined by it. Some boys developed strategies to support and remain in the dominant culture while practicing activities that, if discovered, would place them outside of it. For example, a young gay man may develop his sexual relationships in secret while at the same time work out at the gym two hours a day to give a particular shape to his body, thus reflecting the definitions of the dominant masculinity of the culture.

Hegemonic Heterosexual Masculinity

> Well, you can't be too sensitive or else they'll call you a wimp. I try not to be too emotional or excited. (Mark)

Masculinity is not a unidirectional and uniform consensual process and is always subject to change, but at any given moment the interpretation of what is masculine reveals the personal and collective material and psychological investments of those who have power and those who do not (Connell, 1987). The practice of masculinity in the larger culture saturated the lived experience in classrooms, staffrooms, corridors, and gymnasiums of the schools. The power of individuals and groups of men, both historical processes in themselves, lead to social privilege; a privilege that is paid attention to, worked on, played out, and shared collectively in all social sites, as well as in the most intimate experiences, of most men.

Dominance — regardless of how fragile, how tenuous, how changeable and local it is — is what I and others mean by hegemonic masculinity (Connell, 1987). It consists of specific, concrete and perceived practices of men that give them power over others: heterosexuality, misogyny and sexism, heterosexism and homophobia, physical size and strength through the body, and competition and violence. It manifests itself in numerous and complex ways, from who talks when and in what space, to who gets what job. Masculine heterosexual hegemony is how certain groups of boys, or any one boy, can occupy positions of power and how they can legitimate and replicate the personal and social relationships that generate that power and privilege (Connell, 1987). Anyone who has worked in schools is aware that the most important feature of this masculinity is that it is heterosexual. Bolstered by the everyday homophobia and heterosexism that occupies the social terrain, heterosexuality and masculinity weave themselves together to form what appears as a 'natural' bond.

The possibilities of practice are not granted equal access in a world where hegemonic masculinity is practiced on a myriad of fronts in the wider society. The family system excludes gay men (and lesbians), as do state policies, the medical profession, sociology, sexology, psychiatry, the church, the media, and the school system. Heterosexist or homophobic assertions about the 'naturalness' of heterosexuality and the 'abnormality' of other forms of sexuality are not simply backward ideas held by some of the boys; they are organized through the social relations of masculine heterosexual hegemony (Kinsman, 1987). This heterosexism relates the practices of heterosexual hegemony to the institutional and social settings of the boys (families, church, sports, bodies, schools) and to their sex and gender relations (misogyny, sexism, violence). Things that are seen as personal responses by the boys are organized by the often common heterosexist discourse and practice found in a variety of sites in schools on a daily basis: the 'faggot' jokes, the portrayal of gay men as perverse and sick, the name-calling, the physical and psychological abuse of gay or effeminate men. These incidents are not merely a matter of attitudes. 'Reality' for these boys is interpreted through the schema of what are considered to be 'expert sources' (teachers, coaches, police, policy booklets, government and legal policies), all of which confirm the dominant interpretation of gender and sexuality. Schools perpetuate these relations by supporting violence in sports; failing to recognize and support diverse gender and sexual practices; and by rendering invisible gay men in the curriculum.

For the boys in these studies, heterosexual masculine hegemony was not present in some situations and absent in others. On both the individual and collective level, it was always present and some degree of attention was always paid to it. Although there was a certain contextual fluidity; the boys were 'always figuring it out'. Gender obedience to heterosexual masculine hegemony, was expressed in themes of competition with men, the exploitation and subordination of women and other men, violence towards women and other men, and, of course, homophobia. Most men teachers and boys with whom I talked supported such gender obedience in varying degrees and in various ways according to different circumstances.

Hegemonic heterosexual masculinity received a good deal of assistance in its maintenance. Very large numbers of men, as well as some women teachers and many women students, were responsible for upholding the hegemonic model even though there was a gap and often a great deal of tension between the collective ideal and the actual lived practice of most men. Most men and boys benefit from the subordination of women and other men; the practice of hegemonic heterosexual masculinity in schools is centrally connected to the institutionalization of men's dominance over women and men in the larger society (Clatterbaugh, 1990). Hegemonic masculinity is hegemonic insofar as it exemplifies the successful strategy in relation to women and other men (Connell, 1989a). Without its protection, the privilege of most men would look significantly different.

However, power and its effects did not turn the boys into 'social dupes', simply acted upon by the culture and defined in and through the discourse of the hegemony. Even in schools there was a hierarchy always struggling to establish and maintain its position, and the boys could clearly articulate what it was — heterosexuality, physical size, misogyny, violence. But this hierarchy, in itself, is just as fully historical and relational as any other social process. It shifts and moves: twists and turns. Heterosexuality does not remain dominant without effort or without resistance. Idealized body size does not exist without great effort. Misogyny and violence do not exist without attention and effort.

Possibilities

> Well, I think you get a lot of mixed messages. My father expects one thing, my girlfriend another. Sometimes I feel like I'm not quite sure what I should do. I always try to judge the situation. (Derrick)

Masculinity, as reflected in the interviews, was not a two-layered structure of power, creating a tension between two practices — such as heterosexuality and homosexuality — from which any boy could make a choice. Nor was it a multi-layered structure in which all boys headed in a unidirectional path to the imagined pinnacle: heterosexuality, patriarchy, and physical strength. Rather, masculinity was in a constant state of flux in which the practices changed quite dramatically, even with the same boy.

> I find that you have to be constantly letting everyone know that you're not going to take any shit from anyone; that you're not going to be stepped on. You have to work at it all the time or else someone will be there to take your place. (Trent)

A considerable amount of conflict often resided in the dichotomy between fulfilling internalized needs and meeting standards — standards mostly set by other men and boys (Messner, 1987). For some of the boys, their public practice of masculinity and their private practice differed radically. For others, their actual practice was at odds with their 'internal' practice. Because life was not simply a process of absorption and internalization of ready-made norms, their lives were not without tension and trauma about the split between what they were thought to do and what they actually did (Messner, 1989). Their internal dialogue addressed the conflicts and difficulties that they faced, yet the 'voice inside' that characterized this internal dialogue was a voice that was shared with very few friends, family or teachers. Analogously, just as they developed socially visible strategies to deal with the world around them (a heterosexual public but a homosexual private practice), they also developed private strategies (often a fantasy life at odds with their actual practice) to mediate the disjunction between the public and the private. Any given boy could present a combination of many diverse and wide-ranging practices: heterosexuality with heterosexual fantasies; heterosexuality with heterosexual external practice; a practicing heterosexual with homosexual fantasies; assumed heterosexual practice practicing homosexual sex; or all of the above.

These boys created their masculinity, sometimes successfully and sometimes not so successfully, within and against the social and psychological constraints that attempted to limit the scope of their activity (Connell, 1989). Because there was no culmination to the process of masculinity, there was no end to the process of negotiation. Success was not about 'getting there', but rather was itself a process, always under construction, worked on and struggled for every day. The boys gave meaning to and practiced their masculinity in inner, as well as interactional contexts. The human agency and intentionality of the boys themselves within this practice cannot be overlooked.

Just as the practice of the boys was the locus of tension, conflict, and ambiguities, the institutions and its representatives presented different options for the practice of masculinity. Even though hegemonic masculinity was forever present, a few administrators, teachers, and others who worked in schools resisted and rejected the codes and scripts of hegemony in a variety of ways. The teacher who provided an analysis from a feminist standpoint and changed her curriculum and pedagogy to demonstrate a different approach, and the coach who decided that winning at all costs was not the point of sport, provided students with possibilities for countering hegemony. While the boys strategized around these differing institutional notions, the relation of these options to the dominant hegemonic masculinity illustrated the difficulties encountered in attempts to challenge or question that hegemony.

Needs

I think that a lot of people don't get their needs filled, or they've got the wrong needs, and there's a lot of anger. (Jim)

Some of the boys' practice revealed quite visibly that the choices made were in their interest. And some of their practice also revealed the radical potential of the possibility of a change in how young men live their lives. Other practice was confusing and ambiguous. However, these instances of practice were all instances of human agency and all pointed toward a new language of possibility: self-creation, mediation, re-writing and re-speaking oneself into existence, and resistance. In this way, we can see why some men accepted the possibilities of participating in homosexuality openly, while others felt uncomfortable even with its private fantasies. Or why some of the young men involved themselves in organized sport while others did not. Even if the answer was simply because they 'liked it', liking it did involve a decision based on choice, reflected upon and thought about in relation to broader gendered and sexual circumstances of their lives and their own 'personality' (Connell, 1987).

This does not, and should not, however, mask the dynamics of power found in all contexts. Nor does this reduce the state of the practice of these young men to one of individualism, masking the social structures of men's power and the power relations among men — in particular, the oppression of homosexual men, and class, race, and ability domination among men. The analysis cannot locate itself in simply 'self' or 'social', ignoring the complications of the socially created split. Neither extreme will suffice. As suggested in the chapter introduction, this analysis is an attempt at collapsing past theorizing that perpetuates the dualistic notions of individual and social. What this analysis does do is assign some human agency to young men's lives. It begins to build a theory of masculinity that is fully one of relational practice that at the same time allows for the agency of men within these relations and within themselves, while remembering that the process of power weaves itself in intricate ways in and through both the boys and any social situation in which they find themselves. These relations could not be constructed without the boys and men! We need to 'insert' these boys back into their lives: we need to insert men back into their lives. This means that these young men, like all men, need not be 'let off the hook' or excused from their practices because of what both biology and society confer on or offer them. Their individual and collective practice weave and cement together political struggles of power and self-determination around masculinity. In the complexity of their practice, it was they who mediated and responded to the intersection between their own lived experiences in their everyday/night worlds and the structures of domination and restraint. No-one, no thing, or social process other than human agency did it for them (Connell, 1987).

Yet, and at the very same time, authority and domination were merged into the structure of personality itself. Fear was often the consequence: fear of physical harm, fear of being excluded, of being ostracized or abandoned, fear of persecution and ridicule, humiliation and rejection. For example, some same-sex practice between boys led to self-devaluation, extreme guilt, and even attempted suicide; the gay man often practices his own homophobia and heterosexism. Many teachers fail to realize that the values of the hegemony are woven into the personality structure of the boy who carries out the non-hegemonic practice. This, in itself, is immensely complicated, and becomes increasingly complex if we are to deal with these issues in schooling and change not only the violence between girls and boys and among boys themselves, but also the violence that some men and boys inflict on themselves, including suicide. This type of analysis would suggest that changing curricula, language practices or hiring procedures would not suffice.

The boys stategized and struggled to fulfill their socially constructed needs, but the needs were always tied to these larger structures of authority. In this way, we see why an investment in hegemonic masculinity is so commonplace: intimately tied to the fulfilling of needs, the practice of hegemonic masculinity is not simply a matter of 'boys being mean or bad'. Indeed, an investment in hegemonic masculinity is a highly rational choice, though perhaps costly in other ways, given both the advantage and privilege bestowed on it by schools, as well as by other institutions such as the family (Connell, 1987). Some boys and men may feel a loss of freedom in what they are able to experience because they are men and boys, yet most often, for the majority, the advantages outweigh the disadvantages. The fear of the repercussions of not abiding by the rules can keep many young men within the hegemony.

> Some guys are usually looking to exterminate anything that doesn't fit their idea of the norm. Jocks mainly use jokes, and with some guys it's mainly kicking and beating up people. The main way I can cope is by appearing in public with a girl. If people know you have a girlfriend, then they say 'Well, he must not be a homosexual.' If you dress alternatively and you're not seen with a girl, then you're automatically seen as a homosexual. There are guys in this school who have alternative ideas or dress and they are left alone because they have girlfriends. There are other guys who do the same but don't have girlfriends, and they really get hassled. (Jim)

The resulting process for these young men was one of strategizing to fulfill their needs: a struggle for and a struggle against the authority of the hegemony at any given moment in any given context. There is a tendency to ignore the question of needs and desires and of multiple positionalities in favor of issues that center around ideology and consciousness (Connell, 1987). What is needed is a critical psychology that explores the way in which the authorial voice of hegemony produces an 'un-freedom' and how that reproduces itself in the human psyche (Connell, 1987).

The attempt to collapse the individual/social split of the interpretation of masculinity, moves the issue beyond that of changing the social relations of power, as has been the focus of the literature over the past twenty years. Instead, teachers and educators need to explore ways of instilling in the human psyche a means by which to be rid of the authorial voice so that masculinity can be practiced differently. The search is for ways to allow boys to enjoy 'feminine' things and to engage in practices that may eradicate male power. This is not 'the poor boys' argument that suggests that men's activities are just as curtailed as women's, or that men live in an impoverished state where they cannot express their emotions and thus are repressed and oppressed just like women. This is an argument for an exploration and analysis of the diverse practice of masculinity, focusing on the dominance of men and the degree to which this dominance is tied to the ordinary social structure of the most common of our everyday existence in schools.

Organizing for Change

If you can't be male enough in one area of your life, you can always make it up in another. If you don't have a lot of knowledge, then you can have a girlfriend. You're always working on it so if you fall down in one area, you try to make up for it in another. But you got to work at it. (Thomas)

Much of today's political organizing around masculinity in schools is limited to single issues: violence in sport, sex education, date rape, high school dropouts, AIDS, youth crime, anti-homophobic education. With the daily support of hegemonic masculinity in schools and the lack of support for alternatives to it, it is little wonder that there seems to be little change. Because of the importance placed upon hegemonic masculinity, most young men spend a great deal of time and energy strategizing in relation to it. Until we begin to withdraw support for it, both individually and collectively, and in the structural arrangements of schooling, we will not change much in the gendered and sexed relations of schooling. This is difficult work. Understanding how needs are woven into social structures demands a careful rethinking of how teachers and educators do their work (Connell, 1989b). Changing gendered language, the pictures in textbooks, or the hiring practices by school boards will not change the practice of masculinity.

In my research, there was no lack of interest in questions of masculinity, gender, sexuality, and sexual politics among the boys as topics of conversation. For many, it was a matter of absorbing concern. Within our talk, the practice of masculinity was investigated in critical and reflective ways. We all emerged from the interview process with things to think about, and the possibility of change became a reality for both the young men and for me. It reaffirmed that the possibilities for change do exist for men and boys. We had been making our masculinity as we talked about what it meant to be men; our masculinity had not been made 'behind our backs'. Through our talk, there emerged the possibility that we could begin to live our lives a bit differently. Our talk often carried over to family, friends, and teachers. Many people asked us about our discussions, and we told them that we were talking about what it means to be a man. It may even, in some small way, have changed the relations through which the boys and others constructed their lives.

Both the process and the content of the talk affirm that these young men, like the collective of men, create, mediate, and transform their practice, perhaps most often in what they see as their own best interest. Misogyny, sexism, heterosexism, violence in many forms, and competition all were identified as part of their strategic practice. But the contradictions always surfaced: sensitivity, caring, non-exploitative relationships with women and other men, non-violent sports, acceptance of the diversity of sexuality, non-abuse of power. The life histories and the interviews illuminated many barriers to other possibilities of lived experience that the boys might have chosen if the alternatives to heterosexual hegemonic masculinity had been supported in schools. Some boys felt not simply confined by, but trapped within, the practices of hegemony. Their attempts at standing outside of that practice, in what might be considered minor ways, resulted in uncertainty or fear and confusion, even serious physical and psychological harm. It may be within the marginal spaces of the dominant definitions of masculinity that schools in general, and teachers in particular, need to affirm boys and men as much as possible. The work involves providing 'pauses', regardless of how brief, in the hegemony for men and boys to re-evaluate and reflect; pauses that may be critical to finding a practical way to deal with concerns and issues of gender and sexual politics.

It may be that the spaces in 'between', in places in the very contradictions and tensions of masculinity, allow us a glimpse of how some men and boys have managed, even under adverse conditions, to do it differently. Perhaps it is also in these spaces that we can see how people have stood against the prevailing needs of the masculine hegemony and how they have developed and fulfilled needs that are, in certain ways and to varying degrees, in opposition to the hegemony. This is no simple or easy task, and the forces of resistance can be overwhelming. Every step toward change can represent a 'new man' struggling out of a history, and that struggle has real consequences that may involve loss (Brod, 1987). It might be the loss of a certain profession, teaching young children, for example, for a gay man. It might mean the loss of safety and security, both psychological and social, ensured by hegemonic heterosexual practice.

Even politically experienced men who have been involved in the politics of resistance in a variety of ways (anti-racist education, anti-militarism, and so on) still sometimes fail to see how masculinity operates in and through their own daily lives and their own ordinary routine practices as men, or, if they do recognize it, they still have difficulty standing against or outside of it. Those of us who have worked in schools and in education, including teacher education programs, need to develop courses where issues of gender and sexual politics are central not only to those particular courses, but also to any program of teacher education. We need to encourage research that provides a forum where critical and reflective discussion about their lives can occur. For the young men interviewed, indeed for most boys and men, this would be an exception. It needs to be a given.

The positionality of most men allows us to re-speak, re-write, and re-text the privilege of heterosexual masculine hegemony. In tearing apart the complexities of the postmodern world, we need to be careful that we do not offer up once again some of the reductionistic understandings of the gender and sexed relations (Yeatman, 1993). Theories of victimization have provided us a much needed and necessary analysis of the lives of girls and women; yet they have often not allowed for the visibility of the human agency of women. Nor have they made visible the celebration and possibilities of women's and girls' lives, particularly in relation to the men they care about.

Central to the analysis there needs to be an account of how power operates in and among men, as well as in relation to women (Connell, 1983). Change is not simply a matter of changing attitudes, nor is it located within an individual act of will (Connell, 1987). As long as we value oppression, competition, and the violence that is a necessary part of fulfilling these, we are trapped in the very processes that support the authorial voice of hegemony. As long as we willingly support and reward these processes, especially in our classrooms and in our schools, then hegemonic masculinity will continue to operate because it gets rewarded.

At the centre of change in the daily social terrorism in our schools is coalition politics. Schools, like most social institutions, fuse together race, class, ability, gender and sexual politics (Brittan, 1989). The complexities of the social processes that assist in the maintenance of hegemonies are intermeshed in any one of us, as well as in the broader social structure. For example, we continue to conduct class analysis without paying attention to how hegemonic masculinity weaves itself in and through class practices (Frank, 1987). Or we conduct anti-racist analysis without acknowledging how particular practices of masculinity are interwoven with race. In all of these analyses we need some focus on hope, on possibilities, and on celebration — not in a way that produces a romantic vision of the future, but in a way that leads us away from victimization toward seeing possible alternatives and ways of living them out. Within the stories of the boys' confusion and anger, and hurt and frustration, this research and this chapter is about hope in finding better ways. Perhaps within the complexities of the postmodern condition, there is no one best way (Lather, 1991), but surely there are better ways than the violence that is present in our lives.

Young men spoke about their lives, and in the speaking came reflection and insight. With critical reflection comes the possibility of change in the practice of how these young men, and all men, might live their lives. The solutions for gender-related school problems are often limited to insistence on non-sexist language, balance in textbook pictures, limiting of gender stereotypes, and textbooks that give a more inclusive account of history that recognizes women's contributions. These things are important. However, changing curriculum and pedagogy is not enough. Multiple masculinities are constituted across various sociocultural and historically specific sites. Therefore, problematizing and foregrounding the practices of masculinity and recognizing how the individual and collective needs of boys and men are woven into the structures of the most ordinary of our practices would allow us to make those needs explicit, with a view to changing both the needs and the practices that fulfill them. In the end, as one of the students told me:

> Most people support the masculine guys. So does the whole school set-up, the principals, and the teachers. It's what they value. We need to change more than the boys in this school. (Trent)

References

ALCOFF, L. and POTTER, E. (1993) 'When feminisms intersect epistemology', in ALCOFF, L. and POTTER, E. (eds) *Feminist Epistemologies*, New York, Routledge.

BRITTAN, A. (1989) *Masculinity and Power*, Oxford, Basil Blackwell.

BROD, H. (1987) 'The case for men's studies', in BROD, H. (ed.) *The Making of Masculinities*, Winchester, MA, Allen & Unwin, Inc.

BUNCH, C. (1975) 'Not for lesbians only', *Quest*, **11**, 2.

BUTLER, J. (1990) *Gender Trouble: Feminism and the Subversion of Identity*, New York, Routledge.

CLATTERBAUGH, K. (1990) *Contemporary Perspectives on Masculinity*, Boulder, Westview Press.

CONNELL, R.W. (1983) *Which Way is Up?* North Sydney, George Allen and Unwin.

CONNELL, R.W. (1987) *Gender and Power*, Stanford, CA, Stanford University Press.

CONNELL, R.W. (1989a) 'Cool guys, swots and wimps: The interplay of masculinity and education', *Oxford Review of Education*, **15**, 3, pp. 291–303.

CONNELL, R.W. (1989b) 'An Iron Man: The body and some contradictions of hegemonic masculinity', in MESSNER, M. and SABO, D.F. (eds) *Critical Perspectives on Sport, Patriarchy and Men*, Champaign, IL, Human Kinetics Publishers.

FRANK, B. (1987) 'Hegemonic heterosexual masculinity', *Studies in Political Economy*, **24**, pp. 159–70.

FRANK, B. (1990) 'Reflections on men's lives: Taking responsibility', *Our Schools/Ourselves*, **2**, 3, pp. 69–77.

FRANK, B. (1991) 'Everyday/everynight masculinities: The social construction of masculinity among young men', *The Canadian Sex Research Forum Journal of the Sex Information and Education Council of Canada*, **6**, 1, pp. 27–37.

FRANK, B. (1992 Spring) 'Hegemonic heterosexual masculinity: Sports, looks and a woman, that's what every guy needs to be masculine', *The Institute of Social and Economic Research Papers: Violence and Social Control in the Home, Workplace, Community and Institutions*, No. 3, pp. 271–303.

FRANK, B. (1993) 'Straight/strait jackets for masculinity: Educating for "real men"', *Atlantis*, **18**, 1 & 2, pp. 47–59.

FRANK, B. (1995) 'Masculinity and schooling: Educating for "real men"', *The South Australian Educational Leader*, **6**, 2, pp. 1–11.

HARAWAY, D. (1988) 'Situated knowledges: The science question in feminism and the privilege of partial perspective', *Feminist Studies*, **14**, 3, pp. 575–99.

HARDING, S. (1990) 'Feminism, science, and the anti-enlightenment critiques', in NICHOLSON, L. (ed.) *Feminism/Postmodernism*, New York, Routledge.

HARDING, S. (1993) 'Rethinking standpoint epistemology: "What is strong objectivity?"' in ALCOFF, L. and POTTER, E. (eds) *Feminist Epistemologies*, New York, Routledge.

HOOKS, B. (1984) *Feminist Theory: From Margin to Center*, Boston, South End Press.

HOOKS, B. (1990) *Yearning: Race, Gender, and Cultural Politics*, Toronto, Between the Lines Publishing.

KAUFMAN, M. (ed.) (1987) *Beyond Patriarchy: Essays by Men on Pleasure, Power, and Change*, Toronto, Oxford University Press.

KAUFMAN, M. (1993) *Cracking the Armour: Power, Pain and the Lives of Men*, Toronto, Viking Books.

KIDD, B. (1987) 'Sports and masculinity', in KAUFMAN, M. (ed.) *Beyond Patriarchy*, Toronto, Oxford University Press.

KIMMEL, M.S. (ed.) (1987) *Changing Men: New Directions in Research on Men and Masculinity*, Newbury Park, CA, Sage.

KIMMELL, M. and MESSNER, M. (1992) *Men's Lives*, New York, Macmillan Publishing Co.

KINSMAN, G. (1987) *The Regulation of Desire*, Montreal, Black Rose Books.

LATHER, P. (1991) *Getting Smart: Feminist Research and Pedagogy with/in the Postmodern*, New York, Routledge.

LATHER, P. (1992) 'Critical frames in educational research: Feminist and post-structural perspectives', *Theory into Practice*, **31**, 2, pp. 87–99.

LYOTARD, J. (1984) *The Postmodern Condition: A Report on Knowledge* (Geoff Bennington and Brian Massumi, Trans.) Minneapolis, University of Minnesota Press.

MESSNER, M. (1986) 'Sports and the politics of inequality', *Changing Men*, **17**, pp. 27–8.

MESSNER, M. (1987) 'The meaning of success: The athletic experience and the development of male identity', in BROD, H. (ed.) *The Making of Masculinities: The New Men's Studies*, Boston, Allen & Unwin.

MESSNER, M. (1989) 'Masculinities and athletic careers', *Gender and Society*, **3**, pp. 138–40.

MESSNER, M. (1990a) 'When bodies are weapons', *Changing Men*, **21**, pp. 36–8.

MESSNER, M. (1990b) 'Men studying masculinity: Some epistemological issues in sport sociology', *Sociology of Sport Journal*, **7**, pp. 136–53.

MESSNER, M. and SABO, D. (1990) *Sport, Men, and the Gender Order*, Champaign, Human Kinetics Books.

NICHOLSON, L. and FRASER, N. (1990) 'Social criticism without philosophy: An encounter between feminism and postmodernism', in NICHOLSON, L. (ed.) *Feminism/Postmodernism*, New York, Routledge.

PRONGER, B. (1990) *The Arena of Masculinity: Sports, Homosexuality and the Meaning of Sex*, New York, St Martin's Press.

SABO, D. (1986) 'Pigskin, patriarchy and pain', *Changing Men*, **16**, pp. 24–6.

SABO, D. (1989) 'The myth of the sexual athlete', *Changing Men*, **20**, pp. 38–9.

SANDS, R. and NUCCIO, K. (1992) 'Postmodern feminist theory and social work', *Social Work*, **37**, 6, pp. 489–94.

SMITH, D.E. (1990) *The Conceptual Practices of Power: A Feminist Sociology of Knowledge*, Toronto, University of Toronto Press.

SMITH, D.E. (1987) *The Everyday World as Problematic: A Feminist Sociology*, Toronto, University of Toronto Press.

STEEDMAN, M. (1987) 'Who's on top? Heterosexual practices and male dominance during the sex act', in YOUNG, B. (ed.) *Who's on Top? The Politics of Heterosexuality*, Toronto, Garamond Press.

YEATMAN, A. (1993) 'A feminist theory of social differentiation', in NICHOLSON, L. (ed.) *Feminism/Postmodernism*, New York, Routledge.

Part 3

Pedagogy: Violation or Vindication?

9 Argument as Conquest: Rhetoric and Rape*

Lisa Jadwin

Systemic violence is found in pedagogical practices that are detrimental to some students and prevent them from learning. One pedagogical practice that has been highly valued in the past is the use of argument to sharpen students' thinking and enable them to voice their opinions. In this chapter, the rhetoric associated with argumentative practice is examined for possible bias that might make it pedagogically useful for some students but at a cost to others.

Argument as Conquest

> Until we can understand the assumptions in which we are drenched, we cannot know ourselves. (Adrienne Rich, 1979)

When I was in graduate school in the mid-1980s, my department decided to hire itself a feminist at the tenured rank. That fall, in lieu of the usual public lectures we got a provocative series of 'job-talks' — lectures delivered by six or seven well-known feminist literary theorists. The talks were held late in the day, and by the end of each lecture, no matter how stimulating, everyone was tired. I always stayed to the end because I was fascinated by the psychodramatic question-and-answer periods that followed the lecture.

Question periods appeared to bring out the worst in everybody: the senior faculty postured, the junior faculty genuflected to the senior faculty, and the graduate students loosed all the invective they ordinarily felt compelled to suppress in the seminar room. It was like watching Mike Wallace chase a corrupt bureaucrat across a parking lot. After the lecture ended and 'question-and-answer' began, everybody's body language grew aggressive: the spot-lit lecturer's shoulders invariably squared up; she pushed up her bifocals, wiped her face, crossed her arms, gulped water, squinted up into the blinding lights of the audience. The audience members steepled their fingers, leaned forward and looked straight down their noses, drawling out questions in fully annotated paragraphs.

* I'd like to thank Steve Derné, Gail Gibson, Cindy Ho, and the members of Karen Offen's 1992 NEH Seminar 'The Woman Question in Western Thought, 1750–1950' for their encouragement and their comments on this essay.

More revealing than the body language, however, were the meaty and masterful metaphors that questioners used to skewer the speaker with their penetrating
points. Questioners, male and female alike, tended to cast their conspicuous eru-
dition in metaphors that united sex and violence: they invariably wanted to probe
deeper and penetrate her discourse; they were forceful in their demand for rigor
as they posed their hard questions. The thrust of the argument was that they took
their stabs at her and gradually stripped away her 'face'. The content of the question began to seem less consequential than the rhetoric it was couched in. But to me
this was more than an intellectual exercise in deconstruction. Each of these public
talks was a sobering lesson in what happens to speakers who are strong, arrogant,
or foolhardy enough to expose their ideas to public scrutiny — the intellectual equi-
valent of walking down Bourbon Street at 1:30 am wearing a miniskirt and a
sequined top.

Argument is represented as war in western culture. Lakoff and Johnson (1981),
for example, naturalize the equation of debate and violence by using the trope
'argument = war' to discuss the epistemology of metaphor in general. To them, war
is natural and inevitable — indeed a productive state. It is something we live both
'according to' and 'beside'. Even those who consciously reject the political implications of this paradigm tend to enlist it, consciously or unconsciously. In writing and
in speaking, we rhetorically measure ourselves against others and poke holes in our
opponents' arguments. We scorn wimpy strategies that fail to conquer. We refuse
to take things 'lying down' and strive to 'come out on top'. And while we may not
kill our opponents, our rhetoric implies that at some level we enjoy humiliating
them, silencing them, keeping them off the streets of academe and out of trouble.

Our use and often unconscious promulgation of metaphor affects academics
as scholars and as teachers — in our primary professional capacity as debaters,
critics and proponents of ideas. The metaphor of 'argument = war' has implications for women — a group of people literally excluded from combat duty in the
Armed Services, and figuratively either victimized on, or co-opted by, the battle-
grounds of argumentation. One of the key tactics of both traditional war and traditional argumentation is the metaphor of rape. In this essay, I label as 'conquest
metaphors' those that conflate male sexual violence with successful persuasion or
appropriation.

The *Oxford English Dictionary* (OED) gives 'conquest' two meanings. The
first series of definitions describe 'Conquest by War or Combat' as 'the action of
gaining by force of arms, acquisition by war, subjugation of a country, etc.' (Simpson
and Weiner, 1989, p. 843). The second series of definitions delineate 'Conquest of
Property', referring to 'the personal acquisition of real property otherwise than by
inheritance . . . property acquired during wedlock, and provided for in the marriage
contract' (p. 844). Both senses of conquest involve the taking of 'booty' by force.
The sexualized nature of this appropriation is implied in the first definition (since
women have traditionally been considered one of the spoils of battle) and denoted
by the second. Canonical English writers did not begin to use 'conquest' metaphor-
ically to describe sexual seduction, according to the OED, until the Renaissance

(p. 843). Violent penetration and conquest as a means of enforcing dominance is as much a part of the 'war' epistemology of argumentation as real rape is of real war.

Rhetoric

Metaphors . . . are part of a power structure (or struggle), part of the way in-groups of various sorts delineate their discursive boundaries, name and expel the Other. (Altman, 1990, p. 495)

When Gilbert and Gubar (1979) opened *The Madwoman in the Attic* by asking 'Is the pen a metaphorical penis?', they revealed the power a metaphor can exert. After documenting the popularity of the essentialist penis = tool-for-creating-art metaphor among male artists, Gilbert and Gubar question how this metaphor has affected female artists. They theorize that metaphoric castration has traditionally impeded women's artistic careers. If, as Altman suggests, metaphors are a way in which an 'in-group' names and excludes 'the Other', the pen = penis metaphor certainly helped male artists to 'express and reinforce their bonds', to limit access to their club and to define women as *essentially* unequipped for the production of art.

Phallic metaphors of argumentation resemble phallic metaphors of artistic creation in that both equate pointy-ness and rigidity with the ability to prevail, to pro/create. But conquest metaphors of argumentation differ in four critical ways. First, they are used by a wide variety of speakers and writers regardless of age, gender, or education. Second, metaphors of argumentation tend to be the frame rather than the focus of an argument. They function more subtly than does Norman Mailer's metaphor, for example, when he growls that 'The only thing a writer has to have is balls.' Third, these metaphors have become so standardized and stale that we use them unthinkingly, which enables the metaphors to 'use us', to control the way we know things (Lakoff, 1975). Fourth, and perhaps most important, conquest metaphors of argumentation are simultaneously violent *and* phallic, presenting a union of violence and sex that works by intimidating or silencing an opponent in a specifically sexual way. Conquest metaphors subtly but surely equate rape with intellectual domination by equating phallic sexual violence with successful persuasion, a message hidden beneath the surface of complex, resonant metaphors like 'masterful'.

By removing conquest metaphors from their contexts, we can defamiliarize four groups of metaphors that combine to create the larger 'conquest' image that characterizes argumentation. These four metaphors work in two ways. First, they put a specifically sexual twist on the familiar progression of hypothesis, proof, and conclusion. They incorporate the paradigm of male sexual experience that Peter Brooks (1984) has argued shapes the form of most nineteenth- and twentieth-century novels: tumescence, orgasm, and detumescence. Second, they glamorize the violent usage of these 'appendages' not simply against an opponent, but against that opponent's will. Below I have divided them into discrete groups, the better to evaluate them.

Lisa Jadwin

Largeness

First and foremost (as we hear said), 'Bigger *is* better'. As scholars, we measure works (and ourselves) against each other, labeling the best as 'great', a word whose denotative sense has been all but lost through metaphorical overuse. Canonization imposes valuation! 'The study of literature is evaluation, the passing of judgment on each particular work of art' (Kettle, 1960, p. 12). Whether we accept or resist Kettle's example, most of us still play the game of ranking, comparing Dryden to Congreve, Austen to Dickens, T.S. Eliot to Plath. When we are finished, we label the results of the contest with metaphors of size. The losers are 'minor', 'insignificant', 'trivial', 'lesser', or 'secondary', while we describe the winners as 'greatest', possessed of the most 'wide-ranging' vision or sensibility, the 'giants' of literature. A 'standard', after all, is a pole stuck into the ground, clearly visible to those around it. Anthologies have helped transform the 'great, greater, greatest' game into an immensely profitable industry — an industry whose dictates we echo individually when we create syllabi and departmentally when we establish course offerings. Even those who reject Kettle's preoccupation with canonization — with judging and ranking — are usually interested in measuring their own writing against their peers' work. Judgment and judges have not disappeared in the wake of multivalent texts and guerrilla pluralism; no matter how politically correct we may consider ourselves to be, most of us continue to describe works we admire as 'benchmark' and 'landmark' studies, 'monumental', 'gargantuan', 'towering', even 'Herculean'. Note that our students, also, are preoccupied with 'length'; a too-short or too-small paper is a sign of lesser achievement, and we are more likely to penalize them for failing to produce length than for droning on interminably.

'Bigness' metaphors connote not simply largeness, but a certain conical shape; we want our study to 'loom large' among others, to be 'mountainous', to ascend the 'promontory' of knowledge to a 'peak experience', a 'climax'. No 'low points' or 'crevices' here, reader; only the vantage point, the zenith, the apex, the pinnacle will suffice (advisedly, in the literal sense of 'satisfy'). I guess you could say that size *does* make a difference. What are we to make of 'flesh out' and 'bone up'?

Stiffness and the ability to stab

> With the Ruble Flaccid, Hard Currency is King. (*The New York Times*, December 4, 1991, p. A1)

To be classed as 'great', however, a work or study must not simply be large; it must also possess a certain stiffness, distention, and pointy-ness. At many institutions, it has become *de rigueur* (so to speak) to talk about making our arguments and our undergraduate courses more 'rigorous': that is, characterized by a certain 'stiffness, hardness, inflexibility' (Webster, 1957). (I find it interesting that the argument for 'rigor' seems inevitably to be accompanied by a pronounced fear of 'grade inflation', as though the subversive inflation of the symbol [the grade] is best pricked [and deflated?] by the competing image of 'rigor' imposed by an academic authority.)

We use these turgid instruments quite specifically, to poke things: we aim to 'attack' 'hard' questions with 'probing' discussions couched in 'turgid' prose, discussions that will result in a conclusion so impressive that it is able to 'stand alone'. Ideas themselves we have naturalized as 'points'; armed with these sharp, forceful instruments, we aim to 'take a stab at' (or 'have a go at' or 'have at') a quandary — to play it, as the saying goes, 'to the hilt'. If we possess sufficient 'rigor', we should be able to 'pinpoint' and then 'poke holes in' a 'stiff competitor's' 'soft spots'. Intent on 'honing' our abilities to 'pierce' the veil of illusion, we strive to be 'sharp', 'incisive', 'on the cutting edge', ready to 'slash to pieces' whatever stands between us and what we want to 'pound home'. Finally, in the process of assembling a 'penetrating' or 'meaty' analysis, we must 'push through the muddle', 'firm up' any persistent 'weaknesses' or 'flab'. We aim ultimately to make a 'mark' or 'impression' on the audience with the 'final thrust' of a conclusion designed to make an opponent retreat into silence. We must avoid the fate of being 'poked' ourselves, lest we become mere receptacles, impregnated with the ideas of others, as Paul Willis (1977) implies here in the midst of a critique of Althusser:

> Social agents are not *passive bearers* of ideology, but *active appropriators* who *reproduce* existing structures only through struggle, *contestation and a partial penetration of those structures.* (p. 175, emphasis added)

Willis's rhetoric casts agents of change as appropriators, those who take from others, often without giving due credit, in order to reproduce through 'partial penetration' that involves 'struggle' and 'contest'. Here the phallic contest opposes 'passive bearers', whose position is implicitly feminine, with 'active appropriators', whose position is implicitly masculine, to suggest a re/productive fantasy in which male actors appropriate the process of creation from females through a contest privileging 'partial penetration'. To 'tease out' all the sexual implications of this metaphor may prove an exercise in ideological contraception or polymorphous perversity — but penetration through struggle 'looms large' as the ultimate goal.

Forcefulness

Reinforcing the metaphors of largeness, stiffness, and stabbing is a framework of metaphors that valorize forcefulness, what psychologists sometimes call 'power over', a force we typically characterize with the metaphor 'dominant'. We aspire to create or at least to know what is currently 'dominant' and to 'subdue', 'dispatch', or at least to 'background' the work or claims of competitors. A good argument aims to be 'masterful', 'compelling', and 'forceful' — 'dominant' enough to become a paradigm, to be able to 'take on all (other?) comers'. Moreover, this dominance has a certain outlaw quality. The terms we use to describe the results of successful research and argumentation connote stripping away, breaking and entering: one 'reveals' truth, 'strips away' untruth, 'uncovers' facts, 'unlocks' conundrums, indeed, boldly goes where no man has gone before. (The metaphors we use to describe abandoning such an enterprise also perpetuate the theme of conquest: we speak regretfully of 'pulling out', 'withdrawing', 'backing off', even 'leaving [something] by the side of the road'.) Though such breaking-and-entering can be interpreted as referring to a violation of property — as burglary — the trespassing metaphors, when combined with images of hugeness, turgidity, and forcefulness, strongly suggest brutal *sexual* conquest — that is, rape.

> If there were a *dominant hegemonic* ideology in Sedaka, it would *make its presence known* in several ways. At a minimum, it would require that the beliefs and values of the agrarian elite *penetrate and dominate* the worldview of the poor so as to *elicit their consent and approval of an agrarian order which materially does not serve their objective interests*. Its function would be to conceal or misrepresent the real conflicts of class interests that we have examined and to make of the poor, in effect, *co-conspirators in their own victimization*. (Scott, 1985, p. 318, emphasis added)

In the example above, from James Scott's *Weapons of the Weak*, a 1985 study of peasant political resistance, the author identifies ideology as a weapon the 'agrarian elite' might use to 'penetrate and dominate the worldview of the poor so as to elicit their consent and approval of an agrarian order which, materially, does not serve their interests'. The metaphorical transformation of ideology into a phallus that can be used against the consent of a weaker group, and against that group's better interests, clearly embodies the process of propaganda/persuasion as a dangerous penis that may overcome its victims by force. Scott, whose study focuses on the political manifestations of *ressentiment* in developing countries, seems to be using the metaphor deliberately, advisedly, as if to 'pound home' his 'point' about the consequences of the possible 'penetration' of the unwitting poor. In this case, metaphor follows function, whether the writer or reader recognize it or not; Scott's paragraph is as much an indictment of the metaphor of sexual assault = successful persuasion as it is a critique of cooptation achieved through propaganda. The peasants, his rhetoric suggests, are vulnerable to being coerced into consenting to their own implicitly sexual victimization; the rhetoric highlights the threat of such victimization by making it intimate, implicitly sexual.

Yet other writers use the metaphors with less awareness of their implications. David Harvey, an Oxford geographer writing about postmodernity, uses a rather 'striking' (or 'riveting'?) rape metaphor to describe Nietzsche's 'impact' on nineteenth-century aesthetics:

> [The exploration of aesthetics] *arose* out of the sheer difficulty of translating Enlightenment principles of rational and scientific understanding into moral and political principles appropriate for *action*. It was *into this gap* that Nietzsche was able to *insert his powerful message with such devastating effect*, that art and aesthetic sentiments had the power *to go beyond* good or evil. (Harvey, 1990, p. 19, emphasis added)

Harvey's rhetoric suggests that the study of aesthetics 'arises' out of the process of finding a strategy for 'action', to finding a 'gap' into which Nietzsche is able to 'insert his powerful message' not gently or pleasurably but 'with such devastating effect' as to demonstrate that 'art and aesthetic sentiments had the power to go beyond good or evil'. (Perhaps we should view this rhetoric as out-Nietzsche-ing Nietzsche.) Harvey 'endows' the Uberphilosopher with such superhuman attributes that he is able to penetrate the boundaries of the rather wimpy discipline of aesthetics and to take it violently beyond the realm of moral judgment — beyond good or evil. The moral import of the sentence's final words effectively rationalizes or 'legitimizes' Nietzsche's transgressive act of intellectual rape, placing it 'beyond' the 'reproach' of the implicitly violated field.

Seminality

The culmination of the act of metaphorical persuasion/rape is influence: through 'dissemination' a persuader aims to achieve metaphoric paternity, to become the 'father' of an idea, a document, a field of study. While most of us would consider it preposterously essentialist — not to say sexist — to refer to an important article or idea as 'ovarian', many people still use 'seminal', a word directly related to the Latin for 'semen', to praise important arguments. The seminal nature of ideas is ingrained in educational institutions: as neophytes we attend a 'seminary', or a series of 'seminars', where we learn to penetrate the mysteries of our professions. It is not surprising, then, that the pursuit of truth is so clearly gendered; the word 'testify' derives directly from 'testis', the singular of 'testes'. A testifying Roman citizen held his testicles in his left hand while raising his right hand in an oath before delivering his 'testimony' (derived from the same root). Like the distinctly gendered words that designate academic rank, privileges, and degrees — bachelor, master, fellow — the metaphors that describe the authority of creation inscribe maleness, paternity, the full sense of 'legitimacy', (i.e., having a father), patrilineality, author/ity.

Rape

> To grapple with ideology is to grapple with a phantom, since ideology has neither a body nor a face. It has neither origin nor base which one could recast to provide the battle against it with a precise and well-defined object. Ideology only manifests itself under the form of fluid, or the diffuse, of permanent polymorphism and acts through infiltration, insinuation and impregnation. Ideology does not have a real language, and especially not one of violence. Its total lack of aggression, its capacity to transform itself into everything, its infinite malleability, permits it to assume the mask of innocence and neutrality. And, above all, as I have said, to blend itself with reality itself. (Zimmer, 1978, p. xxi)

Whether you identify ideology with masculine sexual forcefulness, as Scott does in the passage from *Weapons of the Weak*, or with feminine cunning, fluidity, and spontaneous transsexuality (or at least cross-dressing!) as Zimmer does here, you are likely when confronting ideology to accept the need for a 'battle' waged with your own 'well-defined object'. The ideology that frames Zimmer's innovative personification of ideology casts Truth as male, outraged at the feminine shape-shifting ability of the actress 'Ideology' who threatens to change or evade the rules of the conquest game. Conquest metaphors betray the intersection between our view of sexuality and our view of creativity, that overcoming by force is still the preferred way to 'make your point' creatively and procreatively. Their persistence is evidence of two important things: the way language reflects cultural beliefs; and the distance that lies between our understanding of sexual violence and our ability to do anything about it.

Catharine MacKinnon (1989) suggests we need to learn to view rape not as 'an isolated event or moral transgression or individual interchange gone wrong but an act of terrorism and torture within a systemic context of group subjection, like lynching' (p. 172) — part of a continuum that includes less consequential kinds of sexual subjection, such as misogynist jokes and sexual harassment. The persistence of these metaphors 'overwhelmingly' implies that we need to think carefully about *how we say what we say*. Though I have quoted above from arguments written by men, it is important to note that many women use these metaphors as frequently as do their male colleagues. Women's use of rape metaphors puts us in something more than an 'awkward position'; it turns us literally against ourselves, enforcing an alienation from self that is all too familiar to most female academics. Yet, though they readily acknowledge the dangers and the absurdity of this position, many of my colleagues have suggested that it may be difficult to publish or 'make an impression' without enlisting conquest metaphors. These metaphors, after all, are a readily negotiable currency in most academic debates, refereed journals and publishing houses, and perhaps implicit in the essay form itself. If we fail to 'gird ourselves' in conquest metaphors we will appear weak, stripped of our authority, vulnerable to attack. I have only recently noticed the pun in the familiar sports metaphor, 'the best defense is a good offense', a pun you will hear if you place the accents on the nouns' second syllables.

Rhetoric and Rape

What kinds of alternative metaphors and epistemologies of argumentation, then, are available to us? Occasionally we do enlist metaphors that have stereotypically feminine sexual connotations: We 'embrace' or are 'receptive' to an idea. We allow ourselves to 'encompass' a great deal of information, 'dissolve' a reader's assumptions, 'disarm' our critics. Our studies can be 'wide-ranging' or 'inclusive'. We can 'bear witness' to the truth, or question whether an idea is 'borne out' by our experience or reasoning. We can describe our work as 'tentative' or 'open-ended', our teaching style as 'receptive'; we can refuse to conclude decisively, 'with a bang'.

What are the consequences of using such metaphors? First, since there are so few of them, it is necessary to think awhile, retrain the brain to generate them readily. And the language will betray you occasionally; it is hard to fight an enemy that has outposts in your own head. A couple of months ago, for example, I replaced 'rigorous' with 'challenging' only to realize that I was unconsciously clinging to the metaphor of the stag-fight. But it was an ironically appropriate mistake, of course, for the stag-fight is the perfect emblem for the conflation of violence and sexuality embodied by such argumentative metaphors.

You have no doubt noticed that the connotations of fecundity, pleasure, and connection that sexual metaphors ought to arouse are curiously absent from the stereotypically masculine tropes I've itemized above. These 'double-edged' penetration metaphors inevitably connect penetration not to procreation or pleasure, but to violence. Since penetrative conquest in the argumentative paradigm calls for transgression of ego boundaries, the psychic as well as the physical destruction of an Other, it is no wonder that we shun stereotypically feminine metaphors for argument, for the conflation of penetration with violence also equates receptivity with vulnerability, defenselessness.

Perhaps this is why 'egghead' is a derogatory term for a high-powered academic, while 'big gun' is not. We fear the consequences of having 'tunnel vision', of ideas that are merely 'embryonic'. We fear being accused of perceiving things 'in a vacuum', of 'conceding', 'yielding', 'making concessions', of foolishly letting the rapist in through the front door. We live in fear of 'compromising' ourselves — that fate worse than death. To 'take it', 'yield', 'admit something', or 'accept defeat' is to be made to 'swallow' something horrendous: another's eminently more powerful point.

The conquest metaphor of argument places the reader or audience in the stereotypically feminine receptive position by default. Conquest metaphors suggest that the aim of argument is less to persuade than to beget 'concepts' upon the reader, whose role is to 'bear witness' to an unremitting 'onslaught' of reason, and ultimately to be silenced by those final thrusts. I think the aim of scholarship (as it 'stands') is still to 'gain entry', by force or by cunning, to the mind of a 'resisting reader'. Even kinder, gentler essayists strive to 'fill in the gaps' left by earlier, less 'rigorous' critics, strive to 'satisfy' the reader — who signals her satisfaction with silence. As soon as the reader or audience has 'received' the conquistador's message, she becomes caught up in a rape-or-be-raped dynamic that enforces a choice between two stances, both of them (to my mind) unacceptable.

Undeniably our professional reputations suffer when we are publicly 'compromised' by having someone else's points 'rammed down our throats'. Yet the reader may feel compelled to affirm the status quo by adopting the agonistic role of initiating or retaliating by 'mounting' a 'challenge' to an aggressive opponent, hoping that 'the best man will win'. While such a strategy may generate professional accolades and journal acceptances, chances are that a sensitive writer of either gender may find it distasteful or unnatural. (Check out *those* metaphors!) Or the reader may adopt the stereotypically feminine position of accepting and receiving, a position which we unfortunately tend to associate with being 'taken' or 'had'. The stereotypically feminine receptive position is one that many of us, including the speakers being addressed by the questioners during my graduate school days, find to be both an admission of vulnerability and a badge of low status.

Current post-structuralist rhetorical fashion dictates that we replace phallic metaphors with topographical and mathematical metaphors of argumentation. While this substitution certainly signals a heightened awareness of the implications of conquest metaphors, it has its own problems. Peggy Kamuf's 'Replacing Feminist Criticism', for example, asks 'What is the place of feminist criticism in this institution, particularly the university?' (1990, p. 105) and answers that feminist criticism will have the 'greatest force' if it 'shifts the sands of an historical sedimentation [and] leaves its own undecidable margins of indeterminacy visible, readable on the surface of a newly contoured landscape' (p. 111). At the end of the essay, she concedes 'the necessity of replacing [mapping/geographic metaphors] with another and of finding always another place from which to begin again' (p. 111). Though most of Kamuf's metaphors are geo/topographic, she still succumbs to things being left 'intact' (p. 106), 'striking' passages (p. 109), 'pointing to strategies' (p. 109), 'long and potent series of other oppositions which it organizes and commands' (p. 110), and 'pursuing an analogy' (p. 110). Moreover, the mapping metaphor, with which she closes the essay, sounds downright colonialist, redolent of explorers finding the 'lay of the land' of the 'virgin continent'. Finally, literature and theory are not sciences. Why should we pretend they are? Do mathematicians, geologists and cartographers use metaphors from French literature?

My 'point' is that essentialism is always the order of the day, even among expressivists and those who question the epistemological assumptions of traditional academic discourse. In 'The doubting game and the believing game: An analysis of the intellectual enterprise', Peter Elbow (1973) takes issue with the adversarial epistemology of argument. He outlines the impact of the Socratic and Cartesian philosophical tradition of analyzing by doubting, noting that Socrates' favorite term is 'no', just as Descartes' main contribution to argumentative epistemology is the idea of skepticism. Elbow notices that 'the *essential* quality of the Socratic dialogues is reductive and deflating: some belief is shown to be silly or empty or contradictory' (1973, p. 150, emphasis added). The argumentative metaphors Elbow uses to describe what he calls 'the doubting game' are metaphors of conquest. 'Deflating' and 'reducing', like 'putting down' and 'cutting down', all denote reducing an opponent's relative size. Meanwhile, 'silly' and 'empty' condemn another's point of view as a stereotypically feminine 'gap' or void. Elbow suggests that we abandon our faith in this traditional 'doubting game', which proceeds by disbelieving. He suggests we cultivate instead the 'believing muscle' that trusts, absorbs, affirms, and ultimately builds input into 'the gestalt that makes the most coherence out of an ambiguous semantic field' (1973, p. 168). Others, including feminists like Olivia Frey (1990), have affirmed the importance of re-evaluating 'the pervading ethos that stresses competition and individualistic achievement at the expense of connectedness to others' (p. 522).

Though both essays make far-reaching contributions to the debate on what Frey calls 'the adversarial paradigm', it is interesting to note that neither Elbow nor Frey manages to construct an argument free of conquest metaphors. Though much of Elbow's essay focuses on identifying and developing an ability to 'put yourself into the skin of people with other perceptions' (1973, p. 170), the metaphor of '*putting yourself into* the skin of *others*' is itself problematic, as are subtle traces of conquest metaphor elsewhere: 'The believing game does not have its *full power* as a dialectic for *getting to the truth* till you *add* the dimension of time' (p. 170, emphasis added). Frey has the same difficulties, though at first she chooses to accept and defend the position of receiver, with its vulnerability that verges on acceptance of battering in order to achieve a certain goal. 'I have sometimes left faculty meetings *feeling bruised, and I have taken these feelings home with me* . . . I have . . . *taken great pains* to avoid essentialism' (1990, p. 523, emphasis added). Only a few paragraphs later, perhaps weary of 'having taken it', Frey somewhat resignedly flip-flops into the role of the conquistador: 'We need to keep women *very firmly* at the *center* of this issue. To *put it bluntly*, if it were not for women, we might not be questioning the way we write literary criticism' (1990, p. 523, emphasis added).

Perhaps these last examples are oversubtle. I hold Frey and Elbow to too 'high' a 'standard'. After all, I recognize their difficulties; I have encountered the same problems in writing this piece. Essentialism seems the order of the day; one runs away from sexual metaphors only to find oneself staring others in the face. In order to make my propositions stand up to the close scrutiny of an unyielding and possibly hostile editorial board, I've had to fill in the gaps of my argument with rigorous examples and documentation — indeed, cram it full of examples. My aim and methodology are beset by the same ironies that bedevil Elbow's and Frey's essays: though 'the very basis of my essay is adversarial', I claim to 'value other knowledge constructions, other ways of writing' (Frey, 1990, p. 524). Until I manage to wrest myself away from the conquest metaphors that dominate my thinking, talking, and writing, I'm just asking to be stuck with the same old points.

References

ALTMAN, M. (1990, September) 'How not to do things with metaphors we live by', *College English*, **52**, pp. 495–506.

THE NEW YORK TIMES (1991, December 4) 'As the ruble plummets, hard currency is king', pp. A1.1, A18.2.

BROOKS, P. (1984) *Reading for the Plot: Design and Intention in Narrative*, New York, Alfred A. Knopf.

ELBOW, P. (1973) *Writing Without Teachers*, London, Oxford University Press.

FREY, O. (1990, September) 'Beyond literary Darwinism: Women's voices and critical discourse', *College English*, **52**, pp. 507–26.

GILBERT, S.M. and GUBAR, S. (1979) *The Madwoman in the Attic: The Woman Writer and the Nineteenth-century Literary Imagination*, New Haven, Yale University Press.

HARVEY, D. (1990) *The Condition of Postmodernity: An Inquiry into the Origins of Cultural Change*, Cambridge, MA, Basil Blackwell.

KAMUF, P. (1990) 'Replacing feminist criticism', in HIRSCH, M. and KELLER, E.F. (eds) *Conflicts in Feminism*, New York, Routledge, pp. 105–11.

KETTLE, A. (1960) *An Introduction to the English Novel: Defoe to the Present*, New York, Harper Torchbooks.

LAKOFF, G. and JOHNSON, M. (1981) *Metaphors We Live By*, Oxford, Oxford University Press.

LAKOFF, R. (1975) *Language and Woman's Place*, New York, Harper & Row.

MACKINNON, C. (1989) *Toward a Feminist Theory of the State*, Cambridge, MA, Harvard University Press.

RICH, A. (1979) 'When we dead awaken: Writing as re-vision', in RICH, A. (ed.) *On Lies, Secrets and Silence: Selected Prose 1966–1978*, New York: W. W. Norton, p. 35.

SCOTT, J.C. (1985) *Weapons of the Weak: Everyday Forms of Peasant Resistance*, New Haven, CT, Yale University Press.

SIMPSON, J.A. and WEINER, E.S.C. (eds) (1989) *Oxford English Dictionary* (2nd ed.), Oxford, Oxford University Press.

WEBSTER'S THIRD NEW INTERNATIONAL DICTIONARY OF THE ENGLISH LANGUAGE (Unabridged) (1957), New York, G. C. Merriam.

WILLIS, P. (1977) *Learning to Labour*, Westmead, UK, Saxon House.

ZIMMER, C. (1978) *The Civilizing Process*, New York, Urizen.

10   Men's Minds and Women's Matters: Digging at the Roots of Androcentric Epistemologies

Sandra Monteath

> I am the androgyne
> I am the living mind you fail to describe
> in your dead language
> the lost noun, the verb surviving
> only in the infinitive
> the letters of my name are written under the lids
> of the newborn child
> (Adrienne Rich, 1973)

Historically, our educational system has privileged ways of thinking and knowing associated with maleness and denigrated ways of thinking and knowing associated with femaleness. Women, by virtue of their gender, have long been seen as 'the weaker vessel' (Fraser, 1984) insofar as a capacity for learning and scholarship is concerned (Wollstonecraft, 1992). For centuries, women were denied access to higher education. Only in the last few decades have women been allowed to enter the academy. However, many women who pursue higher education find themselves stymied by the academy's requirement that they think and act in ways that are inimical to their culturally prescribed and personally acquired ways of thinking and acting.

To succeed in the academy, women must repudiate the contextual and relational ways of knowing that, at the very least, mark them as having grown up female in our society (Belenky, Clinchy, Goldberger, and Tarule, 1986; Gilligan, 1982). Even those women who have a predilection for abstract thought, or 'Reason', may find themselves marked as 'different', perhaps even as 'unfeminine' (Deutsch, 1973).[1] If they enter the academy, they may find themselves trapped by cultural notions about women's incapacity for Reason. Indeed, some women who pursue higher education may find that having a 'living mind' in a woman's body is at best a mixed blessing and at worst a curse that splits them between two mutually exclusive worlds, the world of men's minds and the world of women's experience.

Gendered Hierarchical Dualities

Gendered dualistic thinking is the association of certain epistemological or psychological dualities — such as mind and body, Reason and emotion, and objectivity and subjectivity — with maleness or masculinity and femaleness or femininity respectively. The syntactical placement suggests a hierarchy of conditions, in what comes first — maleness, mind, Reason, objectivity — is superior to what comes second — femaleness, body, emotion, subjectivity. Within the western epistemic tradition the first set of conditions has long been thought to give rise to Truth; the second never has.

Binary classifications are found in western thought, eastern thought, and tribal thought; and any binary classification is likely to result in an evaluative hierarchy (Rorty, 1991c, p. 109). We separate the wheat from the chaff, the gold from the dross. The dualities that are the problem are not the common-sensical ones, but the philosophical ones. Historically speaking, when men of privilege established classifications of being and thinking, women always got the down side. Women have been the chaff to men's wheat, the dross to their gold.

The western philosophical tradition from the time of Socrates has been marked by 'intellectual homosexuality' (Graves, 1991, p. 11) or 'phallogocentricity' (Derrida, 1985, p. 171). Both terms encapsulate the way that philosophy has disregarded, dismissed, denigrated, or denied the experiences of women (Code, Mullett, and Overall, 1988, p. 4). Philosophy is full of powerful misogynistic statements (Sherwin, 1988). Very few major historical philosophers have had anything good to say about women, and even those that do, such as Plato, Augustine, and Mill, say things that do not always fall pleasingly on feminist ears. Ironically, although Descartes was sympathetic to women, his Cartesian thought made a major contribution to the modernist metanarrative of rationality and objectivity which excludes women as knowers (Lyotard, 1992).

The rejection and exclusion of the female is an essential feature of the way in which philosophy as a discipline (Code, 1991) and Judaism and Christianity as religions were constructed (Ruether, 1975). Early in the first millennium BC, a shift in consciousness from gynocentrism to androcentrism occurred in both Greek and Hebrew cultures. The Mother Goddess yielded to God the Father.

The creation myths tell how the balance of power shifted (Neumann, 1954; Ruether, 1975). The earliest story of the cosmos is that of the uroboros, the serpent eating its tail. In its circularity, the uroboros is also a container, the womb of the Great Mother, from which the gods, both male and female, issue. These gods are the World Parents. They re-order the primal matrix of the Great Mother into heaven and earth, but continue to exist within it. In this matrix, the earth goddess represents settled agricultural nature and social order or wisdom; her consort, the sky god, rules, but gets his power from her. The relationship is complementary, not hierarchical, and recognizes the primacy of the Great Mother.

Feminists typically concentrate on the positive aspects of the Great Mother (Ruether, 1975; Daly, 1975) but male writers like Neumann dwell on the all-consuming, destructive aspect of the Great Mother, and the need for the male to differentiate himself from her, by force if necessary, in order to come to full consciousness (Neumann, 1954, p. 63). How did this masculine ego consciousness living in dread of the emasculating, bewitching, deadly, and stupefying nature of the Great Mother come to pass? According to Ruether (1975), the transition from tribal life to urban life produced a class of idle, privileged men with nothing much to do except sit around, talk politics, and gossip about women. The amount of time and energy that Athenian men in Plato's time spent discussing 'the Woman Question' suggests that women's political inactivity has been a recent thing (O'Brien, 1981). Aided and abetted by their philosophers, the privileged citizens of Athens projected their own gendered consciousness into an image of a transcendent male power that negated and supplanted the power of the Great Mother. This shift in consciousness is also said to relate to the institution of private as opposed to communal property and to the development of technology (de Beauvoir, 1961). Whatever the reasons, nearly three thousand years ago both the Hebrew prophets and the Greek philosophers began elaborating a new duality in which maleness was rational, moral, spiritual, and superior, and femaleness was irrational, immoral, material, and inferior.

One of the first formulations of duality occurred in the sixth century BC. In the Pythagorean table of opposites, qualities associated with determinate form were superior to qualities associated with formlessness (Lloyd, 1984, p. 3). There were ten pairs of opposites: limited/unlimited, odd/even, one/many, right/left, male/female, rest/motion, straight/curved, light/dark, good/bad, square/oblong. This association of maleness with determinate form and femaleness with indeterminate matter has carried through to the modern period. Plato evolved a concept of knowledge that focused on the contemplation of eternal forms in abstraction from unknowable, non-rational matter. Plato's successor, Aristotle, brought forms back to earth: Aristotelian forms could be grasped in the 'particular and the sensible' (Lloyd, 1984, p. 8). Nonetheless, Aristotle still maintained the form–matter distinction: 'The paradigm of knowledge is still the contemplation by a rational mind of something inherently mind-like, free of matter' (Lloyd, 1984, p. 9).

Aristotle was particularly vocal in the denigration of women. He wrote that 'Reasoned Knowledge', which only men may pursue and possess, is the highest human achievement. Thus men, according to Aristotle, were superior to and 'more divine' than women. Aristotle described women in various unflattering ways, as 'monsters . . . deviated from the generic human type', and 'mutilated males'. Women were a lower species, forever captives of their bodies, more like animals than like men. Aristotle thought that even in procreation, women were merely passive vessels for the active principle of the male sperm (Wilshire, 1989, p. 93).

In Greek theories of knowledge, in their original form rather than in later interpretations of them, transcendence of the feminine was implicit rather than explicit (Lloyd, 1984). Furthermore, the 'feminine' that was to be transcended was a metaphysical principle and not the scatter-brained, illogical, highly emotional, unpredictably subjective 'feminine' of today's stereotypes (Code, 1991, p. 118). But the way in which the Greeks associated femaleness with matter — and, *defective* matter at that — influenced later developments in philosophy.

The exclusion of women from 'true knowledge' became less implicit and more explicit when Judaeo-Christian thinkers attempted to combine Greek philosophy with Hebraic scriptural teachings about maleness and femaleness. Philo, an Alexandrian Jew writing in the first century AD, not only associated femaleness with the non-rational aspects of human nature, but used woman as a symbol of the material world, which drags down the human soul (Lloyd, 1984, pp. 23–4). According to Philo, woman, who represented Matter, was responsible for the 'fall' of man, who represented Mind. Women might still achieve knowledge, but only at the cost of their essential womanliness.

In the fourth century AD, Augustine tried to do the impossible by allowing for the spiritual and intellectual equality of women with men, as required in Christian teachings, while maintaining women's natural subordination in accordance with the scriptures (Lloyd, 1984, p. 27). In the thirteenth century, Aquinas drew on concepts of both Aristotle and Augustine in his formulation of Reason. Although Aquinas claimed that women were no less rational than men, and repudiated interpretations of Genesis that described women as being less in possession of Reason than men, he nonetheless saw the subordination of women as an inevitable consequence of their essential nature, which was less reasonable than that of men. Aquinas grouped women with imbeciles and children as being unable to give reliable evidence on grounds of a 'defect' in Reason (Lloyd, 1984, p. 36).

From Aristotle through Augustine to Aquinas, the very formlessness of matter made it essentially unknowable and uncontrollable (Lloyd, 1984, p. 10). The conception of matter, and with it, the conception of knowledge, changed in the seventeenth century with Francis Bacon. He re-conceived matter as being that which conformed to mechanical laws, to which access could be gained through the application of the scientific method. For Bacon, the object of knowledge was the domination of nature and science. Although the epistemic tradition had long associated mind, and its primary activity of Reason, with maleness, and matter with femaleness, Bacon used powerfully explicit sexual metaphors to convey a relationship of domination between a male science and a female Nature (Leiss, 1972, p. 60). He made transcendence over and control of the feminine the very essence of science. Bacon's ideas, building upon the old Greek notion of (female) unknowable matter transcended through (male) contemplative knowledge, played a crucial role in the constitution of the feminine in relation to our ideas about and ideals of knowledge (Lloyd, 1984, p. 17).

It was Descartes, with his idea of Reason as methodical thought, and his radical separation of truth-seeking (which had always been male) from the concerns of everyday life (which had always been female), who opened the way to the idea of distinctive male and female consciousnesses that prevails in today's stereotypes. This was not his intention. Descartes, was, in fact, sympathetic to women. He hoped his method of pure thought would be accessible to all, 'even women' (Lloyd, 1984, p. 44). Descartes wrote his *Discourse on Method* in the vernacular because he recognized that women were mostly educated at home, did not usually learn Latin, and did not therefore have direct access to the Latin-speaking academy. He achieved his end. Cartesianism became the philosophy of choice among women, especially in the salons (Lennon, 1992, p. 53). But Descartes did not seem to realize that even if women pursued his private method of pure thought, the content of their lives, taken up with caretaking of one kind or another, precluded them from full participation in the academy. Descartes insisted on a concept of Reason that excluded the obligations and responsibilities of women's lives and thus further polarized the split between men's minds and women's matters.

Philosophers coming after Descartes had less faith than he in the rational faculties of women. Although Rousseau adulated women as being closer to nature, their very closeness to nature precluded women from participating in the life of the mind. Rousseau prescribed an appropriate education for women that was very different from the one that he proposed for young boys. Women, he said, should eschew abstract thought and strive to attain 'those agreeable accomplishments' that please men (Wollstonecraft, 1992, p. 124n).

Kant also contributed to the notion of complementary male and female consciousnesses. Kant thought that women's essential immaturity of understanding rendered them incapable of rational thought (Lloyd, 1984, p. 67). He also held that ethical consciousness developed from the particular to the universal. Women, by virtue of their essential intellectual immaturity, were caught forever at the level of particularity, but men, by virtue of the superior development of their powers of Reason, could achieve universality, the highest level of ethical development. Kant's ethical theory opened the way for Freud's and later Kohlberg's negative assessments of the moral capabilities of women.

While earlier thinkers like Augustine and Aquinas had seen female consciousness as either somehow derivative of male consciousness or a deficient form of it, later thinkers like Rousseau and Kant saw female consciousness as essentially different from male consciousness. The difference was expressed in opposites like intuition versus intellect, sensibility versus rationality, immanence versus transcendence. These dualities were supposed to be complimentary to women but in fact rationalized their exclusion from epistemic discourse, which was the prerogative of men. Hegel noted that womankind was constituted through suppression (Lloyd, 1984). He remarked that everything that men did not want in their concept of themselves, they projected onto women. They then consigned women to a 'nether world' of the family, where they were to be concerned with 'duties and affections towards blood relatives' (Lloyd, 1984).

Nietzsche pushed to its limits the long-standing polarization of women as Nature and men as Culture (Lloyd, 1984, pp. 2–3). But in pushing something to its limits, we may sometimes break its power. Nietzsche did this to the epistemic metanarrative of the rational and objective knowing subject. In this way he set the agenda for postmodernism, which is so promising for feminism (Hekman, 1990, p. 26). Although Nietzsche engaged in diatribes against women in general, and against feminists in particular, whom he thought foolish to want to be the equals of men, he noted the androcentricity of western rationality, and speculated that if truth were a woman rationality would be the wrong approach to take in winning her (Nietzsche, 1989, p. 1). Nietzsche's conundrum was that he wanted to reject 'masculine' thought characterized by rationality and objectivity, but the only alternative he could think of was 'feminine' thought, which he found just as abhorrent. Nietzsche's problem was that he could not step outside the dualistic thinking of the modernist metanarrative he was attacking. He was caught by its presupposition that men and women have biologically determined rather than socially constructed ways of being and knowing.

The exclusion of women from epistemic discourse and from the academies in which that discourse took place did not happen all at once (Lloyd, 1984). There was no well-thought-out conspiracy to exclude women; rather there was an accumulation of concepts of reason that resulted in the exclusion of women. These concepts simultaneously fed into and were fed by cultural contexts in which women had certain roles, certain selves, and certain stories. The end result has been an enduring dilemma for intellectual women that forces them to choose between the stuff of men's minds and women's matters.

Mending the Split

The dualities of mind/body, objective/subjective, and Reason/emotion have contributed significantly to the chasm that exists between the knowing that ostensibly goes on in men's minds, and the knowing to which women's matters give birth. Mending the split by reconciling the terms of the dualities may lead us to new ways of thinking about knowledge, and hence alternate ways of pursuing and presenting knowledge. Ironically, women are now able to argue for concepts of knowledge that include their embodied experience (Gallop, 1988, p. 7) because, men like Husserl (1970), Heidegger (1962), and Merleau-Ponty (1962), the father and sons of phenomenology, challenged the split between mind and matter that reached its zenith in Cartesian thought.

In his critique of Descartes's concept of the self as pure thought, Husserl reveals the internal contradiction in Descartes's philosophy. Descartes begins his philosophical quest with what Husserl describes as a '*radical skeptical epoche*' (Husserl, 1970, p. 76), that calls into question not only the validity of all other philosophies, but also the validity of the pre- and extra-scientific life-world.[2] His concept of pure thought denied the embodied and subjective nature of Reason. That denial influenced the later development of ideas central to modernist thought about rational and objective knowing subjects and about the unsuitability of women, as people of the body, for the pursuit and possession of knowledge.

Husserl heals the mind/matter split by going back to the 'life-world' and discovering that each of us is an 'embodied subjectivity'. Heidegger (1962) claims that Husserl did not go back far enough.[3] Heidegger's concept of Dasein as an active embodied consciousness of the world goes a long way to collapsing the mind/body split of Cartesian epistemology. However, the embodied subjectivity of Dasein is clearly gendered, and not generic. It is male through and through. No women need apply. If poor Dasein becomes too much enmeshed in what Heidegger calls 'everydayness', and has to deal with 'burdensome and "repugnant"' chores (1962, p. 321) instead of engaging in great public projects, he may experience 'dull suffering'

(1962, p. 345). Dasein needs a wife. The maleness of Dasein is also evident in Dasein's character of being *'thrown'* into existence. Dasein has no mother. Heidegger's idea of thrownness, in its denial of the mother, and the generative power of women, is at one with the Aristotelian idea that the female womb is but the passive vessel for bringing the male seed to maturity (O'Brien, 1975, p. 31). Like Heidegger, Merleau-Ponty (1962) explores the concept of Being-in-the-world. He resolves the Cartesian separation of mind and body by insisting that the two are, and must be, one.

Although in their respective notions of embodied consciousness, Husserl, Heidegger and Merleau-Ponty dissolve the mind/body duality that has historically justified the exclusion of women from the academy, they do not take account of the way in which women's embodiment is different from men's. Neither do they allow for a female Being-in-the-world that is different from a male Being-in-the-world. In phenomenology, men, men's minds, and men's matters remain normative while women, women's minds, and women's matters remain a silence. There is no place for women in the thought of Husserl, Heidegger or Merleau-Ponty (Code, 1991, pp. 147–8). For all the attention phenomenology pays to embodiment, it does not pay quite enough attention to the differences in the experience of male and female embodied subjectivities.

Collapsing the Objectivity/Subjectivity Duality

Phenomenology, whatever its blindness with respect to gender differences in embodied consciousness, gives women, who have been excluded from epistemic discourse on the ground of their lack of objectivity, the means for demolishing the very notion of objectivity. More recently, Eisner (1991) and Rorty (1991c) have developed useful refutations of the 'fetish of objectivity' (Langer, 1967, p. 38) that has ruled epistemic discourse since Bacon and Descartes.

Husserl (1970) argued that objectivity is grounded in subjectivity. Although objective science attempts to grasp the essential reality of the external world and to describe this world as it really is, it inevitably fails to do this. There is no 'external reality', in which we can detach ourselves from subjectivity. There are only the realities that we construct in and through our culturally bound ways of knowing. So-called objective science is one of these ways of knowing. Human beings shaped 'objective' science as a mode of inquiry to satisfy a desire to know more about the world in which we exist. Husserl speaks of scientists themselves as being 'among the components of the life-world which always exists for us, ever pre-given'. In this way, he says, 'all of science is pulled' into the 'subjective-relative' life-world (Husserl, 1970, pp. 130–1). Because objective sciences are the products of a community of human beings who want to know more about their pre-given life-world, they are subjective, or more properly, intersubjective.

The knowledge that these 'objective' sciences produce — what we identify as 'discoveries' or 'findings' — is the result of ongoing collaboration by and within a community of scientists. Scientists are continually coming to some new consensus about what they want to know, how they will know it, and how they will evaluate what they know (Husserl, 1970, p. 131). This scientific consensus is often confused with, but is not the same as, objectivity (Eisner, 1991, p. 47). Eisner makes a nice distinction between what he calls 'ontological objectivity', (the fallacious notion that it is possible to have an accurate representation of external reality), and 'procedural objectivity' (the equally fallacious notion that we can achieve ontological objectivity through a set of practices that 'eliminates, or aspires to eliminate, the scope for personal judgment') (Eisner, 1991, p. 45). According to this notion, were procedural objectivity to achieve its aim of the total elimination of the subjective, we would then have an approximation of ontological objectivity — a true representation of reality.

All that procedural objectivity really does, as Eisner points out, is to get us to come to an agreement, a consensus about what we will accept as being adequate as knowledge of reality, adequate as method of inquiry, and adequate as a representation of reality. We think we are talking about objectivity when what we are really talking about is consensus. Thus, when we accuse people of being subjective, it is really not because they are any less 'objective' than we are or any more 'subjective' than we are. It is because they do not concur with the general consensus that we ourselves support.

The reaching of consensus, moreover, is not a process in which all members of a community participate equally. Historically, it has been men, not men and women together, who have reached a consensus about what constitutes 'true' knowledge, valid method, and acceptable epistemic discourse. Because women, by virtue of being weaker vessels, were excluded from participating in this consensus-making, the consensus that objectivity was both possible and desirable was a male consensus.

Feminist theorists have argued that in the social sciences, objectivity is another word for the 'the masculinist viewpoint' (Hekman, 1990, p. 95). Criticizing objectivity on this ground suggests that the trouble with objectivity is not the notion itself but the way the notion excludes female, feminine, or feminist perspectives (Hekman, 1990). It is far more productive to challenge the idea of objectivity by challenging the idea of the autonomous, non-involved subject on which it rests (Hekman, 1990, p. 96). We can do this in a phenomenological manner by pointing out how true objectivity does not exist because objectivity is grounded in intersubjectivity, or we can do this in a postmodern manner by pointing out that objectivity is really the word we use to describe consensus. Both phenomenological and postmodern refutations make sense.

Collapsing the Reason/Emotion Duality

Emotion is not antithetical to Reason, but an essential aspect of it (Code, 1991; Jagger, 1989; Nussbaum, 1992). Husserl (1970) and Eisner (1991) have made the case for empathy as an important component of knowledge. With the revalorization of emotion as part of Reason, the 'fact' of women's emotionality ceases to be a reason for excluding them from epistemic discourse.

Code (1991) points out that although emotion is the aspect of subjectivity that is most suspect in objectivist theories of knowledge, it is an essential constituent of knowledge (p. 46). In concepts of knowledge that privilege objectivity 'the paradigmatic emotion' is 'uncontrolled hysteria' (p. 47), but we have all sorts of emotions, many of which are epistemically significant. Curiosity and interest are prime among them. Sorrow, anger, frustration, fulfillment, love, hate, grief and joy may start and sustain an inquiry (p. 47). Even something like self-interest may drive an inquiry. 'Emotion and intellect are mutually constitutive and sustaining, rather than being oppositional forces in the construction of knowledge' (p. 47).

Emotions we do not usually associate with knowledge, such as love and empathy, may in fact constitute epistemic inquiry (Jagger, 1989, p. 162). If we approach the human, non-human, and even inanimate worlds with love and empathy, we are going to find out different things than if we regard those worlds and the entities within them with cool detachment. Jane Goodall's contribution to our understanding of chimpanzee behavior would have been impossible without Goodall's empathy; Barbara McClintock's genetic studies show a similar relationship to the objects of her research (Jagger, 1989, p. 162). Empathy also contributes to knowledge creation. Sacks (1990) argues eloquently for the inclusion of empathy in understanding the dimensions of disease, and the capacities of a human being to come to terms with suffering. He speaks of a 'trajective' approach to inquiry in which the physician must 'feel (or imagine) how his [sic] patient is feeling, without ever losing the sense of himself; he must inhabit, simultaneously, two frames of reference, and make it possible for the patient to do likewise' (p. 226).

Husserl (1970) also argued for emotion as an essential component of knowledge. He noted that in the life-world we have a great stock of knowledge about each other and our world that we simply take for granted. We get this knowledge by being born into the world filled with other people. Everyone in this 'subscientific' life-world believes she or he has knowledge of self, of other human beings, and of the world. Furthermore, we also believe that others have knowledge of ourselves (sometimes more than we would like) and of the world (Husserl, 1970, p. 260). Through coming to know ourselves, we become conscious of a world that is simultaneously and paradoxically the same for each of us because we are all in it together, and different for each of us because of our different vantage points. Thus, while we each have our own world-consciousness, that consciousness has what Husserl calls 'empathy experiences' through which we share in the world-consciousness of others. 'Empathy might be every bit as important for cognition as detachment' (Eisner, 1991, p. 12).

Finally, the very duality of reason/emotion may in itself be a cultural construct, part of the story we tell each other about ourselves (Lutz, cited in Jagger, 1989). Once we accept that the separation of reason and emotion is not necessarily an ontological given, then we can allow both reason and emotion to become part of the web of human knowing.

Male and Female Body/Subjects as Second Persons

The assumption that maleness is normative makes marginal women's ways of knowing and women's experience in the world. In a culture such as ours, which is organized along gender lines, these are very different from men's ways of knowing and men's experience in the world. At present, whether a good mind dwells within a male or a female body makes all the difference to the epistemic possibilities open to it and the projects in which it engages. Even if a women does not become a mother, she lives all her life as a woman with all the advantages and disadvantages that come from being so embodied (Overall, 1988, pp. 102–3). We need a concept of knowledge that not only takes account of the differences in male and female embodiment and experience in the world, but that brings those differences together in a conversation between equals about the world in which we live (Rorty, 1991b, p. 206).

It is possible to have concepts of self and knowledge that are flexible enough and permeable enough to allow for different modalities of subjectivity and different modes of knowing. We can together create metaphors about 'human minds as webs of beliefs and desires' (Rorty, 1991c, p. 93) in which gender identity is but a certain type of yarn in the warp, a textured thread in the weft. We need to think of ourselves — both male and female — as born of woman and not as thrown into the world, connected within ourselves as mindful bodies and embodied minds, connected to other human beings genealogically, through our personal and cultural histories, contemporaneously, through our belonging to a community of other persons like ourselves, and linguistically, through our being language users. Then we need to teach to that concept of human being and human knowing.

Baier's (1985) concept of persons as second persons is rich in possibilities for developing an alternate ontology and epistemology that simultaneously takes into account the different embodiment and experience of men and women and reconciles those differences through emphasizing connection and interdependence. 'A person perhaps is best seen as one who was long enough dependent on other persons to acquire the essential arts of personhood. Persons are *essentially* second persons (Baier, 1985, p. 84). The self-consciousness of a second person is by definition a self-consciousness of others; knowledge of self is knowledge of others. To be a second person is to learn from, through, and with other second persons, using our bodies, our language, and the symbolic forms of our culture to do so. As a second person, we can know nothing privately; rather, from the moment of our birth, we share in the communal stock of knowledge. We develop our ways of knowing and acquire our personal stock of knowledge in a world of second persons. At first as young children, we have little choice about the patterns of knowing and portions of knowledge that our caregivers and our teachers inculcate in us; later, as we develop as knowers, we may have more choice about how we know about and what we know. Nonetheless, the choices we make reflect both our personal history, including both experience and education, and our cultural traditions, as acquired through experience and imparted through education. We also contribute to the communal stock of knowledge in everything we do, even if what we do merely reaffirms the status quo, even if what we do appears to be 'only' the stuff of experience and not the stuff of knowledge. Baier's concept of second persons transforms the autonomous, rational and objective knowing subject of the modernist metanarrative, who can only be male, into an embodied subject, who may be either male or female, who exists in relation to and in dependence upon others, and who cooperates and communicates with those others to make sense of a shared life-world.

The roots of androcentric ontology and epistemology run very deep. Even after we have used the spades of phenomenology, feminist philosophy, and postmodernism to expose them, we still have the problem of removing them from our consciousness and our cultural and educational institutions and planting new ideas — notions about body/subjects and persons as second persons — in their place. But until we transform our ontology, our epistemology, our pedagogy, and our curricula, so that they encompass women's ways of knowing, many women will continue to feel that having a living mind in a woman's body is a mixed blessing.

Notes

1   Deutsch (1973) says:

> Women's intellectuality is to a large extent paid for by the loss of valuable feminine qualities: It feeds on the sap of the affective life and results in impoverishment of this life either as a whole or in specific emotional qualities. The intellectual woman is not Antonae, the Wise One, who draws her wisdom from the deep sources of intuition, for intuition is God's gift to the feminine woman; everything related to exploration and cognition, all the forms and kinds of human cultural aspiration that require a strictly objective approach, are with few exceptions the domain of the masculine intellect, of man's spiritual power, against which woman can rarely compete. All observations point to the fact that the intellectual woman is masculinized; in her, warm intuitive knowledge has yielded to cold, unproductive thinking. (p. 298)

2   The essence of Husserl's critique of Descartes is as follows: While I, the ego, may call into question the validity of the world, I cannot call into question my own validity. That is absurdity. As a thinking ego, I have to be excluded in principle from the epoche that I perform on the rest of the world. By placing myself as doubter and negator outside the world that I doubt and negate, I can no longer use the validities of the world for knowledge in a natural way. I am, in effect, standing outside my life as experience and thinking outside myself as a living body. I am split.

In Descartes's formulation of the thinking ego, experience in the world and living bodies in the world have become transformed into mere phenomena, into things about which I have ideas. Descartes asks himself what kind of ego it is that he has discovered, whether the ego is 'the human being, the sensibly intuited human being of everyday life'. Because of his radical skeptical epoche, he doubts and denies that it is. He extends the epoche of the sensible world to include the living body, and defines the ego as something akin to a free-floating mind. But as Husserl says, this is against all common sense. At some point the 'naive validity of the world' breaks through and adulterates the kind of thinking accomplished during the epoche. As beings living in the life-world, we know that Cartesian metaphysics has failed to take account of our embodied subjectivity (Husserl, 1970).

It is, however, important to recognize, as Baier (1985) points out, that Descartes envisioned his radical skeptical epoche as a metaphysical exercise to be practiced occasionally. In his everyday thinking, Descartes did not deny his or anybody else's embodied subjectivity. That would have been a kind of madness.

3 Heidegger calls into question what Husserl's phenomenology takes for granted: the meaning of our Being-in-the-world. Heidegger says that while Husserl speaks of nature-in-itself and psychical being, and introduces a psychological dimension to knowing reality, he still has not made personal Being-in-the-world transparent. Yet as Gadamer (1975) points out, it was Husserl's insistence that the 'absolutely universal working method' of his humanistic science was 'to go back to life' that made it possible for Heidegger to question Husserl, just as it had been Descartes's radical skeptical epoche that had made it possible for Husserl to question Descartes.

Like Heidegger, Merleau-Ponty is also a second-generation phenomenologist, owning to Husserl as the father of his thought. Also, like Heidegger, Merleau-Ponty explored the concept of Being-in-the-world. But with Merleau-Ponty, the body is much more important, so important in fact, that 'I am my body' (Merleau-Ponty, 1962). Merleau-Ponty observes that our experience of our own bodies runs counter to the philosophical tradition of detaching subject from object, which gives us only an idea of the body, and not the body in reality. He notes that Descartes was well aware of the omission of our experiential knowledge of the body from our theoretical constructs about the body, but allowed the omission to stand in order for us 'to experience in ourselves a pure soul from which to accede to an absolute Spirit' (Merleau-Ponty, 1962, p. 199). But this is wrongheaded. There is, Merleau-Ponty says, no inner man [sic], no pure mind: 'Man is in the world, and only in the world does he know himself' (1962, p. xi).

References

BAIER, A. (1985) 'Cartesian persons', *Postures of the Mind: Essays on Mind and Morals*, Minneapolis, University of Minnesota, pp. 74–92.

BELENKY, M.F., CLINCHY, B.M., GOLDBERGER, N.R., and TARULE, J.M. (1986) *Women's Ways of Knowing: The Development of Self, Voice, and Mind*, New York, Basic Books.

CODE, L. (1991) *What Can She Know? Feminist Theory and the Construction of Knowledge*, Ithaca, NY, Cornell University Press.

CODE, L., MULLETT, S., and OVERALL, C. (eds) (1988) *Feminist Perspectives: Philosophical Essays on Methods and Morals*, Toronto, University of Toronto Press.

DALY, M. (1975) *The Church and the Second Sex*. New York, Harper & Row.

DE BEAUVOIR, S. (1961) *The Second Sex* (H.M. Parshley, ed. and Trans.), New York, Bantam.

DERRIDA, J. (1985) *The Ear of the Other: Otobiography, Transference, Translation* (C. McDonald, ed., P. Kamut, Trans.), Lincoln, NE, University of Nebraska Press.

DEUTSCH, H. (1973) *The Psychology of Women: A Psychoanalytic Interpretation* (Vol. 12), New York, Bantam.

EISNER, E. (1991) *The Enlightened Eye: Qualitative Inquiry and the Enhancement of Educational Practice*, New York, Macmillan.

FRASER, A. (1984) *The Weaker Vessel*, New York, Alfred A. Knopf.

GADAMER, H.G. (1975) *Truth and Method*, New York, Seabury.

GALLOP, J. (1988) *Thinking Through the Body*, Gender and Culture Series, New York, Columbia.

GILLIGAN, C. (1982) *In a Different Voice: Psychological Theory and Women's Development*, Cambridge MA, Harvard University Press.

GRAVES, R. (1991) *The White Goddess*, London, Faber and Faber.

HEIDEGGER, M. (1962) *Being and Time*, (J. MacQuarrie and E. Robinson, Trans.), New York, Harper & Row.

HEKMAN, S.J. (1990) *Gender and Knowledge: Elements of a Postmodern Feminism*, Boston, Northeastern.

HUSSERL, E. (1970) *The Crisis of European Sciences and Transcendental Phenomenology*, (D. Carr, Trans.), Northwestern University Studies in Phenomenology and Existential Philosophy, Evanston, IL, Northwestern.

JAGGER, A.M. (1989) 'Love and knowledge: Emotion in feminist epistemology', in JAGGER, A.M. and BORDO, S.R. (eds) *Gender/Body/Knowledge: Feminist Reconstructions of Being and Knowing*, New Brunswick, NJ, Rutgers, pp. 145–71.

LANGER, S. (1967) *Mind: An Essay in Human Feeling* (vol. 1), Baltimore, MD, John Hopkins.

LEISS, W. (1972) *The Domination of Nature*, New York, George Braziller.

LENNON, T.M. (1992) 'Lady oracle: Changing conceptions of authority and reason in seventeenth century philosophy', in HARVEY, E.D. and OKRUHLIK, K. (eds) *Women and Reason*, Ann Arbor, MI, University of Michigan.

LLOYD, G. (1984) *The Man of Reason: 'Male' and 'Female' in Western Society*, Minneapolis, University of Minnesota.

LYOTARD, J.F. (1992) *The Post Modern Explained: Correspondence 1982–1985*, Minneapolis, University of Minnesota

MERLEAU-PONTY, M. (1962) *Phenomenology of Perception*, (C. Smith, Trans.), London, Routledge & Kegan Paul.

NEUMANN, E. (1954) 'The origins and history of consciousness', *Bolligen Series*, **42**, Princeton, NJ, Princeton University Press.

NIETZSCHE, F. (1989) *Beyond Good and Evil: Prelude to a Philosophy of the Future*, New York, Vintage.

NUSSBAUM, M. (1992) 'Love's knowledge', *Love's Knowledge: Essays on Philosophy and Literature*, Oxford, Oxford University Press, pp. 261–85.

O'BRIEN, M. (1981) *The Politics of Reproduction*, London, Routledge & Kegan Paul.

OVERALL, C. (1988) 'Feminism, ontology, and "Other minds"', in CODE, L., MULLET, S. and OVERALL, C. (eds) *Feminist Perspectives: Philosophical Essays on Methods and Morals*, Toronto, University of Toronto Press, pp. 89–106.

RICH, A. (1973) 'The Stranger', Driving into the Wreck'. Poem, 1971–72, W.W. Norton.

RORTY, R. (1991a) 'Inquiry as recontextualization: An anti-dualist account of interpretation', in *Objectivity, Relativism, and Truth. Philosophical Papers, 1*, Cambridge, Cambridge University Press, pp. 93–110.

RORTY, R. (1991b) 'On ethnocentrism: A reply to Clifford Geertz', in *Objectivity, Relativism, and Truth. Philosophical Papers, 1*, Cambridge, Cambridge University Press, pp. 203–10.

RORTY, R. (1991c) 'Pragmatism without method', in *Objectivity, Relativism, and Truth. Philosophical Papers, 1*, Cambridge, Cambridge University Press, pp. 63–77.

RORTY, R. (1991d) 'Two meanings of logocentrism: A reply to Norris', In *Essays on Heidegger and Others. Philosophical Papers, II*, Cambridge, Cambridge University Press, pp. 107–18.

RUETHER, R. (1975) *New Woman, New Earth: Sexist Ideologies and Human Liberation*, New York, Seabury.

SACKS, O. (1990) *Awakenings*, New York, Harper Collins.

SHERWIN, S. (1988) 'Philosophical methodology and feminist methodology: Are they compatible?' in CODE, L., MULLET, S. and OVERALL, C. (eds) *Feminist Perspectives: Philosophical Essays on Methods and Morals*, Toronto, University of Toronto Press, pp. 13–28.

WILSHIRE, D. (1989) 'The uses of myth, image, and the female body in revisioning knowledge', in JAGGER, A.M. and BORDO, S.R. (eds) *Gender/Body/Knowledge: Feminist Reconstructions of Being and Knowing*, New Brunswick, NJ, Rutgers.

WOLLSTONECRAFT, M. (1992) *A Vindication of the Rights of Woman*, London, Penguin.

11 Literacy Tasks and Social Change: Voices and a View from Somewhere

Lorraine Cathro

In this chapter I discuss the possible role of the university as the seat of a changed orientation to knowledge and learning, and, as such, as the place to initiate a change in our understanding of education. School systems are inexorably tied into the premises of the university. Knowledge, as we have known it, is created and controlled at the university; children are educated in the hopes that they will someday access the privilege of a university education as a key to continued privilege and personal power. If we are to change our understanding of what is valuable in education in an effort to make education more relevant to all students, we must re/evaluate the process valued by the university and by all institutions of knowledge.

Institutional Knowledge and Power

All readers and writers begin from somewhere and literacy is always embedded within those contexts. As Richardson (1990) states: 'There is no view from "nowhere", the authorless text. There is no view from "everywhere" . . . There is only a view from "somewhere" an embodied, historically and culturally situated speaker' (p. 27). This chapter is an examination of the effects of the view from somewhere on students who are not situated in the primary Discourse. When I use Gee's (1989) term Discourse, written with a capital D, I do not mean discourse, that is connected language which makes sense. Gee's explanation of discourse includes the larger social contexts of literacy:

> Discourses are ways of being in the world; they are forms of life which integrate words, acts, values, beliefs, attitudes, and social identities as well as gestures, glances, body positions, and clothes. A Discourse is a sort of 'identity kit' which comes complete with the appropriate costume and instructions on how to act, talk, and often write, so as to take on a particular role that others will recognize. (1989, p. 7)

Institutional knowledge and power are played out through academic Discourses in the university setting. The dominant voices in the university are academic Discourses in the various disciplines. The students' voices, and particularly those of marginalized students, are disregarded because their knowledge is not valued.

Devaluation of Experiential Knowledge

Dominant institutions, such as the university, devalue the experiential knowledge expressed as narratives of groups such as First Nations peoples and women. Institutionalized power is maintained by this devaluation of experiential knowledge that is valued in many other cultures. Among the Athapaskan Dunne-za of north-eastern British Columbia, for example, people with power are said to know something and that knowing comes from life experiences (Ridington, 1990): 'They know it [their world] through the authority of experience' (p. 191). Although different among and between themselves, First Nations cultures view living and learning holistically. 'The way of my people is holistic. It does not separate my mind from my heart from my spirit' (Monture-Angus, 1995, p. 37).

As has been pointed out in Monteath's work in the previous chapter, women's knowledge has also been undervalued partly because it is based on 'social realities' that differ from those of most men (Greene, 1986, p. 496). The devaluation of women's knowledge and their exclusion from the construction of what is considered academic knowledge, marginalizes women at all levels of schooling (Apple, 1986; Belenky *et al.*, 1986; Bleier, 1986; Code, 1991; Franklin, 1990; Greene, 1986; Harding, 1991; Smith, 1987).

Marginalized students beginning university are often kept in the role of outsiders through devaluation of their ideas and experiences. This chapter will draw strongly on interviews with 'Lana' and 'Carol', two university students marginalized twice, first by the fact that they are First Nations people and secondly by the fact that they are women. Lana expressed devaluation of her opinions this way: 'That's my opinion so I don't know if I should even put that in.' She had learned that in the university setting, specifically English academic Discourse, her knowledge was viewed as opinion, not knowledge. Carol expressed similar fears: 'I didn't really want to go into elaborate detail on what *I* [her emphasis] thought because I didn't want to bomb out on this one [this essay].' Devaluing students' knowledge, and more importantly creating doubt in their minds that they are knowers, results in maintenance of power by the agencies of the disciplines within the institution. In contrast, when Lana and Carol were allowed to write in narrative form for other courses and to use their experiential knowledge in a familiar form, the writing was perceived as easy because they could use their years of living as a foundation for constructing knowledge, which was then valued in the course work.

Throughout our discussions, there was a strong thread of playing the academic game to gain power within the institution. Institutional power was gained as rules of academic Discourse were learned: 'I just figured that out', is the way Lana showed her learning of a rule for her writing in English class and the resultant increasing sense of power. Once students have figured out rules, they apply them to their work and, in doing so, may also internalize the meaning of the discipline. In Grace's (1990) words, students begin to 'speak correctly' both linguistically and ideologically as they internalize the meaning of the discipline. Lana realizes that 'I don't see it the way he [the instructor] does', but she strives to identify and apply the meaning considered correct or appropriate by the discipline. In taking on the 'correct meaning' of the discipline and the institution, the danger is that a student's own meaning may be devalued, or even lost. When our own meanings are lost, part of ourselves may become lost and our personal power reduced.

Other students fight to maintain their own ways of making meaning, organizing ideas, and creating knowledge. Carol was a fighter, a questioner and did not take on the meaning of a discipline without questioning. In the following example, Carol questions the required format for a compare-and-contrast assignment on two short stories. After completing two different drafts, she went to see the English instructor for help. She described what happened during that meeting:

> I had two typed. One I did . . . in about two pages and I thought it was the better one. And then I went to see him about it and he told me that it wasn't what he wanted. I explained to him that I was doing one similarity [between the two stories] and then a difference . . . He said not that way you can't. It is impossible to do it that way he said. And I did it . . . He also told me to elaborate on a story without retelling it. And I thought, how can you do that?

'And I thought, how can you do that?' are important words. Carol is questioning a rule of English academic Discourse. She is also questioning why her primary Discourse, which would involve elaboration on a story through retelling, is not acceptable.

The disparities in making meaning are greater for students such as Lana and Carol who are marginalized by their gender and race. Their ways of making meaning are also closely linked to their experiential knowledge based in multiple roles. When experiential knowledge is devalued, or undervalued, multiple readings are not accepted within the institution. Marginalized forms of knowledge, other ways of making meaning and sense of texts, are not validated as knowledge. Institutional power is therefore maintained through a perpetuation of the status quo within an academic Discourse, a discipline, and within the university as an institution.

Devaluation of Narrative

Narrative is the primary way in which humans make meaning of their lives (Bruner, 1986; Carr, 1986; Gee, 1989; Mishler, 1986; White, 1981). Narrative is all-pervasive — we live narratives in our lives (MacIntyre, 1984) and it enables humans to view their lives holistically: 'The narrative scheme serves as a lens through which the apparently independent and disconnected elements of existence are seen as related parts of a whole' (Polkinghorne, 1988, p. 36).

Narrative is also transcultural (Barthes, 1977; White, 1981). It not only helps people know and tell their knowledge, but it also assists us to better understand the narratives of others, specifically that of people from other cultures. 'We may not be able fully to comprehend specific thought patterns of another culture, but we have relatively less difficulty *understanding* a story coming from another culture' (pp. 1–2, original emphasis). Perhaps because it has often been associated with fiction, narrative has not been considered appropriate as a form that transmits academic facts and knowledge. It is considered too practical, too common and too rooted in everyday experiences.

Or perhaps narrative was and is not accepted in the university setting because it is too closely linked to cultures in which orality is valued. Lana and Carol represent two such cultures. The imposition of the dominant voice by conquest, colonization and near decimation of First Nations peoples and their cultures, has resulted in devaluation of the narratives of First Nations peoples within the larger society. Narrative is also used and valued by women. The perpetuation of patriarchy in the western definition of literacy was, and is, called scholarship. Narratives have not been considered to be as scholarly as academic treatises. The price of becoming an insider is to devalue our own narratives, to question our experiential knowledge, and, often, to reject self — at least while in the university setting. University students at all levels, but particularly at the graduate level, learn to speak 'correctly' so that institutional power, framed by the dominant voice, can be reproduced.

Narrative has either been, at best, an alternate form of knowledge or, at worst, rejected or subjugated within the university. Partly because of political forces from outside the institution of the university, such as plans for First Nations self-government and concern with all types of equity issues including race and gender, the narratives of First Nations speakers are starting to be considered as legitimate knowledge. If the narratives of marginalized peoples are allowed to carry academic meaning within the institution of the university and not, as has been the role of narrative in the past, just to support academic meaning through anecdote, more people may understand the work of marginalized academics. Their meaning may become accessible to a larger public. First Nations peoples and women may demand equal results,[1] that is validation and valuing of their knowledge, as well as equal access to the institution of the university. Equal access in the past has meant allowing students to learn, but not change, the dominant academic Discourses and to take on the dominant meaning's way of being.

The agencies of the dominant Discourses are the gatekeepers of the institution. Grace (1990) explains:

> In its various manifestations in history and in contemporary societies, the dominant voice or, more precisely, the agencies of the dominant voice, have in general a uniform intention. This intention is the reproduction of the dominant voice within the person and within various subject populations. The intention is to get the person or the community to speak 'correctly', i.e., to speak in the approved form, both linguistically and ideologically. (p. 47)

Lana, Carol, their instructors, and I are all expected to speak and think 'correctly'. In coursework, narratives are devalued, or in some cases rejected. We learn when to write our own narratives, when to write in the dominant voice, and when to be silent. We learn that our narratives are devalued by the agencies of the university as a way of maintaining control to prevent the possibility of academic change. Our narratives are the victims of powerful gatekeeping.

Gatekeeping

Although instructors within the disciplines in the university are perceived by students as having power, they are so only if they are involved in decision-making processes within their disciplines in the context of the institution and the broader academic community outside the institution. Marginalized instructors, such as sessional lecturers and lab instructors, have limited input into decision-making processes and yet are required to carry out those decisions in teaching.

The power relations form a system of gatekeeping. Instructors have some power over students, primarily through grading. As well, instructors control through mentorship, or lack of it. Lana and Carol repeatedly talked about the importance of obtaining good grades, of passing the courses, and the power of the mark. The power of the mark was a constant shadow as Lana and Carol completed literacy tasks.

In turn, the discipline has power over the instructor. The keepers of the discipline determine the syllabi — what is to be taught and by whom. The gatekeepers of the discipline determine which instructors are given power and which instructors are marginalized. A 'culture of power' results, which marginalizes students as outsiders (Delpit, 1988). As Lana said, 'This is my first year, and I don't really know what it's like.' Often students aren't given the rules to this culture of power but learn the rules, or their interpretation of the rules, through trial and error. 'I try it and if he [the English instructor] doesn't tell me differently, I continue it' (Carol). When the rules of the culture of power are made explicit, students can and do use them to succeed. For example, Lana learned to write thesis statements because they were required. Students who are marginalized to begin with, become less marginalized when the rules of a culture of power are made explicit. Marginalized students can then make the decision whether or not to use those rules and begin to take on the academic Discourse. Once marginalized students have learned the rules, they can also choose to critique them. Gaining access to a dominant Discourse forms the basis for later critique (Lazere, 1992).

At the heart of these power relations is language. The degradation of oral cultures and the imposition of literacy as defined by the European invaders is the sociohistorical context within which the institution of the university functions:

> Dominant races, through the process of colonial conquest and imperialism have not only invaded the economic and political space of other peoples, but also their linguistic and cultural space. As part of the imperial process has come the imposition of the dominant voice, the voice of a colonizing power and of its agents. The English language in the context of imperialism has been a classic example of the imposed dominant voice and teachers of English, we must remember, have been historically agents of that process. (Grace, 1990, p. 48)

As well as embedding the dominant voice in racial inequities, Grace (1990) also contextualizes gender power relations:

> The power relations of gender have structured and shaped both language content and language use. The maleness of language has dominated the femaleness of language for centuries and during those centuries men have spoken for much of the time while women have been forced either into the culture of silence, or into marginalized forms of language. (p. 48)

Jadwin and Monteath, in Chapters 9 and 10 of this volume, demonstrated the alienation of women through the use of rhetoric. But the power relations at the university are larger than language: they are the power relations of Discourses that include 'ways of being in the world' (Gee, 1989, p. 7). Written language is just the surface indicator of the larger way of being in the academic Discourse. Taking on ways of being, as required in academic Discourses, requires 'active complicity with values that conflict with one's home and community-based Discourses, especially for many women and minorities' (Gee, 1989, p. 13). For Lana and Carol, adopting the 'way of being' of English academic Discourse often reflected a 'conflict of loyalties' (Stonequist, 1937, p. 69) and 'an unbearable contradiction' (Walkerdine, 1989, p. 277). Institutions such as universities, which perpetuate the dominant Discourses, are often selective of whose voices are heard. 'We want to hear the different voices not too different from ours' (Grace, 1990, p. 52).

Personal Power

'Power is the ability to take one's place in whatever discourse is essential to action and the right to have one's part matter' (Heilbrun, 1988, p. 18). During the study, Lana and Carol both grew in personal power as they learned the rules of the culture of power. They attained short-term goals, such as completion of coursework, and began to attain longer term goals, working toward degrees which would give them some access to institutional power. They took on the 'way of being' (Gee, 1989, p. 7) and learned to 'speak correctly' (Grace, 1990, p. 47) to the extent that their work was acceptable to people on the inside of the Discourse. They showed personal power by being able to juggle their multiple roles, including the learning of the dominant academic Discourses and specifically English academic Discourse, while at the same time struggling to retain their own narratives and to begin to create knowledge using those narratives as foundations.

The second part of Heilbrun's definition of power is 'the right to have one's part matter' (1988, p. 18). As Lana and Carol become employees and decision-makers in their communities, the degree to which their personal power will increase and be felt will be increased. The right to have one's part matter is certainly linked to the potential for social action and change and, as women of First Nations ancestry,

Lana and Carol have traditionally been marginalized. It is within the communities outside of the institution of the university that there is the greatest potential for them, and many others like them, to work for social change.

Personal Power and Social Change

Personal power and social change can occur through validation and valuing of narrative, through mentorship into the culture of power, and through identifying and critiquing the power of the disciplines. Lana and Carol, by learning the academic Discourses required in their various courses, gained the potential to question and critique the dominant voices. As more students of First Nations ancestry and more women — groups traditionally marginalized — enter the professions, there is the potential for social change.

Valuing Narrative

Telling the stories of marginalized peoples, particularly if these stories are accepted as legitimate knowledge within institutions that have traditionally rejected or subjugated these stories, is the first tentative step toward social change. Richardson (1990) views narrative as useful 'in the services of liberatory civic discourses and transformative social projects' (p. 65). If such stories are listened to and understood, power is redistributed among the tellers and listeners (Heilbrun, 1988). The importance of listening carefully to the ideas of women such as Lana and Carol reminds me of the words of Woods (1990) in her discussion of how teachers can be more culturally aware and sensitive in their teaching so that literacy education is more constructive: 'I know of no easy way to make this happen. However, I am convinced that the first step is to listen carefully to other voices' (p. 8).

Perhaps one reason narrative is becoming more acceptable now in academic-based research and writing is that more people who were formerly marginalized have enrolled in universities and are starting to gain in personal power. As the population of the university includes more people from various backgrounds, the processes may gradually change to become more inclusive. 'We need new processes and forms if we are to express ways of thinking that have been outside the dominant culture' (Bridwell-Bowles, 1992, p. 349).

Traditional forms have maintained the status quo, the dominant voices. 'The academic essay is not a vehicle for exploring ideas and making knowledge; it is a vehicle for presenting formed ideas, a didactic, authoritative model rather than an interactive form' (Sanborn, 1992, p. 143). McCracken (1992) also speaks in favor of alternate forms:

> We must help students try to discover how to write about what they know
> that goes beyond where the linear, hierarchical, completely certain mode

of thinking and writing can take them. Where we once listened only for major and minor premise, we must now listen also for truth statements shaped in different patterns such as metaphors and parallel narratives. (p. 123)

Using narrative will mean that the work of academics will be more accessible to people other than academics and that will have implications for social change as people in the community will begin to understand, critique, and perhaps value the contributions of academe. 'Educational research needs a new theory that takes seriously how language and subjectivity intersect with history, power, and authority' (Giroux and McLaren, 1992, pp. 7–8).

Mentorship

Mentoring has not been valued in the university setting as reflected in the large classes at the undergraduate level and devaluation of the importance of teaching and mentoring in tenure and promotion. Mentorship involves risk-taking because as students gain in knowledge and personal power, they will begin to question the knowledge and power of the instructors as agents of the disciplines. Rose (1989) noted that the four mentors he benefited from working with helped students in 'ways that fostered growth rather than established dominance' (p. 58).

Accepting multiple voices, valuing divergent viewpoints, and being willing to take risks are requirements for mentors. Instructors, and specifically instructors working cross-culturally and across genders, need the personal and professional ability to be respectful toward students and to be able to bridge primary and secondary Discourses. Mentors must open doors for people often very unlike themselves in terms of gender and cultural background and hear voices that are often very different from their own. For most people, that is not reassuring.

The sharing of knowledge and power, requires that university instructors make the rules of academic Discourse explicit. Students should not be expected to be experts before they have been apprentices, nor should they be expected to (re)invent the university (Bartholomae, 1985) by guessing at the rules of the culture of power. The more explicit the guidelines for their literacy tasks, the more Lana and Carol gained feelings of control and the more their personal power within the institutional power was affirmed. Gaining access to dominant modes of Discourse is a survival skill and forms the basis for eventual critique (Lazere, 1992). Students cannot critique dominant Discourses unless they acquire knowledge of those Discourses.

Instructors are professionally and morally obligated to provide students with the rules of the 'culture of power' (Delpit, 1988). Members within disciplines need to first allow, and second encourage, instructors to provide rules of the discipline. Making rules of an academic Discourse explicit is not easy for instructors, perhaps because they are often absorbed into the ideological framework of the discipline, of speaking correctly (Gilbert, 1989; Painter and Martin, 1986).

Critiquing the Power of the Disciplines

Students of First Nations ancestry and women will never achieve equal results in comparison to mainstream males unless the rules of the culture of power are made explicit and then actively critiqued. That critique is not just in terms of the discipline critiquing itself which often results in maintenance of the status quo. The critique must come through dialogue between representatives of the groups who have traditionally been marginalized and representatives of the groups who have traditionally been in power. Because people absorbed in the culture of power are often those who cannot identify it, beginners and outsiders marginalized by the Discourse can contribute greatly to the critique. Stuckey's words echo: 'Marginalized peoples can often work to change the system because unlike those in power, they [the marginalized] "can see it"' (1991, p. 127).

Instructors cannot help students critique the implications of how academic Discourses marginalize certain individuals, unless they 'walk what they talk' and can themselves critique the marginalization in their own disciplines. Bridwell-Bowles (1992) suggested that critique begins with examining the language and finding variants of the language used within a discipline. She noted the difficulty of this type of critique: 'All of this is complicated, of course, because we are working within a patriarchal, racist, and classist culture and using a patriarchal, racist, and classist variation of language to try to define something outside the culture' (1992, p. 353). One way to engage in that critique is by using the narratives from our primary Discourses as the foundation for the language of critique, by 'talking back to texts'.

'Historically, universities were developed for the benefit of privileged intellectuals — they were not intended to be instruments of change, but rather were protectors and perpetrators of the status quo' (Brown, 1990, p. 93). No attempt at critique will be to any avail unless people in powerful positions within the disciplines (tenured professors and department heads) and within university administration (deans, vice-presidents, and presidents) engage in and support this appraisal. Critique is essential to reduce and hopefully eliminate the racism and sexism and classism that pervades universities. 'If we think only those thoughts which we already have the words to express, then our presence in history remains static' (Giroux and McLaren, 1992, p. 17). Possible social change, as a result of identifying rules of power and granting it to students, and particularly to marginalized students, is not just allowing access to those disciplines but the right to equal results once they are given access.

As a result of valuing, mentorship, and sharing of knowledge and power, students can learn to use their own voices to bridge their primary and secondary Discourses. Narrative, used as both a process and a product, can be used to achieve this mentorship, this bridging, this balance. Social change is the beginning, and the ending, of this process, however:

Social change is exhausting work and is often done by those who are most oppressed and most overworked. Educating for change is exciting but exacting. While preservers of tradition and the status quo can assume authority simply from their positions, seekers of change must always 'prove themselves'. And resistance can wear out a person. My bones know the places where my soul has been scorched. (LaRocque, 1990, p. 90)

But, in a later passage, LaRocque also offers hope. 'But I was born asking, and with eyes that can never close. The real wishing I do entails the transformation of people and of society' (LaRocque, 1990, p. 90).

Note

1 Equal results refers to the issue of equity that ensures that traditionally marginalized groups such as First Nations people and women receive the same benefits and advantages as the dominant society.

References

APPLE, M.W. (1986) *Teachers and Texts: A Political Economy of Class and Gender Relations in Education*, New York, Routledge & Kegan Paul.

BARTHES, R. (1977) *Image — Music — Text* (S. Heath, Trans.), New York, Hill & Wang.

BARTHOLOMAE, D. (1985) 'Inventing the university', in ROSE, M. (ed.) *When a Writer Can't Write*, New York, Guilford Press, pp. 134–65.

BELENKY, M.F., CLINCHY, B.M., GOLDBERGER, N.R., and TARULE, J.M. (1986) *Women's Ways of Knowing*, New York, Basic Books.

BLEIER, R. (1986) *Science and Gender*, Toronto, ON, Pergamon.

BRIDWELL-BOWLES, L. (1992) 'Discourse and diversity: Experimental writing within the academy', *College Composition and Communication*, **43**, 3, pp. 349–68.

BROOKES, A.L. (1992) *Feminist Pedagogy: An Autobiographical Approach*, Halifax, NS, Fernwood Press.

BROWN, R. (1990) 'Through the fog: Looking at academia', in TURNER, J. (ed.) *Living the Changes*, Winnipeg, MB, University of Manitoba Press, pp. 91–7.

BRUNER, J. (1986) *Actual Minds, Possible Worlds*, Cambridge, MA, Harvard University Press.

CARR, D. (1986) *Time, Narrative, and History*, Bloomington, IN, Indiana University Press.

CODE, L. (1991) *What Can She Know? Feminist Theory and the Construction of Knowledge*, Ithaca, NY, Cornell University Press.

DELPIT, L.D. (1988) 'The silenced dialogue: Power and pedagogy in educating other people's children', *Harvard Educational Review*, **58**, 3, pp. 280–98.

FRANKLIN, U. (1990) *The Real World of Technology*, Toronto, ON, Canadian Broadcasting Corporation Enterprises.

GEE, J.P. (1989) 'Literacy: The solicited work of James Paul Gee', *Journal of Education*, **171**, pp. 3–176.

GILBERT, P. (1989) 'Personally (and passively) yours: Girls, literacy and education', *Oxford Review of Education*, **15**, 3, pp. 257–65.

GIROUX, H.A. and McLAREN, P.L. (1992) 'Writing from the margins: Geographies of identity, pedagogy, and power', *Journal of Education*, **174**, 1, pp. 7–30.

GRACE, G. (1990) 'An overview of conference themes', *Proceedings of Different Voices —* *Aotearoa: The Fifth Conference of the International Federation for the Teaching of English*, Auckland, New Zealand, pp. 11–17.

GREENE, M. (1986) 'Philosophy and teaching', in WITTROCK, M.C. (ed.) *Handbook of Research on Teaching* (3rd ed.) New York, Macmillan, pp. 479–501.

HARDING, S. (1991) *Whose Science? Whose Knowledge? Thinking from Women's Lives*, Ithaca, NY, Cornell University Press.

HEILBRUN, C.G. (1988) *Writing a Woman's Life*, New York, Norton.

LaROCQUE, E. (1990) 'Tides, towns and trains', in TURNER, J. (ed.) *Living the Changes*, Winnipeg, MB, University of Manitoba Press, pp. 76–90.

LAZERE, D. (1992) 'Back to basics: A force for oppression or liberation', *College English*, **54**, 1, pp. 7–21.

MACINTYRE, A. (1984) *After Virtue: A Study in Moral Theory* (2nd ed.), Notre Dame, IN, Indiana University Press.

McCRACKEN, N.M. (1992) 'Gender issues and the teaching of writing', in McCRACKEN N.M. and APPLEBY, B.C. (eds) *Gender Issues in the Teaching of English*, Portsmouth, NH, Boynton/Cook, pp. 115–25.

MISHLER, E.G. (1986) *Research Interviewing: Context and Narrative*, Cambridge, MA, Harvard University Press.

MONTURE-ANGUS, P. (1995) *Thunder in My Soul: A Mohawk Woman Speaks*, Halifax, NS, Fernwood Press.

PAINTER, C. and MARTIN, J.R. (1986) *Writing to Mean: Teaching Genres Across the Curriculum*, Sydney, Australia, Applied Linguistics Association of Australia.

POLKINGHORNE, D.E. (1988) *Narrative Knowing and the Human Sciences*, Albany, NY, State University of New York Press.

RICHARDSON, L. (1990) *Writing Strategies: Reaching Diverse Audiences*, Newbury Park, CA, Sage.

RIDINGTON, R. (1990) *Little Bit Know Something: Stories in a Language of Anthropology*, Vancouver, BC, Douglas & McIntyre.

ROSE, M. (1989) *Lives on the Boundary: The Struggles and Achievements of America's Underprepared*, New York, Free Press.

SANBORN, J. (1992) 'The academic essay: A feminist view in student voices', in McCRACKEN, N.M. and APPLEBY, B.C. (eds) *Gender Issues in the Teaching of English*, Portsmouth, NH, Boynton/Cook, pp. 142–60.

SMITH, D.E. (1987) *The Conceptual Practices of Power: A Feminist Sociology of Knowledge*, Toronto, University of Toronto Press.

STONEQUIST, E.V. (1937) *The Marginal Man*, New York, Charles Scribner.

STUCKEY, J.E. (1991) *The Violence of Literacy*, Portsmouth, NH, Boynton/Cook.

WALKERDINE, V. (1989) 'Femininity as performance', *Oxford Review of Education*, **15**, 3, pp. 267–79.

WHITE, H. (1981) 'The value of narrativity in the representation of reality', in MITCHELL, W.J.T. (ed.) *On Narrative*, Chicago, University of Chicago Press, pp. 1–24.

WOODS, C. (1990) 'Language, culture and identity', *Proceedings of Different Voices —* *Aotearoa: The Fifth Conference of the International Federation for the Teaching of English*, Auckland, New Zealand, pp. 11–17.

Part 4

Legal Violence

12 Suffer the Little Children Who Come into Schools[1]

Ailsa M. Watkinson

Just as democracy in order to live must move and move forward, so schools in a democracy cannot stand still, cannot be satisfied and complacent with what has been accomplished, but must be willing to undertake whatever reorganization of studies, of methods of teaching, of administration, including that larger organization which concerns the relation of pupils and teachers to each other, and to the life of the community. Failing in this, the schools cannot give democracy the intelligent direction of its forces which it needs to continue in existence. (Dewey, 1946, p. 48)

The willingness of educational professionals to move toward democratizing education comes in fits and starts, encumbered, in part, by conflicting values of teacher professionalism and democracy. Amy Guttmann describes the conflict as a tension between the professional autonomy of teachers and the perceived erosion of their competence when students influence the form or content of their own education (1987, p. 88). Thus professional autonomy/authority impedes the democratizing of education. Dewey warned that if schools do not change, do not progress toward democratization, they risk taking refuge in an ark that 'is not the ark of safety in a deluge. It is being carried by the deluge of outside forces, varying, shifting, turning aimlessly with every current in the tides of modern life' (Dewey, 1946, p. 48).

The 'deluge of outside forces' that Dewey described decades ago are pressuring the schools of today. The 'changing current of modern life' is affecting human rights legislation in most developed nations. As an example, I will be discussing the recent legislative changes that came into effect when Canada's *Charter of Rights and Freedoms* (the Charter) became a part of Canada's Constitution in 1982.

Perhaps one of the most substantive and promising changes to be brought about by this human rights legislation was the acknowledgment of student rights.

The *Charter* will provide a vehicle for parents and others to ask for a hearing and, in the *Charter* world of education, educators will have to allow this. The rather select club of educational policy-makers will be opened up to a number of new voices. In that respect the *Charter* may be a democratizing influence. (MacKay, 1988, p. 148)

Over the past decade and a half, a number of important cases have focused attention on the impact of human rights legislation on student life.[2]

Some court decisions, particularly decisions emanating from the Canadian Supreme Court, have expanded the notion of student democratic rights while others have taken extraordinary measures to limit those rights. The later cases show an unabashed deference towards educators, who, as current research has shown, are both unfamiliar with and ambivalent about human rights reform. Attempts to democratize education and change the inequalities and injustices in education are often rebuffed by an education profession bolstered by judicial deference, draconian legislation, and educators' own code of ethics.

The purpose of this chapter is to explore a paradox inherent in teaching. Educational professionals generally consider teaching to be a 'caring profession', a training ground for instilling democratic principles. However, no substantive changes toward the democratizing of education has occurred. The educational status quo is out of step with human rights documents, the courts interpretation of them and the ethical considerations influencing our interaction with children/students. The result is that while children are compelled by legislation to attend school, their democratic rights and freedoms are more at risk in school than out of it. Children who are different because of their race, religion, physical disability, sexual orientation and social status are more vulnerable to educational harm manifested in higher dropout rates, poor grades, lessened post-secondary opportunities and abuse. In addition, the fundamental freedoms and legal rights of students are diminished in school.

This chapter will consider the role of human rights legislation on pushing educational professionals into democratizing education by challenging our understanding of the qualities of a good educator and the training and selection of educational professionals. The focus is undoubtedly Canadian but the impediments to making education more democratic are international.

Authoritarian or Democratic Education

Schools are, by and large, governed in a paternalistic–authoritarian model. They are, as Adler says, undemocratic and antidemocratic (1988). Morris (1980) characterizes the paternalistic–authoritarian mode as based on the premise that students are immature and need to be coerced in certain circumstances. They are given some privileges by the administration but they have no rights. The prevalent attitude of school officials is one of 'discipline first' and 'adults know best' (Morris, 1980, p. 253). The system functions as a bureaucracy with emphasis on strict and comprehensive discipline enforced by extensive regulations of students' conduct. Educators operate in 'a cycle of activities determined and revised by a process of predetermined objectives and continuous testing' (Purpel, 1989, p. 49). Purpel argues that the need to control and have control over personal behavior becomes an obsession which places a higher priority on productivity, efficiency and uniformity than on flexibility, diversity, rights and freedoms. The control/authoritarian model functions with a proliferation of tests — 'a kind of quality control mechanism borrowed crudely and inappropriately from certain industrial settings' (Purpel, 1989, p. 48). Disciplinary rules reinforce the control of the professionals and make it implicit or, if necessary, explicit that 'it is the school that decides, the school that allows, lets, gives permission, waives, makes exceptions. It is the students who petition, request, and plead' (Purpel, 1989, p. 48). It is also the student who has to stand up for her or his constitutional rights. The control/authoritarian model is characterized by rigidity, formal lines of command, unquestioning adherence to rules and school desks all in a row.

This model is in sharp contrast to the democratic model, which places emphasis on a learning environment in which students and adults are seen as equal participants in some of the school activities. Student participation is justified on the grounds that learning is more constructive and beneficial in a democratic context. The democratic model does not imply a value-neutral education but rather one that enables students to discern between good and bad ways of life. Guttmann states that 'children are not taught that bigotry is bad . . . by offering it as one among many compelling conceptions of the good life' (1987, p. 43). A democratic education continues to cultivate in children the character that feels the force of right.[3] A democratic education encourages and values critical deliberation of 'the good life and the good society' (Guttmann, 1987, p. 44).

The democratic model is the essence of human rights legislation. The *Charter's* purpose is to ensure that 'Canadian society is free and democratic' (*R. v. Oakes*, 1986, p. 125). And to uphold the *Charter's* purpose, the Canadian Supreme Court said:

> The court must be guided by the values and principles essential to a free and democratic society which . . . embody . . . respect for the inherent dignity of the human person, commitment to social justice and equality, accommodation of a wide variety of beliefs, respect for cultural and group identity, and faith in social and political institutions which enhance the participation of individuals and groups in society. (*R. v. Oakes*, 1986, p. 125)

The education system, which is bound by human rights legislation, values and principles, has the same constitutional obligation — that is, to embody respect for the inherent dignity of each student, to commit to equality and social justice, and to adjust the education system to accommodate a wide variety of beliefs and group differences. Democratizing education is a constitutional obligation.[4]

Some Canadian courts have played a role in challenging the control/authoritarian mode of school governance by applying human rights documents to the education setting. For example, the Supreme Court has ruled that the public's interest in public education is an overriding interest and cannot give way to a parent's wish for non-approved religious home-schooling (*Jones v. The Queen*, 1986); that the use of corporal punishment will be viewed with suspicion (*R. v. Ogg Moss*, 1984); that employees of school boards whose religion is different from the majority must be accommodated by adjusting the workplace so as to allow them to maintain their

Sabbath (*Renaud v. Board of Education of Central Okanagan No. 23 and Canadian Union of Public Employees, Local 523*, 1992); and that a teacher's freedom of expression does not include the right to promote hatred against a protected class (*R. v. Keegstra*, 1991). Other courts and tribunals have ruled that the reciting of the Lord's Prayer and readings from the Bible are unconstitutional (*Zylberberg et al. v. Sudbury Board of Education*, 1988; *Canadian Civil Liberties Association v. Ontario (Minister of Education)* 1990; *Russow v. British Columbia (A.G.)*, 1989; *Manitoba Association for Rights and Liberties Inc. v. Manitoba (Minister of Education)* 1992); that students with disabilities have a right to integration within their neighborhood schools (*Eaton v. Brant (County) Board of Education*, 1995); and that harassment in schools violates the equality provisions of human rights laws, and school authorities have an obligation to combat harassment by undertaking substantive educational measures to neutralize an environment that condones it (*Quebec Human Rights Commission v. Board of Education of Deux-Montagnes*, 1994). But despite the increased activity among students, their parents, and advocates in expanding the rights of students, educators continue to be ambivalent.

Who Knows What? . . .

Educators' ambivalence is due in part to their lack of knowledge, acceptance and understanding about the democratic educational reforms being heralded by human rights legislation. A recent study found that '. . . only a small number of educators in the western provinces have a good grasp of the law as it pertains to various rights in the educational area' (Peters and Montgomerie, 1994a, p. 13). Perhaps more troubling was the study's finding regarding educators' attitudes toward student rights. Educators show a lack of support for the mainstreaming of students with disabilities and the abolition of corporal punishment, but are willing to 'provide selective support for particular rights, generally in those areas which don't appear to impact directly on their own operations in their classrooms or schools' (Peters and Montgomerie, 1994b, p. 17). An earlier American study found that educators are more conservative about the application of civil liberties to students than the courts had been but that educators were as liberal as the courts about expanding the rights of educators (Menacker and Pascella, 1984). In other words, rights and freedoms are acceptable if they improve the life of the educator but not if they interfere with their practices. The authors of the Canadian study concluded by saying that:

> . . . there should be concern that the level of knowledge regarding rights by educators in this study is as low as it is. Until educators acquire a more accurate knowledge of the constitutional and statutory rights which individuals enjoy in the educational area, human rights and Charter oriented endeavors are likely to be less successful than public policy makers might wish. (Peters and Montgomerie, 1994a, p. 18)

A 1990 study on the perceptions of school authorities (teachers, principals, superintendents, Department of Education officials, and school board trustees) regarding the rights of students and parents reported that, among other things, 98 per cent of the respondents believed that principals should have the right to choose the appropriate punishment of students; 79 per cent said corporal punishment can be justified; and 66 per cent agreed that school authorities should have the right to refuse a parent's request for the admission of a learning disabled child in a regular program (Bergen, Gour and Prichard, 1990). Salient in all these studies is the continued reliance on the traditional — 'adults know best' — mode of school governance, despite the 'deluge'.

... and Who Cares When?

Other research has found that Canadian courts have aligned with the 'care' perspective rather than the 'justice' perspective in dealing with issues that affect minorities and other disadvantaged groups (Watkinson, 1993). The care perspective or ethic of care is defined as taking care of others and one's self. It entails knowing others well and discovering the context of their lives. Caring celebrates connectedness and interdependence (Gilligan, 1982). The justice perspective, or ethic of justice, is more formal, abstract and universal. Within the justice perspective of moral reasoning, 'every person's claim is to be treated impartially, regardless of the person' (Kohlberg, 1981, p. 39).

The courts have repeatedly instructed other decision makers to take seriously the context surrounding those who are claiming a human right and to avoid the rigid and formalistic interpretation (the ethic of justice) that historically characterized legal decision making (Watkinson, 1994). But while the court's moral orientation in considering equality rights claims is care, educators are more likely to employ the justice orientation (Watkinson, 1993). Thus educators are not synchronized with the Supreme Court in their moral orientation and decision-making roles.

The court's repeated direction in urging a more contextual approach to interpreting the human rights legislation is evidence of a rejection of rigid or blind adherence to the black letter of the law. What is needed, the courts have said, is more caring, more humanity, more empathy born of contextual listening. The courts stated preference for a contextual, caring approach in determining rights is 'grounded in the identification of historical and current disadvantaging [which] constitutionalizes a contextual approach' (Sheppard, 1989, p. 230). Educational professionals, as well as other decision makers who fall within the rubric of the human rights legislation are obliged to conduct the work they do from a caring perspective. It is not enough to ensure that rights, in a universal, abstract sense, are upheld but we need to extend and expand our understanding of equality and fundamental freedoms to include 'a fundamental obligation to be kind and considerate in dealing with children — to care for them — and to put ourselves out in ways that differ from those in which we must put ourselves out for adults' (O'Neill, 1992, p. 24).

O'Neill cautions against relying too heavily on the notion of children's rights/ students' rights because of the rigidity of the obligation. She argues that those who only meet their obligation of living up to a student's right will meet the 'perfect obligation' but not the 'imperfect obligation'; the distinction being that 'perfect obligations' correspond to legal rights, 'they specify completely or perfectly not merely who is bound by the obligation but to whom the obligation is owed' (O'Neill, 1992, p. 26). They do not rely on specific social or political conditions. Perfect obligations correspond to the justice perspective or the ethic of justice. Imperfect obligations are inherent in caring, or the ethic of care, as they strive for inclusion of and connectedness with others. Imperfect obligations, O'Neill notes, are often trivialized as 'frightfully nice', a matter of 'decency' or of being 'morally splendid'. Imperfect obligations are considered supererogatory (O'Neill, 1992, p. 28). But 'parents or teachers who meet only their perfect obligation would fail as parents or teachers' (1992, p. 27). A single focus on a rights-based approach, O'Neill warns, cannot take full account of the ways in which children's lives 'are particularly vulnerable to unkindness, to lack of involvement, cheerfulness or good feeling. . . . Cold, distant or fanatical parents and teachers, even if they violate no rights, deny children "the genial play of life": they can wither children's lives' (1992, p. 28). Some educators appear willing to meet their perfect obligations in dealings with students but are more tentative in meeting the imperfect obligations. As a result, inequality pervades the education system and students who partake in critical discourse of the system do so by placing themselves at risk.

Inherent Inequality in Education

Contemporary schools are designed as bureaucracies and influenced greatly by the business model (Sergiovanni, 1996; Hodgkinson, 1991). Ferguson compares bureaucracies to authoritarian political regimes. Both bureaucracy and terror she writes, 'depoliticize society by crippling public life, reducing individuals either to passive agents of the system or to inmates of it, and denying them the status of responsible actors capable of rationally giving consent and acting in concert toward shared ends' (Ferguson, 1984, p. 17–18). Lapham (1993) sympathetically compares workers to the courtiers of George III who find themselves forfeiting their capacity to speak and think and their willingness to argue their case, all for the sake of maintaining their economic stability (Lapham, 1993, p. 2).

A dehumanized learning environment contributes to student feelings of isolation and alienation. Fine (1991) argues that the anonymity and enforced isolation of large bureaucratic schools push students to dropout. A large percentage of these students are members of minorities, lesbians, gay men and the poor (Fine, 1991, pp. 19–22). Fine notes that most studies on dropouts are obsessed with finding the characteristics of individual students rather than on the characteristics of the schools from which they flee. The studies that do question the characteristics of schools from which students flee, show that students report a lack of faculty interest, unfair discipline procedure, rigid retention policies, tracking procedure and competency examinations — characteristics inherent in the traditional mode of school governance. The effect of dropping-out is poverty. The poverty is layered according to race, gender and class (Fine, 1991, p. 23).

Bureaucracies are incapable of seeing the student. A student's peculiarities, circumstances and needs are lost in the rigid process of running bureaucracies. Empathy, caring, contextual knowing are stripped from educational decision making (Watkinson, in press). The unwillingness or inability of educational decision makers to empathetically understand the particular circumstances of those who are disadvantaged socially, politically and legally has dehumanizing consequences. A Canadian survey reports that in 1991 only 12 per cent of aboriginal students completed Grade 12 compared to an overall graduation rate of 78.2 per cent (Saskatchewan Education Indicators Report Update, 1995, p. 5). A 1985 study on inner city dropout rates found that only one out of every ten aboriginal students who starts Grade 7 will complete Grade 12 compared to six out of every ten non-aboriginal students (Saskatchewan Department of Education, 1985). The study was never released publicly because the findings were considered too political. An American study reported that the profile of students dropping-out of school was 23 per cent Native Americans, 19 per cent Hispanic students, 17 per cent African-American and 12 per cent whites (Fine, 1991, p. 22). Other studies detail the failing of girls and young women by an education system designed by and for men. Research has shown that traditional pedagogy favors boys' learning patterns more than girls', teachers interact more with boys than girls and the interaction is more meaningful (Lather, 1991; Sadker and Sadker, 1994). The effect is that the learning environment stunts the intellectual growth of girls. Girls start school ahead of boys in reading and basic computation skills, but by the time they graduate from high school, boys have higher scores in both areas (White, 1983, cited in McLaren, 1989, p. 184). As well, girls encounter a learning environment poisoned by sexual harassment (Watkinson, 1995; Stein, Marshall and Tropp, 1993).

The impact of systemic inequalities in schools is increased dropout rates, damaged self-esteem, diminished post-secondary educational chances and the real risk of living in poverty. Schools are the one institution that everyone is compelled to attend. It is appropriate, then, that education should be the leader in eliminating societal inequalities. Instead, schools mirror and reinforce the inequalities and injustices. Rosemary Brown, a former Canadian Member of Parliament, considers education to be 'an institution [that] plays at maintaining the status quo. . . . Education is indeed part of the reason why sexism and racism flourish' (Brown, 1990, p. 233).

Student Resistance and Student Risk

Questioning authority, a laudable principle within a democracy, is undertaken by students at their peril. They face obstruction from judicial deference, draconian legislation and educational profession's code of ethic.

The Canadian Supreme Court's interpretation of the equality rights and fundamental freedoms enshrined in human rights legislation have been expansive and contextualized. The interpretation of student legal rights by the lower courts has been anything but. Two areas demonstrate clearly the courts' unabashed deference to educators: the lack of rights for students who are in trouble with the law; and the legally condoned use of physical force on students. Before I consider these issues, however, it is important to consider the role of Section 1 of the Canadian *Charter* and its potential for promoting a democratic education.

The Promise

The rights and freedoms promulgated in the *Charter* are not absolute rights. Section 1 of the *Charter* allows governments and, through them, school authorities to limit the rights and freedoms of students and staff if the limits meet the criteria set out in Section 1. Section 1 states:

> The Canadian Charter of Rights and Freedoms guarantees the rights and freedoms set out in it subject only to such reasonable limits prescribed by law as can be demonstrably justified in a free and democratic society. (1982)

A Section 1 analysis begins once the court has determined that an infringement of a *Charter* right has occurred. At this point the onus is shifted to the teacher or educational administrator to justify their actions by providing relevant information, which only they have, to support the need for limiting a right or freedom. The attractiveness of this process for students should be that those in positions of authority now have to answer, with cogent and persuasive evidence, why they have done what they have done (*R. v. Oakes*, 1986). Section 1 promotes talk or deliberation 'essential for realizing the ideal of a democratically sovereign society' (Guttmann, 1987, p. 52). Proving that a limitation is reasonable and justifiable is to be accomplished against the backdrop of a legal system which, in the words of former Justice Wilson, is committed 'to uphold the rights and freedoms set out in . . . the Charter' (*Singh v. M.E.I.*, 1985, p. 68).

Section 1 has been described as 'distinctively Canadian because it fits well with parliamentary democracy by trying to reconcile individual and community rights' (Colker, 1992, p. 84). Justice McLachline compared the Canadian approach to restricting rights with the American experience under their Bill of Rights. One of the major differences, she said, was that the Canadian approach provides a method of analysis that permits:

> [A] sensitive, case-oriented approach to the determination of their constitutionality. Placing the conflicting values in their factual and social context when performing the Section 1 analysis permits the courts to have regard to special features of the expression in question. (*Rocket v. Royal College of Dental Surgeons of Ontario*, 1990, pp. 246–7)

The importance of factual circumstances in undertaking a Section 1 analysis is vital 'as they shape a court's view of both the right or freedom at stake and the limit proposed by the state, neither can be surveyed in the abstract' (*R. v. Keegstra*, 1991).

Neither the defining of a right or freedom nor the limiting of a right or freedom can be viewed in the abstract. Former Chief Justice Dickson described the relationship between the values the *Charter* is intended to uphold and the circumstances of a particular case as 'synergetic' and central to judicial interpretation. He stated that 'a rigid or formalistic interpretation to the application of Section 1 is to be avoided' (*R. v. Keegstra*, 1991, pp. 38–9).

The limits on rights and freedoms are to be justified within the values and principles of respecting the inherent dignity of others, a commitment to justice and equality, accommodation of a wide variety of beliefs, and respect for group and cultural differences (*R. v. Oakes*, 1986, p. 125). The same values and principles that underlie the rights also underlie the limiting of rights. The determination of whether a limit meets the principles and values of a free and democratic society requires an examination of the context of an individual's or group's circumstances. Thus Section 1 both limits rights and contributes to the democratizing of education by forcing those in authority and with the power to limit rights to clearly and cogently explain the reasons for limiting a right or freedom.

Shifting the onus of justification to school administrators who limit rights and freedoms by way of policies and practices moves toward the democratizing of education. The principle has generally worked for students claiming equality rights but not for students caught in the criminal justice system or in issues of 'law and order' in the school.

Judicial Deference

In 1986, the Ontario Supreme Court heard the case of *R. v. G.J.M.*, which dealt with the search and seizure of a Grade 7 student who was seen outside the schoolyard placing drugs in his sock. The principal and vice principal summoned the student to the principal's office and asked him to remove his footwear. The student took something out of his pant cuff and ate it. After some time, the principal obtained what he considered to be suspicious matter and called the police. The student was charged with possession of marijuana. At trial, the student argued that his right to be secure against unreasonable search or seizure had been violated.[5] The student also argued that since he was detained by the principal, and subsequently charged with an offense, he had the right to retain and instruct counsel and to be informed of that right.[6]

The judge responded to the student's argument by relying on an American case, *New Jersey v. T.L.O.* (1985) and applied the American two-fold test to determine the reasonableness of the search. The American case involved a 14-year-old student who was found smoking in the school washroom. The student denied smoking and as a result the principal searched her purse whereupon he found illegal drugs. T.L.O. argued the search had violated her fourth amendment right (*New Jersey v. T.L.O.*, 1985). The application of the American test, conceived under the *American Bill of Rights*, effectively circumvented the justification stage of a Canadian Section 1 analysis. By applying the American test, the judge usurped the principle of reverse onus, which would have required school authorities to justify the search within the values and principles of a democratic society. The judge supported the principal's handling of the matter by referring to the provincial education act which requires the principal 'to maintain proper order and discipline in the school'. This was a strange turn of events considering that the *Charter*, as part of the supreme law of Canada, governs the scope of provincial legislation rather than provincial legislation governing the scope of the *Charter*.

The judge stated that a strict adherence to the principle of 'reasonable expectation of privacy' was relaxed since it was the principal and not a police officer who conducted the search. The justification was that 'the principal has a substantial interest in the accused student' and secondly 'society as a whole has an interest in the maintenance of a proper educational environment, which clearly involves being able to enforce school discipline efficiently and effectively' (*R. v. J.M.G.*, 1986, p. 710). But as MacKay points out, 'the consequences for the student . . . are the same regardless of who conducts the search' (MacKay, 1995, p. 193). The impact of this ruling is that a student's right to be secure against an unreasonable search and seizure is diminished by virtue of being in school. The consequences of not being secure against an unreasonable search and seizure, however, are not diminished.

The judge also ruled that the detention of a student is not the type of detention considered under the human rights legislation since 'the accused was already under detention of a kind throughout his school attendance' (*R. v. J.M.G.*, 1986, p. 712). The analogy of schools to jail cannot be lost. By attending school, students can be detained without being informed of their rights and face possible criminal justice consequences. If the same student had been detained by a police officer on the street, he would have had to be informed of his right to retain a lawyer and nothing that he said before he was read his rights could be used against him.

The judge found, using the American case as a precedent, that it was not necessary to apply the Section 1 analysis. But, he added, if he had been forced to use Section 1, he 'would have no hesitation in finding the right [of the principal to maintain proper order and discipline] . . . to be "demonstrably justified in a free and democratic society"' (*R. v. J.M.G.*, 1986, p. 713). Leave to appeal this case was refused by the Supreme Court of Canada.[7]

Draconian Legislation

The other area in which student rights are superceded by the teachers' need to maintain order is in the area of corporal punishment. Students in Canada are vulnerable to the possibility of physical assaults by educators in school because Canada's *Criminal Code* allows parents, teachers or persons standing in the place of parents to use force on children to correct the child's behavior. Normally, if a person applies intentional force on another it is considered an assault. The assaulted can either charge the perpetrator with assault under the *Criminal Code* or pursue a civil action and sue for monetary damages. However, children do not have the same recourse because a physical assault perpetrated by a teacher (euphemistically called corporal punishment) is condoned by Section 43 of the *Criminal Code*, which states that:

> Every school teacher, parent or person standing in the place of the parent is justified in using force by way of correction toward the pupil or child, as the case may be, who is under his [sic] care, if the force does not exceed what is reasonable under the circumstances.

This section is crucial because it is almost always employed as a defense whenever a teacher is charged with assault. It is also a very effective defense. A recent case exemplifies its impact on student life. A 9-year-old girl described as 'a difficult child' with a history of behavioral problems was spanked once on the buttocks, over top of her clothes, by her teacher. The child cried and wanted to leave the class but was not permitted to do so. The child's mother reported a 'bright red hand mark on her left side' about 2 hours after the incident (*R. v. Graham*, 1994). The teacher was charged with assault. *The New Brunswick Schools Act* provides that 'a teacher shall not discipline any pupil by administering corporal punishment' (R.S.N.B., 1973). However, the judge ruled that the *New Brunswick* legislation, prohibiting the use of corporal punishment, takes away a 'right' that all teachers have pursuant to Section 43 of the *Criminal Code* (p. 204). Further, the judge warned school authorities against trying to discipline the teacher for breaching school policy. Implicit in the ruling is the message that it is acceptable to physically assault a child for breaking school rules but it is not acceptable to discipline teachers for breaking school rules. The judge quoted the biblical passage 'spare the rod and spoil the child' and justified the use of the Bible with reference to the *Charter*'s preamble which states: 'Canada is founded upon principles that recognize the supremacy of God and the rule of law.' The judge said, 'It is difficult to recognize His supremacy without giving import to His words.' The judge concluded that the assault was not unreasonable and stated that he failed to see why the Crown had proceeded with the case at all. He quoted with approval the following passage from another case:

> It is important for the teacher to make sure that there is respect for authority; this is part of his responsibility as teacher and educator. The teacher represents authority and it is his duty to make sure he is shown respect. This is part of the duty he owes to the student who lacks respect for him and especially the duty he owes to the rest of the class . . . If corporal punishment is used, it is necessary to make it effective to a certain degree. Otherwise, far from being a measure salutary to the child, it will become, on his part, a cause of indifference, even more than that, of independence and defiance; hence the fault for which the punishment was intended will be repeated to satiety, since his chastisement is lenient (*R. v. Plourde*, 1993).

The judges in these cases were sitting comfortably with the views of educational professionals, who hang tenaciously to the authoritarian mode of school governance.

Judicial approval and the extension of a teacher's 'right' to use force on students is a powerful alley for the traditional forces.

Even the objection of students to the use of force can justify its use! In this case, the defendant, Mr Plourde, was the homeroom teacher of a Grade 8 class. It was his duty each day to check attendance and have the students listen to the day's announcements before they left to attend their respective classes. On the morning of 1 April 1992, some students entered the class talking and bickering with each other. One student, Pierre, turned to talk to another. Mr Plourde told Pierre to listen and, as described by the judge, 'put his hand on the student's shoulder and turned him around toward the front of the class' (*R. v. Plourde*, 1993, p. 276). Another student, Eric, told Mr Plourde that he should not act that way. Mr Plourde told him to be quiet. Eric kicked a metal cabinet and was ordered to leave the classroom. Eric refused to do so and Mr Plourde 'grabbed him by the arms, lifted him from his chair and escorted him outside in the hallway' (p. 276). In the process, Eric's back was pushed against the blackboard. Eric sustained a red mark on his back and red marks on his forearm. When Mr Plourde re-entered the class, another student called out to him and told him he was crazy to act that way with Eric. Mr Plourde 'reminded him that he was indeed the teacher and that students should not talk to him that way' (p. 277). This student got up from his chair and Mr Plourde 'slapped him on the head while grabbing him by the shoulders to make him sit down' (p. 277). Yet another student also told him he was crazy. He 'grabbed her by the arm, brought her to the intercom in front of the classroom and informed the principal's office that she would shortly be going there for purposes of discipline' (p. 277). The first two students unsuccessfully charged Mr Plourde with assault. The judge said, 'I do not believe there is one homeroom teacher who would not have reacted in such a situation' (p. 277). He ruled that 'the defendant had to deal with the insolent behavior of two students in order to maintain his authority and order in the classroom' (p. 280) and that the 'correction' seemed to have made an impression because there was no evidence to say that the disruption caused by the two boys continued. He found that the force did not exceed what is reasonable under the circumstances and, relying on Section 43, determined that it was not an assault.

The effect of Section 43 is that that it deprives Canadian students of the equal protection all other Canadians have. It legalizes assaults against students while, elsewhere in the *Criminal Code*, it makes it an offense to assault an adult. In other words, Section 43 discriminates on the basis of age in that it allows adults to use physical force on children but not on adults (Watkinson, 1988). It eliminates both a perfect obligation not to cause physical harm to others and the imperfect obligation to protect the weakest among us.

Elsewhere in the *Charter* it is declared that 'every individual is equal before and under the law and has the right to equal protection and equal benefit of the law without discrimination . . . based on age' (Section 15). There is little doubt that a student does not receive equal protection nor equal benefit from legislation that prohibits assaults and applies punitive measures on those who assault but which, in its next breath, sanctions the assault of children.

In 1992, Canada became a signatory to *The Convention on the Rights of the Child* which specifically calls on all state parties to take appropriate legislative measures to protect children from all forms of physical and mental violence, injury or abuse while in the care of parents or others who care for them. The pervasive view that teachers somehow have a right to discipline children as they see fit, continues to place children at risk. Nearly twenty years ago, Englander, an educational psychologist, wrote that 'statutes now prohibit wife beating, the flogging of sailors, the owning of slaves, the hanging of witches, and the whipping of prisoners and the insane. The only remaining group that is not protected is children in schools' (1978, p. 531). In May, 1995, the Canadian government was criticized by the UN Committee on the Rights of the Child for this very section allowing the use of force upon children.

Codes of Ethics

In Canada, by means of various provincial laws, a person is obliged, if he or she suspects that a child is being abused, to report the suspicion to the appropriate social agency.[8] If you are a teacher and you suspect that a student or students are being abused by another teacher you must report your suspicions to that teacher. The Codes of Ethics for various Teachers' Federations in Canada, which are quasi-judicial documents, direct teachers to: 'make valid criticism of an associate only to appropriate officials, and then only after the associate has been informed of the nature of the criticism' (Saskatchewan Teacher's Federation Code of Ethics, 1994). In one recent case, a teacher, Jane, was concerned about the treatment of children in Mary's classroom. Jane spoke to the principal, who did nothing about it. Parents in the community were also concerned and eventually went to the police. Mary was charged with assaulting children in her care. Jane was summoned to testify at the case and reported what she had observed. Mary was found not guilty, using Section 43 as her defense. When the case was over, Mary charged Jane with breaking the Code of Ethics because Jane had spoken to the principal without talking to Mary first. Jane's misdemeanor was placing the care of children before the preservation of the profession's reputation. Jane was called to appear before a teacher's disciplinary committee and was subsequently acquitted, but not without much physical and emotional distress.

There are several areas in which students receive less legal protection than do other members of society. Students are more protected from assaults in their homes or on the streets than they are when they are in schools. They are the only members of society who can be assaulted with impunity by other members of society. If anyone else has reason to believe that a child is being abused by someone in authority over them, they are obliged by law to report their suspicions, but if other teachers are concerned about the legalized assaults they may witness and fulfill their perfect and imperfect obligation to the students by reporting it, they run the risk of being punished for 'professional' misconduct.

Education and Democracy

In 1932, Counts (1969) implored teachers to take power and fashion their curriculum and the procedures of the school so as to positively influence the social
attitudes, ideals and behavior of the coming generation. He urged teachers and
administrators to build a new social order, one that would challenge the forces of
conservatism epitomized in capitalism, 'with its deification of the principle of selfish-
ness, its exaltation of the profit motive, its reliance upon the forces of competition,
and its placing of property above human rights' (Counts, 1969, p. 47). Counts'
vision included the development of a democratic society that would:

> [C]ombat all forces tending to produce social distinctions and classes;
> repress every form of privilege and economic parasitism; manifest a ten-
> der regard for the weak, the ignorant and the unfortunate; . . . transform
> or destroy all conventions, institutions, and special groups inimical to the
> underlying principles of democracy; and finally be prepared . . . to follow
> the method of revolution. (1969, pp. 41–2)

I would direct Counts' education manifesto to students, parents and their advocates as well, encouraging all groups to insist on democratic participation, to repress
every form of educational privilege used by educators to maintain their control and
power and to fashion a new school order imbued with the values and principles of
a democratic society. In tandem, I would also challenge educational professionals
to dismantle the forces of authoritarianism in education and transform educational
design from a bureaucracy to a web of interconnectedness, a place of community.
Sergiovanni (1994) proposes that we change the metaphor which describes educational institutions as an 'organization' to one of 'community'. I agree. Communities
promote familiarity, a sense of knowing the other well. Familiarity improves the
breeding of compassion and caring.

One place to begin would be by ensuring that education training programs
reflect these same democratic values and principles. That would include reconstructing teacher training so as to inform student teachers and administrators of the
inequalities inherent in education, teach them the methods necessary to rectify the
inequalities, apprise them of the need to provide compensatory curricula to overcome past inequalities and provide them with a clear understanding of the perfect
and imperfect obligations required of educators. As MacKay (1988–89) wrote:

> I think it would be reasonable for a student to say that the system whereby
> adults, and largely white male adults, have defined the best interests for
> students and for everybody else in society has not worked well. And
> perhaps if we give more rights to students, if we give more recognition
> to women in society, if we give more recognition to minorities, homo-
> sexuals, or others, we are going to produce a different kind of society, one
> that will make more rational decisions for adults, as well as for students.
> (p. 149)

Counts' new school order, MacKay's vision of a different kind of society and Dewey's charge to educators to move forward will be advanced through the selection of caring, compassionate educators who, recognize completely, and fulfill absolutely, their perfect and imperfect obligations towards students. With the 'critical mass'[9] of professionals such as these, there is a good chance of change, of moving schools forward in step with our democratic society: 'Failing in this, the schools cannot give democracy the intelligent direction of its forces which it needs to continue in existence' (Dewey, 1946, p. 48).

Notes

1 This is a revised version of a paper presented at the Third International Conference on Social Values, St Catherines College, Oxford University, July 19–23, 1995.

2 *R. v. Keegstra*, 1991; *Zylberberg et al. v. Sudbury Board of Education*, 1988; *Jones v. The Queen*, 1986; *Mahe v. Alberta*, 1990; *Canadian Civil Liberties Association v. Ontario (Minister of Education)*, 1990; *Russow v. British Columbia (A.G.)*, 1989; *Manitoba Association for Rights and Liberties Inc. v. Manitoba (Minister of Education)* 1992; *Eaton v. Brant (County) Board of Education*, 1995.

3 See, Rushworth M. Kidder, 'Universal human: Finding an ethical common' (July–August, 1994) *The Futurist* 8. Interviews were carried out with two dozen women and men of conscience. The interviewees were asked 'If you could help create a global code of ethics, what would be on it?' They identified eight common values: love, trustfulness, fairness, freedom, unity (community), tolerance, responsibility, and respect for life.

4 Section 32 states that: (1) This *Charter* applies (a) to the parliament and government of Canada in respect of all matters within the authority of parliament including all matters relating to the Yukon Territory and Northwest Territories; and (b) to the legislature and government of each province in respect of all matters within the authority of the legislature of each province.

5 Section 8 of the *Charter* states: 'Everyone has the right to be secure against unreasonable search and seizure.'

6 Section 10(b) of the *Charter* states: 'Everyone has the right on arrest or detention (b) to retain and instruct counsel without delay and to be informed of that right.'

7 I have come to expect that when I talk about the *Charter* and student rights with educators they will generally be uninformed. The exception is this case. Educators are aware of the leeway given to them and how it differs from that of the police.

8 For example, Section 12 of the Saskatchewan Child and Family Services Act, 1989, states '. . . every person who has reasonable grounds to believe that a child is in need of protection shall report the information to an officer or peace officer.'

9 A critical mass was defined as 'the number of designated group members within the unit sufficient to challenge the rule, to provide aid and support to one another in redefining issues and expanding horizons' in Gene Anne Smith (1991) 'Affirmative action in faculty hiring: A reply to J.E. Miller', *Vox*, **8**, 1.

References

ADLER, M.J. (1988) *Reforming Education: The Opening of the American Mind*, New York, Collier Books.

BERGEN, J.J., GOUR, N.P. and PRICHARD, B.W. (1990) 'Perceptions of school authorities regarding the rights and freedoms of students and parents', *The Canadian Administrator*, **29**, 4, p. 1.

BROWN, R. (1990) 'Overcoming sexism and racism — How?' in CHOLEWINSKI, R.I. (ed.) *Human Rights in Canada: Into the 1990's and Beyond*, Ottawa, Human Rights Research and Education Centre.

CANADIAN CHARTER OF RIGHTS AND FREEDOMS, CONSTITUTION ACT (1982) as enacted by *Canada Act*, 1982 (UK) c.11, s.1.

CANADIAN CIVIL LIBERTIES ASSOCIATION V. ONTARIO (MINISTER OF EDUCATION) (1990) 71 O.R. (2d.) 341 (Ont. C.A.).

COLKER, R. (1992) 'Section 1: Contextuality and the anti disadvantaged principle', *University of Toronto Law Journal*, **42**, p. 77.

COUNTS, G.S. (1969) *Dare the School Build a New Social Order?* New York, Arno Press.

DEWEY, J. (1946) *Philosophy of Education (Problems of Men)*, New Jersey, Littlefield, Adams and Co.

EATON V. BRANT (COUNTY) BOARD OF EDUCATION (1995) 22 O.R. (3d.) 1.

ENGLANDER, M.E. (1978) 'The court's corporal punishment mandate to parents, local authorities and the profession', *Phi Delta Kappa*, **60**, p. 529.

FERGUSON, K. (1984) *The Feminist Case Against Bureaucracy*, Philadelphia, Temple University Press.

FINE, M. (1991) *Framing Dropouts: Notes on the Politics of an Urban Public High School*, New York, State University of New York Press.

GILLIGAN, C. (1982) *In a Different Voice: Psychological Theory and Women's Development*, Cambridge MA, Harvard University Press.

GUTTMANN, A. (1987) *Democratic Education*, New Jersey, Princeton University Press.

HODGKINSON, C. (1991) *Educational Leadership: The Moral Art*, Albany, State University of New York.

JONES V. THE QUEEN (1986) 2 S.C.R. 284.

KOHLBERG, L. (1981) *The Philosophy of Moral Development: Moral Stages and the Idea of Justice*, San Francisco, Harper & Row.

LAPHAM, L.H. (1993) *The Wish for Kings: Democracy at Bay*, Grove Press, New York.

LATHER, P.A. (1991) *Getting Smart: Feminist Research and Pedagogy*, New York, Routedge.

MACKAY, A.W. (1995) 'Principles in search of justice for the young: What's law got to do with it?' *Education and Law Journal*, **6**, p. 181.

MACKAY, W. (1988–1989) 'The judicial role in educational policy-making: Promise of threat?' *Education Law Journal*, **1**, p. 127.

MAHE V. ALBERTA (1990) 1 S.C.R. 342.

MANITOBA ASSOCIATION FOR RIGHTS AND LIBERTIES INC. V. MANITOBA (MINISTER OF EDUCATION) (1992) 5 W.W.R. 749 (Man Q.B.).

MENACKER, J. and PASCALLA, E. (1984) 'What attitudes do educators have about student and teacher civil rights?' *Urban Education*, **19**, p. 115.

MORRIS, A.A. (1980) *The Constitution and American Education*, Minneapolis, West Publishing Co.

NEW JERSEY V. T.L.O. (1985) 105 S.Ct.733.

O'NEILL, O. (1992) 'Children's rights and children's lives', in ALSTON, P., PARKER, S. and SEYMOUR, J. (eds) *Children's Rights and the Law*, Oxford, Oxford University Press.

PETERS, F. and MONTGOMERIE, C. (1994a) 'Educators' knowledge of rights'. Paper presented at the Canadian Association for the Practical Study of Law in Education (CAPSLE), Saskatoon.

PETERS, F. and MONTGOMERIE, C. (1994b) 'Educators' attitudes towards rights'. Paper presented at the Canadian Association for the Practical Study of Law in Education (CAPSLE), Saskatoon.

PURPEL, D.E. (1989) *The Moral and Spiritual Crisis in Education: A Curriculum for Justice and Compassion in Education*, Massachusetts, Bergin & Garvey Pub. Inc.

QUEBEC HUMAN RIGHTS COMMISSION V. BOARD OF EDUCATION OF DEUX-MONTAGNES (1994) 19 C.H.R.R. D/1.

R. v. J.M.G. (1986) 56 O.R. (2d)(O.C.A.) 705 at 710.

R. v. KEEGSTRA (1991) 117 N.R. 1.

R. v. OAKES (1986) 65 N.R. 85.

R. v. OGG-MOSS (1984) 54 N.R. 81.

R. v. PLOURDE (1993) 140 N.B.R. (2d) 273 (Prov. Ct.).

R.S.N.B. (1973) c.S-5.

R. v. GRAHAM (15 August 1994) (N.B. Prov. Ct.) [unreported], referred to in Ian Fellows, (1995) 'Spare the rod and spoil the child', *Education and Law Journal*, **6**, p. 203.

RENAUD V. BOARD OF EDUCATION OF CENTRAL OKANAGAN NO. 23 AND CANADIAN UNION OF PUBLIC EMPLOYEES, LOCAL 523 (1992) 141 N.R. 185.

ROCKET V. ROYAL COLLEGE OF DENTAL SURGEONS OF ONTARIO (1990) 2 S.C.R. 232.

RUSSOW V. BRITISH COLUMBIA (A.G.) (1989) 35 B.C.L.R. (2d.) 29 (S.C.).

SADKER, M. and SADKER, D. (1994) *Failing at Fairness; How America's Schools Cheat Girls*, Toronto, Maxwell Macmillan Canada.

SASKATCHEWAN DEPARTMENT OF EDUCATION (1985, February) *Inner City Drop Out Study*, Regina, Queen's Printer.

SASKATCHEWAN TEACHERS' FEDERATION CODE OF ETHICS (1994) Regina, Saskatchewan Teachers' Federation Printer.

SASKATCHEWAN EDUCATION INDICATORS REPORT UPDATE (1995, May) Regina, Saskatchewan Education, Training and Employment.

SERGIOVANNI, T.J. (1996) *Leadership for the Schoolhouse: How is it Different? Why is it Important?* San Francisco, Jossey-Bass Publishers.

SHAKESHAFT, C. (1989) *Women in Educational Administration*, Newbury Park, Sage.

SHEPPARD, C. (1989) 'Recognition of the disadvantaging of women: The promise of *Andrews v. Law Society of British Columbia*', *McGill Law Journal*, **35**, 207 at 230.

SINGH V. M.E.I. (1985) N.R. 1 at 68.

SMITH, G.A. (1991) 'Affirmative action in faculty hiring', *Vox 8*, **1**, Saskatoon, University of Saskatchewan.

STEIN, N., MARSHALL, N.L. and TROPP, L.R. (1993) *Secrets in Public: Sexual Harassment in Our Schools*, Massachusetts, Center of Research on Women Wellesley College and NOW Legal Defence and Education Fund.

THE CHILD AND FAMILY SERVICES ACT (1989) c. C-7.2, Regina, Saskatchewan.

WATKINSON, A.M. (1988) 'Corporal punishment: Apply the charter, spare the child', *Canadian School Executive*, **8**, 5, p. 15.

WATKINSON, A.M. (1992) Caring and justice in education: A Charter challenge. Unpublished doctoral dissertation, University of Saskatchewan, Saskatoon, Saskatchewan.

WATKINSON, A.M. (1993, June) Inequality and or hormones. Paper presented at the Canadian Association for the Study of Educational Administration, University of Carlton, Ottawa.

WATKINSON, A.M. (1994) 'Equality, empathy and the administration of education', *Education and Law Journal*, **5**, 3, pp. 273–304.

WATKINSON, A.M. (1995) 'Hostile lessons: Sexual harassment in schools', *The Canadian School Administrator*, **34**, 1.

WATKINSON, A.M. (in press) 'Administrative complicity and systemic violence in education', in EPP, J.R. and WATKINSON, A.M. (eds) *Systemic Violence in Education: Promise Broken*, New York, State University of New York Press.

WHITE, D. (1983) 'After the divided curriculum', *The Victorian Teacher 7*. Cited in McLAREN, P. *Life in School: An Introduction to Critical Pedagogy in the Foundations of Education*, New York, Longman, 1989.

WILSON, JUSTICE B. (1990, February) Will women judges really make a difference? The Fourth Annual Barbara Betcherman Memorial Lecture, Osgood Hall Law School, York University.

YOUNG, I.M. (1987) 'Impartiality and the civic public', in BENHABIB, S. and CORNELL, D. (eds) *Feminism as Critique: On the Politics of Gender*, Minneapolis, University of Minnesota Press.

ZYLBERBERG ET AL. V. SUDBURY BOARD OF EDUCATION (1988) 29 O.A.C. 23 (Ont. C.A.).

13   Postscript: Making Central the Peripheral

Juanita Ross Epp

In this book we have reiterated twelve people's research and thinking on aspects of systemic violence. This has not been an integrated analysis, but rather a series of isolated probings at the extremities of what we consider a vast malignancy choking the growth of individual students and of society itself. What is this thing we have called 'systemic violence'?

Put simply, systemic violence is the denial of democracy as described by Watkinson in Chapter 12. But it is more than a state of being that pits all students against all teachers in a losing battle against bureaucracy. Systemic violence is more complicated than that. It emerges as the apparently equal treatment of students that allows privilege for some and subordination for others. It is the denigration of individuals based on visible characteristics; the entrenchment of privilege through a smoke-screen of seeming equality.

Systemic violence reaches into every corner of the school and the school system, from elementary and secondary education, as noted in Parts 1 and 2, to the postgraduate setting described in Chapters 9, 10 and 11. Beginning with the initial struggle for the loyalty of a 6-year-old, when he or she must accept the authority of school and relinquish the focused attentions of parents in favor of the distracted, diffused attentions of a teacher, the potential for systemic violence is unconstrained (Chapter 4). The rights of the school are entrenched in tradition, teacher perceptions and legal obligations (Chapter 12). Children are treated as the property of the state (Chapter 2) and yet the state is loath to intervene between child and parent if the child is at risk (Chapter 3).

When compulsory schooling was introduced, children were forced into the schools and parenting became a secondary societal role. Although children are forced to be separated from their parents through compulsory education, schools are not required to provide parental substitutes at the emotional level. Schools remain unwilling to intervene in the new dynamics of child raising, unwilling to relinquish their narrowly defined role as purveyors of cognitive knowledge. Neither are they compelled to examine the role of the parent or engage in intellectual discussion on what a parent is or does. When teachers are suspicious that parents are not providing properly for their children, they call in a third agency, either the police or social services, to try to repair the damage. The children become nobody's problem and everyone's problem.

It is not as if the schools are not full of parents. Many teachers are also parents, but the structures of the school encourage them to separate the domestic from the professional. Parenting teaches people valuable lessons in time management, personal relations and understanding of the human condition. When teachers are discouraged from connecting the personal with the professional, the valuable skills that teachers learn by becoming parents are wasted. These learnings should be valued by the institution and promoted throughout the school system. Teacher-parents, as Abbey explains in Chapter 4, are valuable assets that are often dismissed and overlooked.

As the child advances through the grades, the power of the school is undiminished. Children remain at the mercy of their teachers and administrators and become increasingly at-risk from their classmates because schools are unable or unwilling to intercede in 'childish' conflicts (Chapter 5). The winners of such conflicts are usually students with social capital within the system. Children who have been betrayed by their parents, ignored by their teachers, and left to fend for themselves, are the ones most likely to become the targets of their classmates' violence (Chapters 6 and 7). They are the ones least likely to find allies in their teachers. They cannot expect teachers to help them cope with the real issues of their lives, because the teachers are too busy teaching; too busy reinforcing the value of the cognitive at the expense of the affective. This is, after all, the current definition of a teacher's job. For many students the most important thing they learn from school is their station in life. The pecking order has long been established to place 'real men' (white, heterosexual, athletic) at the top (Chapter 8), and other males, white females and non-white females in the ranks (Chapters 6 and 7).

This ranking is reinforced by pedagogical practices that allow the ordering to become obvious in the classroom. Eventually, at the university level, the violence of rhetoric (Chapter 9), the dominance of masculine constructs (Chapter 10) and the exclusion of the voices of those who are Other (Chapter 11) ensure continued positions of privilege for some students and failure and frustration for others. Although these later chapters (9, 10 and 11) are philosophical in that they examine the way in which we understand knowledge and the processes by which we identify that which we value as knowledge, they are not removed from the practical implications of systemic violence. They provide a backdrop to understanding why we allow the dominant–subservient structures to survive in our schools, and why we value the objective over the subjective, the cognitive over the affective. Without this philosophical deconstruction of what we value in schools, we cannot deconstruct the things we do in schools, and nor can we envision what we must do to re/value the things we now ignore.

It is in the process of re/valuing that we are able to address systemic violence. No one is responsible for the violence, it is not intended or malicious, it is rather ingrained in our thinking and, until we can change that, we cannot change our schools or our society. Systemic violence is so much a part of the fabric of our society, and therefore of our educational system, that the exclusionary and biased aspects of our educational processes have not been immediately obvious even to the authors of this book — especially since we are among the successful adult products of this system. It is little wonder that students are unable to understand and reconcile the apparent and verbalized commitment to equity espoused in the schools with the pain in their own lives. Why, then, are we forever surprised when they resort to acts of defiance and violence?

But the contributors to this book are not without hope. In our analysis of the problem, we have been able to find ways in which systemic violence can be reduced and have attempted to make suggestions for countering it in the areas that we have examined. These recommendations are not comprehensive, nor are they integrated, yet the impetus for them came from our diverse topics in a strangely coherent way.

Systemic violence could be reduced if we could co-opt the focus of education to encourage teachers, administrators, and students to become in touch with each other and with their own affective selves. The dichotomy between the cognitive and the affective, which places value on cognition over personhood, is inherently violent. Although school rhetoric often proclaims a child-centered approach to education, a truly child-centered approach can only be achieved if the child's emotional, social and physical well-being is placed above intellectual development. This is not to say that intellect will suffer because of the emphasis on the emotional. There is much research to indicate that attention to the affective is prerequisite for the development of the cognitive (Brookes, 1992).

How would the emphasis on the affective play itself out in our schools? First it would remove the conflict between home and school by recognizing that the child's personal interests are in the school's best interest. By leaving the affective to the home, the school has abdicated the opportunity to intervene in cases where the home is not fulfilling children's needs (Chapter 3). Teachers are aware of their duties as reporters of child abuse but they are encouraged not to become involved in intervention processes. In order to become effective in intercepting abuse cases, teachers and administrators must treat abuse as a terrible yet commonplace event. If curriculum materials and classroom discussion examined the issues of abuse, and recognized the related issues of domination and control, teachers and their students would be in a position to discuss abuse and deal with its realities.

The same process of making central a formerly peripheral topic applies to the treatment of school violence. School violence is an important component of the daily lives of children in schools (see Chapter 5). It affects where they walk, how they dress, where they go and who their friends are. As long as teachers treat violence at arms' length, as something that should really be someone else's problem, they will continue to neglect the opportunity to intervene in a crucial aspect of the children's lives. By ignoring school violence, the name-calling, the shoving, the fighting, the harassment, they are condoning it. Children see teachers walking by, pretending not to notice, and they learn that the way we treat others, the way we interact on the street or in the playground, is nobody's business but our own. Teachers must talk about violence, they must recognize it, examine it, dissect it, let children see and understand its secrets and its sources. Without this examination it remains an ugly secret that society cannot understand or control.

Making central peripheral subjects, would also be effective in countering racism, which is often operationalized in the form of violence. A process for bringing issues of violence, racism and abuse into everyday spaces in the curriculum is described by Wason-Ellam in Chapter 6. She witnessed the transformation of a racially oppressive classroom through a circle of 'talk about books'. Such open discussion of real issues allows children to find their places in society and to understand the contextual meanings of what is happening to them in their lives.

As important as it is to bring issues of abuse, violence, racism and sexism into focus in school curriculum, the importance of all of these is superseded by the need to talk about the meaning of masculinity as it is practiced in today's society. As Frank has pointed out in Chapter 8, much of what is systemically violent about our schools is tied up in the systemic structuring and reordering of people that begins with the competition for who will be counted as a man. When boys can talk about what it means to be men, the taboos keeping all other groups at a distance from power will be challenged and eroded. The essential key to change lies in addressing this, the ultimate taboo.

Of course, none of this will be easy. This process of allowing tabooed subjects to become central to the curriculum in an analysis of social oppression is dangerous to those teachers willing to address it and to the children in their classrooms. In the current social order, there are punishments for those who would listen for children's voices in the process of re/centering the curriculum. As Leroy points out in Chapter 7, children and teachers alike know that discussions of abuse may lead to apprehension and, as Frank has explained in Chapter 8, boys must go to great pains to adopt masculine stances or pay the consequences. Recognition of privilege and inequity makes the classroom an uncomfortable place (hooks, 1994).

It was not that children are loath to talk about these subjects. In all our studies, students were eager to talk, whether it was about violence, masculinity, racism, homophobia, sexuality, abuse or anger. They often thanked researchers for giving them an opportunity to think and talk about these issues. Even those students who chose not to talk, because they feared the consequences of exposure, would have liked to have talked, if the dangers could somehow have been eliminated.

But the dangers cannot be ignored; we do not know the pitfalls that await the process of bringing systemic justice to our school systems. The complexities of a changed view of education are already focusing critical and feminist pedagogy on the difficulties of doing what is just in a world of many voices. It is tempting to draw back into the safety of a system that has 'worked' for generations; but safety and privilege are gained only at great cost. We must find a way for our schools to become crucibles for change. Unless we can do that, we, with our children, are trapped in a repeating violence of our own making.

References

BROOKES, A. (1992) *Feminist Pedagogy: An Autobiographical Approach*, Halifax, NS, Fernwood Press.

HOOKS, B. (1994) *Teaching to Transform*, NY, Routledge.

Notes on Contributors

Sharon M. Abbey holds an EdD degree from the Ontario Institute of Studies in Education. She is currently an Assistant Professor in the Pre-service Faculty of Education program at Brock University in St Catharines, Ontario where she teaches curriculum courses in Personal and Social Studies and supervises students in their field practicum work. She is also a founding member of the Center on Collaborative Research at Brock University and a member of the editorial board of 'Brock Education.' Her extensive background in education also includes teaching all levels of elementary school, work as a curriculum consultant and leadership roles as an elementary scool principal. Her major research interests also include gender equity issues, narrative inquiry and women's studies related to mothers and daughters.

Lorraine Cathro is presently the Adviser to the President on the Status of Women, University of Saskatchewan. Lorraine was a sessional lecturer, term appointment and out-of-scope assistant professor with the Indian Teacher Education Program at the University of Saskatchewan. Her research interests center on narrative enquiry, literacy and gender issues. She is presently engaged in a study with two teacher co-researchers on 'Two Teachers' Classroom Practice of Gender Equity.'

Juanita Ross Epp taught for fifteen years at both the elementary and secondary levels before obtaining her PhD in Educational Administration from the University of Saskatchewan. She now teaches at Lakehead University in Ontario, Canada. Her research interests arise from her concern about child abuse and issues of gender and pedagogy are the focus of her publications.

Blye Frank holds a PhD in Educational Foundations from Dalhousie University. He is an Associate Professor in the Department of Education at Mount Saint Vincent University in Halifax, Nova Scotia where he teaches courses in Educational Research Literacy, Inclusive Education and Gender. His research interest is in masculinity and schooling.

Lisa Jadwin teaches in the English Department at St John Fisher College. She has published essays on pedagogical theory and on Victorian and contemporary literature. She has just completed a book on cognition and writing development and is currently co-authoring a study of the works of Charlotte Brontë.

Carol Leroy has been a teacher in Kenya and in First Nations communities in Alberta and British Columbia. She obtained her PhD at the University of Alberta and became interested in inner-city children's literacy through work that she carried out with local social agencies. She is now an assistant professor in the Faculty of Education at the University of Regina, where she teaches courses in Language Arts and Literacy. Her current research involves the use of ethnography and narrative inquiry to develop a better understanding of social issues that affect the teaching and learning of reading and writing in elementary education.

Irene M. MacDonald is completing her doctoral work at the University of Alberta's Department of Educational Policy Studies. A former school board trustee, she is currently involved in four research studies funded by the government and the university, all dealing with school violence. She is on a special project with the Alberta Ministry of Education titled, 'The Safe and Caring Schools Initiative', a collaborative three-year project involving researchers and educators from across the province. Her main area of focus is junior high students, and legislative responses to violence in schools.

Sheila Martineau is a PhD candidate in Educational Studies at the University of British Columbia. Her research involves qualitative and interdisciplinary sociology, and focuses on child abuse, gender socialization, and adolescent advocacy. Sheila is involved with the Society for Children and Youth of BC and their Rights Awareness Project (RAP), established to disseminate information and monitor compliance and implementation of the UN Convention on the Rights of the Child in BC.

Sandra Monteath is a writer who holds a Masters of Environmental Studies degree from York University and a PhD in Education (Sociology of Education) from the University of Toronto. She once taught art and English at the secondary school level and spent many years as an editor in educational and academic publishing. She has also designed educational games. Sandra's mode of inquiry is at once analytic and ethnographic, and she writes from an embodied, feminist standpoint. Currently she is working on a children's book on Arya Tara, a Buddha who vowed always to appear in female form, and is also completing a study, 'No strangers to sorrow: Conversations with children about suffering', on children's understanding of, and talk about suffering.

Rosonna Tite is an Associate Professor in the Faculty of Education at Memorial University of Newfoundland. Besides teaching sociology of education in the undergraduate teacher education program, she teaches research methods and policy studies at the graduate level. She is also involved with the Women's Studies program. Her research interests include child abuse, gender and schooling and feminist pedagogy.

Linda Wason-Ellam is an ethnographer who researches the 'social lives of children in cross-cultural literacy classrooms'. She is a Professor at the University of Saskatchewan teaching courses in Reading, Language Arts, and Children's Literature. A former teacher and consultant, she has published many articles in educational journals and is the author of the following books: *Start with a Story, Literacy Moments to Report Cards, Sharing Stories with Children*, and co-author of *Horizons in Literacy*. Her forthcoming book addresses teaching and learning in cross-cultural classrooms.

Ailsa M. Watkinson is a researcher and equality consultant with a special interest in the area of education and human rights laws. She received her PhD in Educational Administration from the University of Saskatchewan in 1992. Prior to returning to University in 1989, she worked for twelve years with the Saskatchewan Human Rights Commission. In 1987, Ailsa received a national award from the Canadian Association for the Study of Educational Administration for her master's thesis entitled *Student Discipline and the Canadian Charter of Rights and Freedoms.*

Index

ability grouping, 6, 18
abuse, child
  agency responsible for, 55
  and moral development, 36
  bullying as, 83
  historical construct of, 30–1
  lack of reporting, 19, 59–61
  of feeble-minded, 29–30
  punishment as, 12, 29, 182–5
  school practice as, 19, 37–8
  social construction of, 30–3
  see also reporting abuse, 50–64
abused children
  and atrocities, 41
  and criminality, 13
  and neglect of affective, 9
  apprehension of, 106
administrator
  must report abuse, 51
  perceptions of violence, 84–5, 90
  response to violence, 89
advantaged students, 2–6
affective learning
  as aid to cognition, 10
  emphasizing in schools, 193
  neglect of, 8
age-graded classrooms, 7, 11
alienation, 11, 179
anger, student, 8
apparent equality, 191
apprehension, 59–60, 106–8
  child's fear of, 107
argument
  as rape, 139–40
  role in Western culture, 134
assault cases, 183–4
at risk students
  and full service schools, 43–4
  and student resistance, 179
  pathologized, 44

authoritarianism, 174–8
  child questioning of, 179–81

bias
  against gay students, 19, 119–21
  against girls, 18
  cultural, 5, 100, 163–4
  in standardized tests, 5
  unintentional, 19
binary see dichotomy
blame
  culture of, 30, 35, 40
  internalized, 16
  of mothers, 72
  system over individual, 2
body and masculinity, 116–19
body and 'second persons', 154
book circle, 101
boys
  and attention deficit, 42
  and emotion, 8
  and masculinity, 113–27
  and power relations, 13
  and sexual preference, 121–2
bullying, 83–4
  by girls, 99–100
  interventions into, 101–2
  racial, 94
bureaucracy in schools, 174
  as dehumanizing schools, 179

care
  ethic of, 177
  of teacher-mothers, 75
Charter of rights, 173, 180
children
  as political actors, 28
  as property, 37
  over protection of, 39
Christianity and women, 146–8